"I found this book to be fascinating and informative. It is filled with the information that is supportive of the best principles of dance training and performance and clearly outlines the dangers and pitfalls that plague the profession. I believe this should be required reading for all aspiring dancers and dance teachers."

—Dame Sonia Arova, Artistic Director, Alabama Ballet

"[*The Dancer's Survival Manual*] should be read by every professional dancer—immensely useful and sensible."

—Maina Gielgud, Artistic Director, Australian Ballet

"An excellent book which every dancer should read—a wonderful encyclopedia for dancers."

—Todd Bolender, Artistic Director, State Ballet of Missouri

"[*The Dancer's Survival Manual*] is beautifully written and should be an excellent reference book for parents and young aspiring dancers, as well as being helpful for teachers and directors of schools and companies."

—Robert Barnett, Artistic Director, The Atlanta Ballet

"In this golden age of dance, performers face new demands in their professional and personal lives. The authors address these problems with courage, compassion, and from experience. As we applaud the performer's talent, let us also give a helping hand to his survival."

—William Como, Editor in Chief, *Dance Magazine*

"As a dancer who has gone through pain, injury, and anguish, it is comforting for me to know that because of this survival manual, today's dancers—those beautiful thoroughbreds, fragile and vulnerable—will no longer feel alone in their search for solutions to physical and emotional stress."

—Violette Verdy, Teaching Associate, New York City Ballet

MARIAN HOROSKO and
JUDITH R. F. KUPERSMITH, M.D.

The Dancer's Survival Manual

Everything You Need to Know About
Being a Dancer
. . . Except How to Dance

PERENNIAL LIBRARY

Harper & Row, Publishers, New York
Cambridge, Philadelphia, San Francisco, Washington
London, Mexico City, São Paulo, Singapore, Sydney

Portions of this work originally appeared in somewhat different form in *Dance Magazine*.

FIRST EDITION

Designed by Laura Hough
Drawings by Henry Fera

Library of Congress Cataloging-in-Publication Data

Horosko, Marian.
  The dancer's survival manual.

  Bibliography: p.
  Includes index.
  1. Dancing—Vocational guidance—United States.
  2. Dancers—United States—Case studies.
  I. Kupersmith, Judith R. F.   II. Title.
  GV1597.H67   1987   793.3′023′73   87-45057
  ISBN 0-06-055084-8   87 88 89 90 91 RRD 10 9 8 7 6 5 4 3 2 1
  ISBN 0-06-096199-6 (pbk.) 87 88 89 90 91 RRD 10 9 8 7 6 5 4 3 2 1

Contents

Foreword

Twenty-five years ago dance in America was poorly funded, seldom mentioned in the media, and considered an unreliable source of income. By the 1970s dance was America's fastest growing art form and its most important cultural export. Although dance is relatively new to America, we have just witnessed a meteoric rise in its popularity unprecedented in the history of the art.

Today in the 1980s dancers perform in remarkable variety and the United States can boast of twenty major national companies, six in New York City alone, the dance mecca of the world, where we teach 15,000 to 20,000 students in our schools. Along with the swift proliferation of interest in dance has come improved technical training, more opportunities for employment, higher incomes, society's respect for the dancer, a significant body of dance literature and criticism, informed management, a comprehensive library of books and films to preserve the dance of our time, and a warm, responsive, and appreciative audience.

In addition we have gained a new system of dance medicine to heal our injuries and to perform new surgical miracles. There are therapists to rehabilitate us without a loss of muscular strength, accessible nutritional information, and specialized treatment in sports/dance clinics throughout the nation. With the formation in 1981 of PACH, the Performing Arts Center for Health, of which Marian Horosko and Judith Kupersmith were cofounders, New York City acquired the first of many psychiatric clinics restricted to performing artists to alleviate the stress of performing and save our talent from emotional despair.

The dance profession has gained much yet has more to do. Our technical advances must not be permitted to become physicality. The education of the dancer must include the development of artistry and his or her ability to communicate that artistry. We need to consolidate our methodologies of teaching dance into fluid yet valid and accredited science. Choreographers need to be given a structure in which they can study the masterworks of the past while they explore new forms for the future. Talent and creativity need not be lost after a performing career has ended. A means of channeling and redirecting the experience gained on stage should be found.

There is much yet to do in educating young audiences, in discovering and supporting new talent, and in encouraging composers and designers to become part of the dance world. And whatever form the theater of the next century will take, dance must surely be a part of it.

I have faith that the next generation of dancers is equal to the task, as dancers have been in the past. What a beautiful and rewarding future dance holds for all of us.

ROBERT JOFFREY
Artistic Director, The Joffrey Ballet

Acknowledgments

Our thanks to Helen Moore, our editor, who tactfully kept us from indulging in technical dance terms and psychological jargon.

And to *Dance Magazine,* for publishing our inside-outside view of the dance world no matter what our subject or how frank we became.

Not least, we are grateful for the patience of family and friends who permitted us to disappear on Sunday mornings into our special world of dance health as we wrote this book.

The Dancer's
Survival Manual

Introduction

It would be remarkably fortunate to have a career in dance without difficulties—without a search for the best dance education, without financial strain, or without obstacles in a career or emotional upheavals.

Most professional dancers, no matter how successful they seem, have had many moments of doubt, disappointment, and insecurity mixed with the excitement, enjoyment, and sense of accomplishment that using one's talent to the fullest can bring. They have been able to maintain enough stability to overcome disruptions in their professional and personal lives, yet remain dedicated to their art without its costing too much in their progress and happiness. But so much talent is lost through incorrect training, insufficient support from family and friends, and through psychological disturbances.

The growth of dance in the past two decades to a respected place in our society has resulted in higher levels of dance training in most cities throughout the United States and in more performing opportunities. But along with that growth, competition and physical and psychological demands have increased as well. Without a clear picture of those demands in becoming a professional dancer, a good amateur, or a satisfied lifetime student of dance, the cost in time, talent, and emotional security may be too high.

We do not presume to know the answers to every problem. And we have delighted in knowing those dancers—the exceptions—who have not followed any norm or rule. But for most dancers, there is a general pattern of events that everyone faces to which we offer some general solutions that bear investigation until an individual resolution is found.

To demonstrate the general pattern of events and the general solutions, we have created a scenario, a fantasy of the perfect conditions in dance for a young student, Ann, and her friends, Bea, Cissy, and Danny.

Through Ann's young life we can see the stage set for her adult experiences as a successful and emotionally supported professional dancer. Through the actions of her friends, we may discover where progress may be postponed, and emotional security delayed.

Ann was born into an arts-minded, middle- to upper-class family in a cosmopolitan city with sophisticated dance/music/museum activities. Her parents consider the arts upgrading, and while they understand the hard work and insecurity involved in choosing a profession in the arts, they still consider it a valid choice.

Although there are dance dynasties, Ann's family is not one of these, nor is there a family history in the arts. But as second-generation European-Americans, her family members respect artists.

Ann's mother, in addition to caring for her family, has many outside interests. She is not a caricature of femininity or a feminist. She regards women as independent persons. In dress she has taste and her choices are suitable to the occasion. Body beauty is encouraged in cleanliness and awareness of attractiveness without undue emphasis. She has no unresolved ambition for the arts and because she is not rigid or constantly seeking perfection in herself or anyone else, she will not choose a rigid, inflexible, or stern school for Ann when the time comes.

Ann has sufficient self-esteem, joy, and reward in her accomplishments and enough approval from both parents to give her pleasure in her activities. Ann's relationship to her father includes no overpowering craving for attention by showing off.

As a child, and as all children do, Ann responds to music and moves as if to dance. But because of her innate talent, she responds emotionally to changes in tempo and mood. She changes herself into a bird, an animal, a tree, or the wind, drawing from her own imagination and as the music suggests, without prompting from others.

Ann runs, slides, swings, and tests her physical capabilities at the playground without being warned with too much emphasis on the dangers of falling or injury. Her coordination develops and, since she continues to express her feelings in dance, her parents consider lessons. They are wise enough to know that a child of three or four years of age does not have sufficiently ossified bones to withstand the rigors of dance technique. However, when Ann is five, she is enrolled in a weekly eurythmic-type class where she can respond to rhythms, skip, run, and jump as demonstrated by her teacher and performed by the other pupils.

Ann enjoys sharing some of the duties in caring for her baby brother and, because her interest in dance classes is sustained, her parents decide to select a ballet school for her. (If Ann were to become a modern dancer or choose musical theater dance, ballet would be the best and preferred first choice before changing disciplines.)

Ann's willingness to attend a new school and her continued strong interest in dance enforce her parents' choice of school with graded classes, a history of producing professional dancers, and performing opportunities. They know that it costs as much to go to a professional school as a small, local one, and that time spent in poor training can never be regained.

But Ann's life, now that she is eight years old, changes completely. She is no longer encouraged in any physical activity except bike riding and is no longer the talented baby upon whom her relatives doted. It is explained to her that what she accomplishes between the ages of eight and twelve will set the pattern for her dance life physically, technically, and in her sense of discipline. Although there is time for extra activities, including arts-related subjects, and time for personal expression in sharing ideas and games with other girls her age, Ann has a sense of growing up and having to become more responsible.

The first class in the new school is very different as well. She cannot do except what she is told in holding her body in correct positions, in being exact and limited to the class material. She, like the other girls, passed the physical test to enter the school. They all have long legs, a short body, long neck, small head, and strong, naturally arched feet. Their hips rotate easily and they are flexible, conforming to the current aesthetic physicality. Ann is harmoniously proportioned and has an attractive face. (Her parents are not exceptionally tall—her mother is under 5'8".) The other girls in Ann's class are of mixed ethnic backgrounds and status.

Ann is somewhat fearful in this class of peers and is somewhat annoyed at not being free to do as she would like in class. But soon she takes pride in the restrictions and the discipline because they separate her from the "babies" in her earlier classes. She has the ability to postpone pleasure knowing that someday dance will result from the discipline. Soon, she no longer cares what the others are doing—she enjoys her twice weekly lessons in every way.

Ann makes a friend in the class—Bea. Bea and her mother are very ambitious for a career. Ann admires her friend's spunk, her energy, and obvious knowledge of the theater and gossip about professional dancers. They both pass the yearly exams of the school, keep up their academics, and dance in the small productions of the school over the next two years.

When they are both about ten years old, they know there is a chance for them to appear in a professional production (*The Nutcracker,* a spring recital, or other production). The audition for this appearance is in the form of a class. Ann is sure that Bea will get into the production and hopes that she will too.

The directors of the production come to watch their class but Bea surprises Ann by going into a "spaz" (hysterics). She wears the required class uniform of leotard, pink tights, and shoes, but has added colorful leg warmers, put a flower in her hair, and wears sparkly earrings—all totally against the rules. Bea's "spaz" continues throughout the class as she suddenly breaks out into a cartwheel, fast and unsteady turns, and big jumps behind the other students.

The steps seem difficult, wild, and exciting. Although there is a look of dismay on the teacher's face over Bea's attention-getting tactics, Ann admires her courage and desire to win a role in the production. It never occurred to Ann to do anything but classwork; she would have been unwilling to take such a risk.

When the class audition is over, Ann is called into the school office and is told she has been chosen to fill the role. Elated, Ann returns to the dressing room to share the good news with the others. But there is a stunned silence in the room. Some of the girls show indifference to her success, some put it down, some give polite good wishes. Some imply that Ann got the role because she is "teacher's pet" (not true), because she is the right size, or hint at unknown reasons for her success.

Ann tells her mother, who is waiting, her good news. Her mother says she would have been proud Ann did well at the audition even if she had not won the role. When Ann tells her about the reaction of the other girls, her mother explains that some are envious, which will make them work harder to succeed, but others are jealous, which is a destructive emotion that is unreasonable and teaches nothing.

When Ann and her mother leave the school, they hear some of the mothers scolding the students because they did not win the role. "Were you lazy?" they ask. "Did you remember to smile?" They are angry at their children for not succeeding.

Ann's first rehearsal for the production is frightening. The cast is older than she; some are pleasant, others ignore her. The director shows her the choreography. Ann makes mistakes but tries again without prompting until she understands the movements, the pattern, and the counts. She is in awe of the dressing room and can hardly wait to rehearse again but wonders at the same time why she is exposing herself to all this strangeness. When a wardrobe mistress passes by, Ann sees the costumes and knows that one of them will be hers. The orchestra rehearsal is thrilling, and the lights hot but cheerful. When the performance time arrives, it never occurs to Ann that she will forget her role or be frightened, only a bit anxious. She has repeated her part to herself so often, she knows she will be able to do it.

After the performance, the director tells her she did well and must do the same at each performance. Ann is overwhelmed by the applause and the bows. Her parents, relatives, and Bea congratulate her and she is very happy.

When Ann returns to the dance class, her friends are not the same. Those who never paid attention to her now shower her with questions and friendliness. Cissy, for instance, who always appeared to be so mature, cool, and aloof in everything, told her: "You were very good in the performance. I admire anyone who does anything well." The entire class seems to be trying harder. Only the teacher remains as before.

At school, her academic friends think nothing at all about her good fortune. Some think it all silly and not worthwhile. One of her school friends invites her to a birthday party on a performance night. She tells her friend that it is not possible for her to miss a performance but that she is still her friend and, at her mother's suggestion, makes a date with her friend for a special birthday celebration at another time. Ann doesn't want to lose her school friends but she has to make a choice.

The students who now attend class three or four times a week are twelve or thirteen years of age. The dressing room conversation is about the physical changes becoming apparent in the girls. Both Ann and Bea reach their menarche (beginning of the menstrual cycle) but discover they have few facts about the phenomenon. Each family handles the information in a different way: Ann's mother explains that the cycle is a sign of growing up and leaves further discussion open for the future; Bea's mother tells her it is called "the curse." Cissy's mother does not discuss the changes at all. Cissy is not pleased with the changes in her body and feels she is unattractive. Cissy gets a lot of attention from her mother, although it seems to others that she is insinuating herself into Cissy's life. Cissy is disgusted by the slight bloat before a cycle, and magnifies the difference, which fills her with horror.

Cissy complains about water retention, fatigue, and a craving for sweets. The family doctor gives her a diuretic, which both she and her mother take. Cissy begins to watch her diet to the extreme and hoards bits of food, claiming to be too busy to eat dinner with her family. Her main interest in life is to please both her parents in dance and at school. They want her to be outstanding in everything she does.

The class is largely the original group by the time they reach the age of thirteen or fourteen. Pointe work has been added and they have gained good placement of the body, strength, flexibility, and stability in movement. But Bea is becoming more and more impatient with her progress. She conforms, but her personal life is taking on more sparkle. She goes out on dates, to parties, and stays up later than Ann and sometimes comes to class quite tired.

One day during the class Bea twists an ankle. The teacher determines that she should not continue because of pain, and a staff person in the school puts ice on the swelling and sends Bea home. The teacher warns the class about landing improperly after a jump and about giving injuries proper care without undue emphasis.

Ann feels badly for her friend, then suffers an accident herself. She thinks she was tripped during a rush at her school assembly. Could she have been tripped on purpose, she wonders. In any case, her knee is badly skinned, and because classwork would open the wound again, she is not permitted to dance until it heals. The two girls compare injuries on the phone. Ann is not going to follow her instinct to blame another person. She will go to class to watch the lessons and to learn what she can by watching. Bea is not going to attend the class. She blames the slippery floor as the cause of her accident. She complains, too, that the other students were too close to her, and she will not admit that she was not listening to directions from the teacher, nor that she was very tired that day. She places blame on others instead of assuming responsibility.

Eventually, boys become part of the dressing room discussion. Ann has a crush on Danny, a boy in a sports program. As an athlete, he understands Ann's need for sufficient sleep and no fast-food binges, as well as giving up other pleasures. They go out on group dates and she watches him practice. He, however, like no one else, is permitted to watch a dance class. They understand each other's commitments.

Bea finds it fun to have several boyfriends and goes out alone with her dates. Cissy will have nothing to do with dating. She has added extra courses in math to her schedule because it comes easily to her and satisfies her father's request that she consider college as an alternative to dance. Her thinness becomes a concern to the teacher and the school, but her mother tells them "she will grow out of it."

The school offers Ann a scholarship and her wish to become a professional dancer seems to be confirmed by the encouragement of the school. Bea has no doubts about her own future stardom but has been told by the school she is not ballet company material. Cissy is encouraged to decide upon a career but cannot make up her mind.

The girls add another class to the schedule—pas de deux, or partnering class. Danny makes friends with Cissy and Bea. He began to dance after sports began to bore him, and with parental support obtained a scholarship from the school and began his study at the age of fourteen. He and Ann have many things in common, but they are no longer attracted to each other. As friends, they think alike about their future careers, about study, and about their goals. Bea thinks he is a nice kid. Since she is not going to be in the company, she begins to take classes in other forms of dance elsewhere. Bea thinks she knows how to get ahead, and sex has come up in her conversation as a means of getting ahead.

Bea persuades Ann and Danny to go with her to an audition for a regional company. Ann has reservations because of her scholarship but is so curious to know where she stands in comparison to others that she cannot resist. Cissy will have none of it.

At the audition, Ann suddenly loses confidence in the presence of so many good auditionees and fails. She is encouraged by the directors, however, to continue her study and develop herself. Bea is full of confidence and tries every step with energy and gusto. She looks older than sixteen in her standout dressing and more mature attitude. She is offered a job. Danny is offered a job as well. But Bea, now confident that she is ready for bigger things, turns down the offer. Danny says he really wants to wait for his own school's company and both are pleased with themselves. All but Ann, who is shocked that she failed and wonders how this happened.

Ann knows that Bea has added individuality to her work and

she has not. Despite her good body and good training, her talent and love for dance remain hidden. She asks her mother, who cannot help her, but her teacher can and tells her to "find herself." She is encouraged to expand her awareness by reading more and going to museums and plays and to show more inner content in her classwork, her variation class, and the pas de deux class. She talks philosophy with her school friends and boyfriends, risks some emotional content in her work, and is corrected when it is not suitable to the movement or role. She becomes more aware of music as a contributor to her classwork, begins to understand characterization in her school acting class, chooses more sophisticated clothes for her wardrobe, and begins to take care of her skin and hair and to wear makeup.

Cissy works herself to a frazzle. She becomes too weak to rehearse for the final school performances. Bea has left the school but Ann and Danny work hard for the "graduation" performances, knowing that there will be agents attending and directors from the company. Cissy gets physical and psychological help and attends the performances with Bea.

Ann is chosen to become a member of the company. Danny is told to study two more years and he will join as well. Ann leaves home to live on her salary, rooms with two other dancers, and changes her life-style to meet the needs of company class, rehearsals, and performances. Her boyfriends write from college and her travel with the company is her big joy. She's on the bottom of the corps but she has achieved her goal.

Bea is still a friend and visits whenever she is in town. She seems always to be looking for a new job and trying to make contacts. Cissy writes from college where she continues to dance—the best one in her class.

Ann at this point can be tempted to remain where she is and enjoy the pleasures of her life. Or, when she sees some discontent or bitterness among the members of the company, she may decide to pursue solo roles. Her best chance is to progress as she did before—finding herself but this time asking to understudy roles and asking for a chance to do them.

Bea might find her big chance—but it is not likely because

"luck" is rare. If she gets her big chance, she will never feel she earned her right to it whatever price she pays. She is a good candidate to find a crutch like alcohol or drugs to keep her on top.

Danny, because male performers are still desperately needed in dance, will do well if he doesn't become a victim of so many open doors. His career will be shorter because he did not begin at an early age, and he therefore will have a lesser technique and more inclination to injuries. But his career will probably be longer as the open door continues to swing him into choreography, artistic directorship, or teaching.

Cissy has the most options if she can overcome the fact that she will probably never dance. Should she become a modern dancer at this point (or had she become one earlier) her chances of a career would be getting better all the time. If she does not dance and does not become bitter, she can become an excellent teacher, a physical therapist, or enter any arts management office. Then, again, she may become totally academics minded.

As for happiness: Ann and Danny can have a happy life if they meet challenges and look for long goals. Bea may never find happiness, while Cissy, if she accepts the loss of her early years and becomes emotionally healthy, has a very good chance.

Few dancers have had the advantages of an Ann—early recognition of talent, excellent education, support at home, friends from whom to learn, and healthy emotional outlook. Many dancers are, at various times, a combination of the characters in our fantasy, with gaping holes in their dance education, less-than-golden opportunities, and many wounds from emotional fallout.

For this reason, we will explore ways education can be amended, injuries avoided, and risks and challenges faced with more rewarding attitudes.

The Dancer
as Student

1

The Realities of Dance Education

CHOOSING A SCHOOL

The first step to take in choosing a school for dance education is to know when to take that step. The age of eight is generally considered the time when mind and body are ready to begin the serious study of dance.

Often, with the best of intentions, many parents enroll their child in dance classes at the age of three or four, expecting an advantage from a very early start. Granted, an early start is better than a late one, but until a child is five or six years of age, vigorous playground activities—running, jumping, and climbing—provide sufficient physical and creative exercise for the developing young mind and body.

Most young children have a natural desire to move and dance. When they react to music and rhythms parents, assuming their child is talented, decide the time has come to consider dance classes. A young child's concentration, however, lasts only a few moments before slipping into play. Organized classroom play, such as easy gymnastics, tumbling, or easy yoga exercises, has a place in early physical education, but organized dance classes that place a burden on the body can do harm.

Nonetheless, because so many parents think their child an exception, predance, preballet, and creative play classes are full of these very young exceptions. Some classes even include the mother, who, instead of concerning herself with helping her young child become physically independent of her, includes herself in her child's dance class. This prolongs the child's emotional dependency and encourages the child's physical imitation of adult movements instead of encouraging individual self-expression.

A predance class may be considered for a child who is truly an exception—one who has shown a sustained interest in dance and demonstrated that interest in movement on every possible occasion, not just to gain parental approval but for the pleasure it gives the child.

Youngsters five, six, and seven years of age who have shown this sustained interest may benefit from a weekly class that should last no longer than forty-five minutes, provided that class is more structured than an expensive baby-sitting session. The range of predance classes available in this category extends from improvised play to invaluable contributions in educating the physically handicapped or emotionally disturbed child. Somewhere between the two extremes a predance class that teaches coordination of music with movement is the best one to choose. The classwork should be based upon a syllabus (vocabulary) of demi-pliés (half bends of the knees), small jumps from two feet, stretches *sitting on the floor,* and dance steps such as the polka or galop, done on a diagonal across the floor. The music may be recorded at this level of study. In no way should the child be forced into any position that is not a running-jumping-skipping movement other than the floor stretches. While gymnastic and acrobatic classes begin more intensive stretching at this level, the dance school should be more concerned with correct standing alignment and placement of the child's body.

Most children lose interest in these classes in a short time and have to be coaxed to attend. But if interest does not wane and the child goes to class willingly, accepting no excuse to miss a class, the study should continue.

One way to determine if the interest is genuine or simply obedience on the child's part is to notice if the child responds to the class material by making a contribution not suggested by the teacher. In better schools, a period for improvisation is permitted at the end of each class. Each child is given a few bars of music to choreograph outside the classroom or to use for an improvisation. The teacher observes the child to determine the extent of the student's imagination, musicality, performance sense, and dramatic ability. No comment is made. If the child has talent, there is no better way for it to be demonstrated. The choreography chosen by the child is usually a mixed bag of steps from television or ice shows, but how it is performed and assembled shows the child's potential and guides the teacher in correcting weaknesses.

When the child is eight years of age, it is time to consider a beginner's class, for dance will no longer be play, but must be understood to be the beginning of serious study.

EVALUATING THE FIRST SCHOOL

When the eighth year is reached, the bones are sufficiently ossified for sustained physical work and the ability to concentrate equals the span of a one-hour class. If, in addition, there is an acceptance of discipline over play as a sign of emerging maturity, the child is ready for a dance education. Between the ages of eight and twelve, the basic physical and mental patterns of dance are set. The choice of a school should be made carefully. Even if the child prefers to become a modern or jazz dancer at a later time, two years of previous ballet training will be required.

The choice of a first school should not be made on the basis of personally knowing a teacher, on geographical convenience, or economic or social status, or because of recruiting efforts made by the school's marketing or publicity person.

The best choice is an official school that trains dancers for its professional company—hopefully a successful, flourishing, and acclaimed dance company. Such a school has an obvious success ratio. But if your options do not include a school that has such an affiliation, be sure the director can prove that former students have entered the ABC or XYZ professional company in the past. A suitable reason for choosing a school without a company affiliation would be in knowing that the school's gifted students are passed along at the right time to a school with a company affiliation.

Ask right from the start about the use of a syllabus, a codified method of teaching technique and vocabulary of dance, by the school. In many cases, the syllabus will be described as a combination of several accepted techniques such as French, Russian, England's Royal Academy of Dance, or Cecchetti. American schools tend to mix techniques unlike state-run institutions in other countries. These schools all teach the same technique chosen by tradition as their aesthetic preference. Study in a school that teaches a pure or single method is an advantage in that it provides a strong structure in which stylistic changes may be made as different choreographies demand at a later time in a dancer's career.

Whatever the technique, pure or mixed, the use of a syllabus by the school at this point implies that the school uses a grading system and has a yearly or semiannual measure for the material given in the classroom. Before a child advances to the next level of study, the principles of technique and the vocabulary suitable to each level must be mastered to assure a strong and safe basis for continued study. A school that has a testing schedule, even a test that is a discussion among the teachers about a student instead of a formal demonstration test, is less likely to be a school influenced by parents who insist upon advancement based upon their own evaluation of their child, rather than by the school.

If the school has no syllabus, make sure the classes are given on several levels of instruction. Be sure beginners are not dumped into classes with older children to pick up whatever drops into their awareness. Careful body alignment and personal attention are the cornerstones of the first few years of study. It's a slow, one-to-one, persistent task for the teacher. These early classes must be taught, not merely given.

On your visit to the school under consideration notice the surroundings. Is the classroom clean? Airy? Light? Is the dressing room well-kept? Is there a water fountain or only a soda machine? Is the neighborhood safe for after-school or weekend rehearsals? Check the floor. Is it a good wood floor or linoleum-covered concrete? Is the bathroom in the school or down the hall? Showers, lockers, eating facilities, and boutiques are recent health club extras not necessary to a dance education.

Many schools require a physical entrance examination. There may be two reasons for this: The school may want to teach only the most talented with the fewest physical faults—it's easier—or only those who are born with a configuration in current aesthetic vogue. The best reason for a physical exam should be to detect possible physical faults that would endanger the child and disappoint the child and parents at a later time. A good school will also attempt to keep classes small by selecting the physically suitable in order to maintain good communication between students and teachers. You have only the reputation of the school to make this judgment.

The physical examination is usually in the form of an audition and consists of a few steps to determine musicality and coordination. It is possible to determine if a young child's body will become harmoniously proportioned, is flexible, strong, and if there is easy rotation of the joints, particularly the hip joints. As the examination continues, the ability of the entrant to react to instruction and to remember a sequence of given movements is revealed. It is not unusual for a child at this point to be somewhat knock-kneed, swaybacked, or weak in the ankles and still be accepted into the school if the talent warrants the efforts necessary to correct these faults. But if the condition persists even with good instruction and after the age of ten years, the body is most likely not suitable for dance. But here again, there have been notable exceptions who benefited from corrective therapy and became fine dancers.

If you are in an area where there are no schools with company affiliation, you may be near one of the small, remote schools that have trained winners at major competitions and members of professional companies. Because the school is in a small town or remote area, and if the teaching is good, the school often has a special advantage. The teacher can insist upon daily correct work and teach small classes with greater care. Without large schools nearby to tempt or confuse the students, the training can be thorough. Large cities with many schools frequently have classes too large for careful teaching, mixed levels of instruction, and pupils unwilling to take correction. Talent is provided by the pupil, but the small town teacher in the United States has produced excellent dancers. Again, ask about former pupils entering the professional world before deciding to be the one to create the small school's reputation.

Ask to observe some of the classes. Look at the body alignment of the pupils. All forms of dance require that the placement of the torso be in a nonrigid yet supported position. The pelvis should not be tilted forward arching the lower back, nor should the buttocks be tucked under. The spine should be dropped straight down and the pelvis and stomach held in and up toward the rib cage. (Appendix B provides a list of textbooks with descriptions and photos of the basic principles of ballet which you should review before observing a class.)

As the pupils execute their first exercises at the barre, notice if their ribs protrude during the movements. Are the shoulders raised? Do head and shoulders stoop forward? Are the feet placed firmly on the floor and not rolling inward? Do the knees bend directly over the feet instead of inside the arches? If any of these positions are obvious in the pupil and not corrected by the teacher, do not accept an explanation that the students are just beginners. These faults are very hard to correct at a later time and may be physically damaging. Walk immediately out of the school and do not consider it as suitable.

Notice, as well, if the students are permitted to wear layered clothing instead of tights, leotard, and shoes. Are the students permitted to hide the muscular mechanics of their movements in fashion outfits more suitable to a health club workout than a dance classroom? Adding attractive leg warmers, sweaters, pants, or skirts before or after the class can assist in the warm-up and cool-down periods. But the pupil should not be permitted to hide behind layers of clothing from the corrections the teacher must make. An exception would be to keep an injured area protected and warm. But in a good school, a uniform dress is required and all additional clothing removed when the class begins. If the school is properly heated in winter, it is not uncomfortable to wear just a leotard, tights, and shoes. Air conditioning in the summer is not necessary if there is good ventilation in the room. Schools usually close during the very hot months of July and August.

A recent trend is the false notion that all windows must be closed, thus depriving muscles of the oxygen needed to function properly and efficiently. The perspiring body throws off carbon dioxide—another reason for keeping the windows slightly open even in the coldest weather.

Along with the current fashion for layered clothing in class, many students wear rubberized sweat pants to induce perspiration, thinking they can reduce weight by sweating it off. Unfortunately, the loss will only be in water and the weight regained as soon as the liquid is refilled in the body. The degree to which a school permits its students these trendy additions indicates its level of discipline over the pupils in their human and young desire to try something new and magical to achieve a desired effect.

Another question that should be asked is about the school's policy concerning pointe work. When is the study begun in the school? The child should not be permitted pointe work until she is strong enough, with two or four years of training behind her. No matter how a school may excuse having a very young child on pointe, there is no physical way before the age of eleven, twelve, or thirteen the strongest student can have legs, ankles, and feet ready for pointe shoes. Damage to bone structure and very bad habits in technique can be the result of wearing pointe shoes too soon. The student who is overweight as well should not be given pointe work. Feet must be correctly placed in pointe shoes, aligning with ankles and knees in every movement. Barre exercises are all that should be permitted if the student is ready for pointe work during the first year.

Observe if boys are taught in the same class with girls. Although it is not economically sound for most schools to separate boys and girls until the intermediate level, a separate class for boys from the beginning classes would be an advantage. Even at a young age, the physical and psychological differences should be considered in the teaching of boys. If the school under consideration teaches both boys and girls together at first, a men's class should be added when the boys are twelve or thirteen years of age. At the same age, girls will have a pointe or variation class added to the regular technique classes both will continue to attend as the schedule becomes more demanding. Then the study of partnering (pas de deux classes) may begin. But again, these extra classes depend upon the size of the school and its financial resources. Boys frequently begin the study of dance after the age of twelve when boredom or disinterest in sports leads them to dance. An earlier start, at eight or ten, would be a distinct physical advantage.

Participating in yearly recitals or performances with the affiliated professional company provides joy and release from class discipline and is an invaluable part of the education. Learning to make a commitment to a rehearsal schedule, to cope with performance anxiety, to overcome jealousy, and to face competition are part of the learning process. These trials will make performing and auditioning seem less threatening at a later time in the student's future.

EVALUATING THE TEACHER

Famous dancers seldom make good teachers for beginning students. Later in the training, famous dancers make invaluable coaches. But every retired or still-performing artist who teaches must be willing and able to give up the limelight in the classroom and not set an example, but demand one. A good teacher is not one who requires imitation, but one who has an ability to analyze movement, a knowledge of correct methods of teaching, and who can communicate these principles to the student. The best teacher is one who has been taught to teach, an unfortunate rarity in America. Teacher training courses are given in some countries to dancers who have served twenty years or more onstage in a national company. They are then trained for four years to teach either the first four years of the country's syllabus or the last four years.

There is no guarantee that a famous teacher/artist has trade secrets to pass on. The only secrets are in the mastery of the material and the development of the individual talent at the right time and in the methods that have taken three centuries to perfect in ballet, and that form the basis of modern dance early training.

There is a category of teacher to be avoided—the one who is the center of a personality cult, the "in" teacher followed for a time as the guru of a group until it finds another. These teachers are found mostly in large cities teaching intermediate or advanced levels. Their classes are usually very large and few corrections are given. A personal dependency is cultivated and expected between teacher and pupil. The high cost of studio rental in big cities tempts teachers not to weed out those who should not be in the class because they act unsuitably, or because they only want praise and to be left alone. This kind of pupil would have been asked to leave the studio at one time. But no more. Everyone dances.

When choosing the first school, ask permission to watch a beginner's class. Observe the teacher. Are corrections made in a pleasant and impersonal manner without a scolding or ridiculing tone? Is the pace of the class a slow warm-up, increasing to a quickened pace, then eased down to a gentle ending? Does the teacher demand full attention all the time from each pupil? Are the combinations (class material) repeated a sufficient number of times for the pupils to comprehend? Is there an explanation of the principles involved in the material or does the teacher just expect the pupil to imitate the steps? Does the teacher make personal remarks? Is the teacher so consoling or personally involved that an emotional dependency is created as if he or she were a parent? A teacher may be supportive and respected, but must stimulate independence, individuality, and the desire to master the principles of dance.

THE TURBULENT TURNING POINT

There is a considerable dropout rate among dance students at puberty. The pressures of academics, increasing social interaction, and parental demands make a decision necessary at this point. It might well be the first big trauma for some.

The professional school, if it has an economic structure that permits total honesty, will reevaluate the student at the age of thirteen or fourteen. Many talents simply do not develop beyond this point, no matter how excellent the training or how great the desire to dance.

The school should make it clear that, in their opinion, the child will probably not become a professional dancer and the option to leave or stay should be discussed. These discussions are traumatic for child, parent, and teacher. But the teacher must be totally honest with the parents about their child's chances. There are always exceptions—late bloomers. If the teacher thinks that the talent is there but obscured by temporary emotional disturbances, the child should be given a chance to continue in the class until a more definite decision can be made.

If the child has the makings of a professional dancer, the number of classes will increase per week and the academic structure of the student's life will change. Professional children's schools and secondary arts schools can provide academically accepted courses with as much time for dance as for academics. A scholarship is frequently provided at this time if the tuition becomes prohibitive for the parents and the child clearly shows talent.

Regardless of the parents' reaction, the child is usually the one to be least confused, stunned, or disappointed with the decisions. If there is a desire to dance, the changes in scheduling are welcomed and anticipated with pleasure. If the parents are told the child is not sufficiently talented to warrant further training or hopes for a career, the child has probably known it all along and puts up very little fuss. After all, he or she has been exposed on a regular basis to the obvious talents of the other students and has a personal evaluation based upon daily comparison.

If the parents and child disagree with the teacher, it might be worthwhile to change schools entirely and find a less demanding teacher.

It is the parents whose child is judged to have less than adequate talent who need the most counseling at this turning point. Many react in anger over "lost" years and tuition. Many become angry with the child for not trying hard enough. Most will not believe that a child who was considered talented enough to be chosen for a school and who has worked hard is no longer talented as a teenager. Some blame bias on the part of the teacher or the school, not realizing that every school and every teacher wants talented pupils to prove their reputation. The decision in the end should be made mutually and lovingly between parents and child and the student given uncritical support. Not an easy task. There is no need to sacrifice academic studies at this point even though some professional schools permit it. It is not a wise move because the student needs the interaction of peers from the academic structure for emotional growth as well as the opportunity to develop other interests. Some of the student's time should be set aside to include other arts, music, drama, and visual arts. There will be worthwhile benefits in cramming the daily schedule at this point without applying pressure or taking shortcuts.

If there is still some doubt about a decision to continue, it would be a good idea for the child to enroll in one of the many summer school courses offered throughout the country. Summer courses of six or eight weeks attract students the world over and provide an opportunity for well-known teachers to give classes to new students in new environments. Without academic pressures of the school year, students study with more freedom, and exchange ideas with dancers other than their regular class friends. Eventually they find a new basis for self-evaluation.

Summer courses give a taste of life away from home in safe and worthwhile programs. Search committees comb the country for students to sponsor. Check trade papers and magazines for listings of auditions for summer scholarships and competitions.

Part of the self-evaluation will be in seeing others with different training. There will be a temptation to consider fast turns, high extensions, or wild jumping about as desirable traits. The student may find tricks, affectations, and bad taste attractive. The good teacher will quickly put these attempts at gaining attention into perspective and the course will have added value in providing the first judgments in taste and style.

If the student stays in the first school, there will be a change of teachers in the new classes to experts in teaching intermediate levels of dance. As earlier, the teacher's comments should be impersonal, directed to the appropriate individual student, and not mimick the sensitive adolescent. Respect for the emerging individual must be kept. The student may not like the teacher personally. That is unimportant. It is only important to take good teaching personally. It is not uncommon for an adolescent to feel a sexual attraction for the teacher of the opposite sex. The attraction must be thoroughly discouraged by the teacher. A teacher who is abusive and intimidating should be reported to the school head. Parental visits to classes when permitted should not be abandoned. It is still the best way to observe the interaction of the class and the progress of the pupil.

The intermediate student develops a curiosity about other schools and teachers in order to test his or her own talent. In large cities, this can lead to studio hopping like supermarket shoppers searching for a bargain. If the student leaves the regular school to indulge in a search for the trendy or the "best" teacher, the serious training is pretty well at an end. The value in continuing with one school is advancing within a syllabus to the finishing level. There is no syllabic progression in hopping from studio to studio and permitting the student to become his own adviser and teacher.

Some young dancers move from famous school to famous school, from well-known teacher to well-known teacher, learning little. They have the mistaken belief that impressive names on a résumé will reflect their dedication and worth. Although an extensive education looks good in press material, the real test is not where a student has studied but what he or she can do at an audition to show the thoroughness of the training and the talent.

Auditions are the next challenge for the young student as he or she approaches the late teens. If the student has remained in the first affiliated school, the graduating performance becomes the audition for the company. The artistic director of the company usually makes his choice of new members long before that moment, but a performance reveals what the classroom cannot—the dancer's ability to communicate with an audience. The artistic director is very often the director of the school as well, and knows the enrolled students for several years—their personality, technical ability, and suitability to the company's repertoire.

Competitions throughout the country offer prize money to young students to continue their study. These are listed in trade papers and magazines with the conditions, times, and prizes. Look for competitions that are held by professional organizations such as the Dance Masters of America or the Dance Educators of America. The conditions should be suitable and the judges qualified. The student may need permission from the school or teacher to enter a contest. And it would be wise to observe the competition a year before entering in order to determine whether it presents sufficient challenge and whether winning an award from the organization gives prestige. The best schools offer scholarships if there are financial problems. Be honest with the school in this matter. All will be held in confidence. Scholarships should be given because of talent and financial difficulties, not expected to indicate talent alone and therefore entitlement to the school's support.

International competitions require the performance of variations from the classical repertoire, a new piece of choreography under one minute's duration, costumes, music tapes, travel expenses for the student, a parent, and/or teacher or coach. Entrants often think competitions will bring them fame and fortune or, at least, a job. Occasionally, a director will agree to an apprenticeship for a competition entrant, but the competition showcase is not as comprehensive an audition as most directors prefer. A professional dancer is very often given roles on the basis of a performance seen by a choreographer or director. But that dancer has probably passed so many auditions, another audition is unnecessary and the director has seen enough to be convinced of the dancer's suitability for his or her needs. The young student is not at that stage and should not become depressed or too disappointed if no job or award is the result of entering any competition, large or small.

After the dancer finishes academic studies, and if that dancer has not performed professionally, passed auditions, or is waiting for an opening in a specific company, the decision of whether or not to go to college may be presented. There may be good reasons to compromise a career for a college education. Although modern and jazz dancers may have a career after college, it is too late for the ballet dancer because of lost stamina and the lost apprenticeship years most companies provide before membership.

The student who wants to go to college, however, may be more interested in choreography or other disciplines such as physical therapy, notation, or arts administration as taught in the universities and colleges. The training years are well spent as a basis for these studies and there are some performance opportunities in colleges as dance majors, or in affiliated companies.

The young dancer taken into apprenticeship or as a member of a company will find psychological differences between himself and herself and nondancing friends much as was found in the adolescent years. While other adolescents were going to parties, games, and weekends, the dancer was meeting a rehearsal schedule that deprived her or him of social interaction. A young dancer may appear to be amazingly mature when interpreting roles onstage, but be withdrawn, shy, and undemonstrative offstage. A lack of emotional maturity based upon a lack of social interchange may be corrected at a later time.

Finding friends of the opposite sex can be a problem unless the dancer finds others committed to an art, sports, or other time-consuming effort. Although our society is very permissive in presenting sexual implications in advertising and television, and the very young discuss their popularity and sexual confrontations freely, being part of a popular and sexually aware group is not necessarily a valid pursuit for any young person. Interaction and emotional growth can be postponed until a later time when there is less need to devote all one's time to study and when friends are mature enough to appreciate a life-style different from their own. Travel and the frequent changes in jobs experienced by dancers will bring new friends and experiences. There will be time for emotional growth to catch up. Then again, some dancers do not seem to suffer too greatly and manage to grow up on a heavy schedule with interaction on a healthy and sustained level with the opposite sex despite rehearsal and performance schedules.

Each person must settle for a different balance of work, play, and study. Balance is the key. Overuse of the body can be harmful if fatigue or dangerous conditions are present such as poor performing surfaces and too many strenuous performances. Too much concentration on academics can be stimulating but instill a desire to please too many masters. In general, the student with a balanced program will do well in all aspects of life, but that balance has to be self-regulated and flexible.

Whatever the cost for those crucial years of training, it will pay off well in a career. The result will be freedom and joy in performing, safety, and a long career. Wherever the talent leads, if the structure is sound, ambitions can be reached and challenges met on a firm basis.

TUITION COSTS
In East Coast Areas

For beginners in company-affiliated school: $525 for two weekly lessons of one hour each, October to June.

For intermediates: $845 for four lessons weekly of 1½ hours.

For advanced students: $1035 for eight lessons of 1½ hours.

In nonaffiliated schools cost per class ranges from $6.50 to $8.00 with number of classes a personal choice.

Summer sessions, six weeks, cost approximately the same as regular school year.

Cost of accommodations in New York City about $150 per week in approved homes. Some sessions are in nearby college and university sites with dormitory accommodations at far lower cost. Food not included. Total cost for academics, tuition in professional school, food, clothes: $12,000 per year.

In West Coast Areas

For preballet five- to seven-year-olds in affiliated school: $80 for six weekly classes, one quarter of the school year.

For beginners: $85 for weekly classes, one quarter of the school year.

For advanced students: eight classes weekly, $600 per one quarter of the school year.

In Southwest Areas

All costs slightly less

Every school, affiliated or nonaffiliated, has a requirement for the number of classes per week necessary to achieve a specific level of accomplishment. In nonaffiliated schools the age of the student is not a factor in placing the student on a beginning level. Scholarships are available in most schools on almost every level. Professional dancers may study daily in a school of their choice or in the classes given to members of the company affiliated with the school at "professional rates" or no cost.

CLOTHING FOR CLASSES

Basic cotton leotard: $10.50 in color school level requires (two minimum)

Fashion leotards may cost up to $38 (permitted in nonaffiliated schools)

Tights: $7 to $21 depending upon size (three)

Shoes: ballet $14.50 to $28 (two per year)

Pointe shoes: $29 (American); $40 (imported)—three pairs per year

Leg warmers, sweaters, and socks may be hand-knitted or purchased at various prices.

2

Auditioning

Auditioning is part of a performer's life. From the first examination to gain entrance into a dance school, through trials for scholarships, competitions, and contests, and throughout a career for new roles or new companies, the performer—beginner or famous star—faces a seemingly endless round of auditions.

Auditions always bring a degree of anxiety, but if the performer knows what to expect, auditions can become more than a learning experience—they can be stimulating and enjoyable, even if you don't win the goal. The important thing to remember about auditioning is that the more you audition, the more skillful you become and that winning or losing an audition does not mean the beginning or the end of your career. Auditioners can be wrong in their decisions.

Auditions are necessary. No matter how well you perform in class, no matter how well you are known for your work onstage, no matter what your level of accomplishment, there is a time when decisions have to be made by producers or directors to fill a role that is *in harmony* with the rest of the company, cast, or production.

Union rules (AGMA, the acronym for American Guild of Musical Artists, and other unions) require that union members as well as nonmembers be permitted to audition for professional work in order to restrict unfair competition. This kind of audition is called an "open" call and is advertised in trade papers and magazines.

All-important is your attitude toward auditions. If you assume that auditions are only a formality, that the choices are predetermined, that you have to be a great beauty, good at playing politics, or "know the right people," you have a negative attitude that will be hard to overcome. While all those unfair conditions do exist in some audition situations, the audition itself is still the moment of truth.

The important questions to ask yourself are: (1) Do I really *want* to audition for this goal? (2) *Why* do I want this goal? (3) Am I *prepared* to audition?

If your school has had regular examinations for grading purposes, you know that trials are a test for advancement and that they indicate your level of accomplishment. These tests get harder each year, but if your concentration and efforts have been good between tests, you know that there is less to fear from the exam. Auditions work the same way. After the easy ones, the harder ones are easier.

If your first audition is for a scholarship to begin or continue your dance education, your auditioners will expect you to show an eagerness to learn, good potential, and a sense of responsibility toward that scholarship. A scholarship is not given for talent alone but for financial need as well. Many students feel entitled to a scholarship because they are talented. The cost of tuition for the school or group presenting the scholarship is involved, and is the basic reason for the privilege of study—it is not solely an award of merit. If you are talented but have no financial need for tuition, don't be disappointed in not receiving a scholarship.

Some school scholarships are short-term and involve studio maintenance. Get a clear answer on the extent of your scholarship and the responsibilities involved. It doesn't help your self-esteem to be given tuition-free classes because you are good at desk work, cleaning mirrors, or washing the floors.

The bottom line for every audition, test, or examination is in your answer to the question *Why do I want to audition?* Are you auditioning because you are expected to do so by your family, friends, teacher, or classmates? If you can't see yourself in the role for which you are auditioning, don't take the audition. If you need just a bit of coaxing, ask your teacher for advice. He or she is in a better position to evaluate your prospects than anyone else. Not wanting to let down the people who have been instrumental in your training when you don't want to go to an adution is a heavy load to carry with you. Have a talk with the person or persons involved in your feelings. It may be just too soon for you to feel confident in a test against others. Then again, maybe those persons don't really want you to do anything you are not comfortable doing.

REAL AUDITIONS

While tests for grading and scholarships involve overall performance, real auditions are for auditioners who have never seen you perform and who know nothing about you—not even, in some cases, your name.

In order to become prepared for this kind of audition you have to check the source of your audition information.

You are auditioning for a reasonably secure job if your information about the audition came from trade papers such as *Variety, Show Business, Hollywood Drama Logue, Dance Pages, Backstage,* or *Dance Magazine,* or if a notice was posted on your studio billboard. Established companies are listed frequently in these outlets. If a company is new, you can check its solvency by calling a union, where a bond must be posted before auditions begin.

Although there is far less chicanery in the management of theatrical productions than in the past, there are still nonagreement, nonunion, and poorly financed speculations on every level of production. Even with sufficient backing, a large production may cancel a run during tryouts and dance companies full of recognized talents can fail. We also know that small, low-budget groups often perform successfully for years. Size is not a factor in longevity.

Lured by the possibility of traveling to exotic places or just another town, many dancers have found themselves stranded—victims of nonunion contracts and unfulfilled promises. No matter what assurance you have from a producer, a return ticket home and your passport kept firmly in your own hands are your best protection. If you have any doubts, call the appropriate union and ask these questions:

- Has the producer posted a bond with the union for the protection of the performers?
- Does the producer have a good reputation or has he or she been placed on a "bad faith" list?

Even if you have been informed that the producer is reliable and has posted a bond with the union, be sure your contract includes specific payment for rehearsals and a per diem for hotel expenses and food. Don't accept a promise that you will be paid on a "we'll-see-what's-left" basis. Nothing is often left for the performers. You don't need experience or a job so badly that you need risk your safety and well-being.

Always make sure that auditions are held in a theater or studio with several people around. If you are the only one to audition, suggest your auditioner watch your class. You can always get a few moments afterward in the studio to perform whatever your auditioner feels was not included in your classwork for a specific role.

If the production for which you are auditioning meets minimum standards of acceptability, research is your next step. If the choreographer for whom you are auditioning creates for his own company or has created works for other companies, your local library or newspaper office may have reviews of his work. Even better would be to locate a videotape of his or her work in the Dance Collection of the New York Public Library at Lincoln Center in New York City. If you are not near that viewing source, write or call them for copies of the reviews. If you are not suited to the choreographer's requirements, don't go to the audition.

While doing research, you might discover other choreographers for whom you would like to audition in the future. Write them asking to be notified when vacancies occur. When their company comes to your town, you may be permitted to audition. If a company you like visits your town, go backstage and ask if you may be permitted to audition or take a company class. Whatever the outcome, it will be a valuable experience.

Read the notice of the audition carefully. Don't be early or late. Auditions run on a schedule even when they seem endless. Be sure to bring pointe shoes, tap shoes, sheet music, and a photo or résumé if the notice asked for those items. Don't be encumbered by your pet, your mother, your Walkman, or your best friend, or wear expensive fashion items such as jewelry.

Did the notice for the audition tell you to mail a photo and résumé ahead of time? The photo should be in simple practice clothes in a simple pose with unexaggerated makeup, a head shot, and, if you want to include modeling in your future, a fashion shot in casual clothes. The photo should be a composite 8 × 10 glossy print that *does not have to be returned.*

The résumé should recount your performances no matter when or where, and give your dance school background (famous names will not help you at the audition), your academic schooling, your honest height, weight, and a brief physical description. If you are to hear from the producers by mail, you might include a self-addressed stamped envelope to speed an answer and as a courtesy.

Between the time you go to the audition and send in your information, or until the date of the call, there are some things to do:

- Maintain daily class schedules with the following things in mind: Check how quickly you comprehend new material, how quickly you make corrections, how well you take directions. All those things will be important for you to do quickly at an audition.
- While working on technical elements check your musicality, your comprehension of the characterization of the given material, the ease and artistry or individuality you bring to your work. You will find these qualities more important than the level of your technique.
- Retain your stamina by not going on a strict reducing diet

and by maintaining a good sleep schedule untroubled by worry over the audition. Your career does not depend upon one audition, one role, or one company no matter how important it seems at the moment.

THE BALLET COMPANY AUDITION

The audition for a ballet company trainee or company position usually takes class form: barre, centerwork, combinations, and diagonal crossings.

Many large companies hold auditions in several cities before making a decision.

The Dance Theatre of Harlem offers this advice: "Rehearsal clothes must be neat, clean, in two pieces, with no leg warmers or outlandishness. No pushy behavior will help you."

You can tell by that advice that the atmosphere at auditions is businesslike, impersonal, and that the proceedings move along at a good clip.

"I want to see the dancer through the combination," many choreogaphers say. They feel they are buying a commodity—a person, to be sure, but onstage a commodity that must have audience appeal.

For the most part, the barre will be a good warm-up. Correct placement is an important factor with clean and exact execution of each exercise. Coordination of the arms and head, and a sense of finish in each movement without indulgence, are the mark of a well-trained dancer.

"Basically," the Cleveland Ballet tells us, "we look for a strong, clear technique. One that is not fussy. It should be without mannerisms like an arm in second position, for instance, that flails about, dissipating the energy and making it difficult to see if the dancer has a sense of line. Musicality is a must. But the biggest fault is in the auditionee's not doing what is asked. For example, if an écarté or croisé position is asked, there is that moment of hesitation that tells us there has been a lack of schooling and a lot of imitating going on

AUDITION PLAN OF ACTION

1. Make sure your source of information concerning an audition is reliable.

2. Send résumé and photo if required with self-addressed envelope for confirmation of your acceptability.

3. Continue your classes with special attention to quick comprehension of the class material.

4. Choose a becoming, neat outfit and hairdo for your audition.

5. Get plenty of regular sleep and eat wisely before going to the call.

6. Pack your things in one inexpensive bag, and keep everything together at the audition.

7. Be courteous, attentive, cheerful, adaptable, and willing to talk to your directors.

8. If called back, wear the same outfit and hairdo, and assume your first-day attitude of enthusiasm and energetic cooperativeness.

9. No matter what the decision, remain courteous and outgoing.

10. If possible, ask why you were eliminated, if that happens.

11. Regard your audition as a learning experience and go over in your mind where you could have done a better audition.

12. If you are asked to come to rehearsals, remember there are still three days in every contract during which you may be dismissed. Keep up your best efforts.

---

in classwork, and that the dancer does not know *how* to dance, but just dances."

Centerwork requires stability for all extensions. Balance in turns and especially in final poses is important. Many dancers are eliminated in auditions not because there are a limited number of jobs, but because there are a limited number of dedicated dancers. Many young people dance because of its current popularity without realizing it is more than technique. There must be talent present in order to communicate, intelligence, a desire to express oneself in dance, and a special quality that makes a dancer fascinating to watch.

While class is not exactly the time to go around expressing yourself, in a way, the advanced classes are a time when you must have the *quality* of your work in prominent view. That may be a lyrical, dramatic, cool, or highly energetic quality—but it must be there or you will bring only your schooling to the audition.

Sometimes sheer fear hides the quality or the pose of indifference is adopted as a protective stance. It won't get you a job. Don't wear a mask; be yourself. Show that you like to dance and don't be indifferent. Take corrections and make changes immediately and with good humor. Don't act out your personal feelings about the director or the audition. They are there to judge you. If you have trouble understanding the combinations, look at the overall exercise. Get the basic counts, then fill in the details. Keep going and doing the exercise until it gets better and better each time. Of course, this means that you must be courteous, stay in the place given you by the director or dance captain, and learn the combinations without talking about it or asking questions. It's a silent art. You learn through your eyes and ears. There is no time during union rehearsal time to talk movements no matter what your favorite teacher or choreographer may have told you.

If you are rejected, respond with a courteous acceptance and leave with a "thank you." When you are dressed to leave, and if the audition is over, you might ask why you were eliminated. Very often you will be given good reasons that will help you in your next call. Don't come to your own conclusions. Thinking you were "too fat," "too tall," "not tall enough," or "the wrong type" may be entirely wrong. Consider the opportunity to get good criticism valuable and accept it without argument even if you disagree.

THE MODERN DANCE COMPANY AUDITION

Unlike ballet company auditions, the modern dance company auditioner will tell you exactly what qualities are expected in the movements. In some cases, ballet steps will be required. If you have done your research, you will know the general style of the company/choreographer: classic, contemporary, or avant-garde. You will know too if your outfit should be simple or trendy.

In some cases, the way into a company is through the official school of the group, but there are open auditions held by large modern groups throughout the country.

You may expect a barre of sorts, or a warm-up series of exercises, centerwork, crossings, and improvisations. Listen carefully for the shading that should be involved in the movement as well as observing the physical shape and rhythm of the given material. Ask yourself: What is the approach, thrust, breadth, or concept of the movement? Should it have energy? Is it an intellectual approach? Balletic? Lyrical? Humorous? If you have any doubt, ask. The modern audition needs an explanation. Respond immediately to the directions and without personal mannerisms. The auditioners want to see if you can do their work, not if they like yours.

West Coast choreographer Bella Lewitsky tells what she seeks in a dancer: "I look for someone who will blend in strength, speed, flexibility, and good jumping technique with my other dancers. If the dancer comes to my audition overweight, I know that is the least she is ever going to weigh. If he or she is in disarray in clothing, he or she can't get it together and, right off, that is not fair to my other dancers. If I think the dancer, after an interview, is emotionally unstable, going to injure herself by incorrect work habits, I do not accept that dancer. That also is unfair to the others."

If you are called back at any audition, be sure to wear the same clothing and the same hairdo. Bring the same enthusiasm and alertness. If you are not called back but did your best, remember that many famous dancers have stories about being called at a later time "out of the blue" because they were remembered.

Paul Taylor, founder-director of The Paul Taylor Dance Company, adds another element to his final decisions on a dancer: "I look at the eyes. Provided the dancer has all the qualifications for the job, the thing that determines it for me is the look in the eyes. The question in my mind is: 'Can I live with this person through rehearsals, performances, tours?' I've never worked with a mean person. I watch during auditions to see if there is an 'excuse me' when one dancer bumps into another. If there isn't, that person is too competitive and I don't want that. We work together."

THE MUSICAL THEATER AUDITION

Many dancers who try out for musical theater auditions are insufficiently schooled in a number of styles to fuel a long career. It is possible to be the right type, at the right time, at the right call, and succeed in getting a job in musical theater. But unless your training has included serious work in drama and singing, your dancing ability will not see you through a very long career. The capacity to perform in several styles suitable to the many revivals musical theater shows enjoy will enhance your usefulness, enlarge your scope of work, and extend your career.

Here, again, what you wear and how you present yourself are all-important. This call will be a longer test in time than the ballet or modern dance audition. You may be required to return two or three times in lineups to see how you measure up in size and type with others who have successfully passed the previous auditions. These call-back lineups may be on successive days so be sure to get plenty of sleep. No use staying up worrying about your audition the next day; you have to look fresh and rested to cope with the next day's challenges. Be sure, as well, to eat a good meal several hours before you arrive—it may be a long day. Find a place for a warm-up since you will not be given a barre for this audition.

Joe Tremaine, in the Professional Dancers Society newsletter *The Gypsy Chorus,* gives this advice: "Dress tastefully, don't overdress, and always wear something very identifiable. For the girls, a simple French-cut leotard, tights, and danceable heels. For the men, jazz pants, jazz shoes, T-shirts. Never wear 'garbage' to an audition— sweat pants, plastic pants, parachute pants, etc. Do not hide your body. Be honest and show it all as it is."

Need glasses to see the choreographer's demonstration? Twist several rubber bands around the end of each ear rest. Glasses won't move when you do. Keep your purse, belongings, and a piece of fruit or a water drink all in one large bag, and underdress—it will save time and be easier than dressing in a crowded room. Above all, don't pop a pill to get yourself "up" or "down." You need your wits about you and your body will supply extra adrenaline as needed. If an audition is that hard on your emotions, you are not ready for the audition.

At an audition for a musical or jazz show, you are likely to find several producers, a director or two, a choreographer, and a dance captain as well as a pianist ready to watch you. That means someone has an eye on you at all times, so don't talk unnecessarily after you've been given a number or place by the stage manager. Be friendly, but don't gossip. Don't make remarks about the material, dancers, or the directors. Above all, don't offer excuses about feeling poorly or having an injury. If you begin to feel panicky, take a few deep breaths.

Keep looking confident during the repetitions of the material even if you feel you are doing badly. Keep doing what you are asked, not what you think you do best.

Be prepared for the unexpected—being asked to sing or read a scene. Request a moment to read over the script to yourself, then ask for direction on the reading. If you don't get advice, use common sense and take your time with the lines, making them loud enough to be heard and clear enough to be understood.

Gwen Verdon has advice on preparing a song for an audition: "Choose an upbeat song and know the key signature for the accompanist. Don't act like you're trying to sell a hot Oriental rug . . . don't subvert yourself and be apologetic. Just go for it. Sing it fast, then sing it slowly. Most of all, be open and just do it."

Another unexpected part of the audition may be a talk with a choreographer. Marvin Gordon, director/choreographer of musicals and fashion shows, says this: "When it comes to a final decision at an industrial show, for instance, I have a conversation with the dancer. I want them to look at me, to come down to the front of the stage where we can meet on a one-to-one basis. I want open, honest answers. The questions are innocuous, but the answers tell me if the dancer is intelligent but not a smartie, has charm but is not cutsie, has a sense of humor, is 'together' and professional."

CONTESTS AND COMPETITIONS

The contest and competition is an audition in a sense, since it awards a monetary prize instead of a role; it has judges—several; and although many times it is held before an audience, the material is performed in competition with others doing the same thing.

If the contest requires a solo number arranged by your teacher or another choreographer, the same rules apply as for the audition. Give it your all, cheerfully, completely, with confidence and as much ease as you can muster. While you may not win anything in a contest, the event is a good showcase and gives you performance experience.

The competitions, national and international, are another matter since they go on for three or more days, require tremendous stamina, and are open to the public. All the questions about why you are entering the competition and to what extent you are prepared apply here twofold. The scope of your talent must be wider, your desire to compete and excel stronger, and your stamina and individuality closer to that of a soloist than a corps member of a company.

If you compete in another country, remember relaxing and resting are important. Take your support with you, at least one person you trust, coach or teacher, preferably not a parent. The choice of your entrance variation and your "free" variation (a classical solo from one of the masterpieces of ballet repertoire and a solo of about ninety seconds created for you with a more contemporary vocabulary) should be chosen carefully. The investment in a coach, music, costume, and travel to one of these competitions *begins* at $3000. The gain is a year's free tuition in a major school attached to a company (Prix de Lausanne), winning recognition for your company (you may already be a member in the sixteen-to-nineteen age bracket required by the competition rules), or you may want to gain soloist stature for yourself in another company. Remember, with the exception of the Prix de Lausanne, which gives awards for further schooling, most competitions are highly political.

The competition begins with a class, judged by several jurors from various countries, and is given on high professional standards. Age of the contestants is not considered here. Individuality is highly considered as are appearance, musicality, stage presence, capacity to do more than one kind of dance, stamina, and training. Few Americans have won international competitions. One of the reasons is that few have entered, preferring to try for one of the national companies that provide secure and challenging work. Another is that American training is less traditional than that of European and even Oriental dancers and the competitions require passing that mark before going on to contemporary work.

The second, or "free," variation is usually the downfall of contestants who pass the classes, given variations or other material taught at the site, and perform their classical work well enough to proceed to the semifinals. The second variation should be choreographed by a recognized name if possible, not by a teacher, and above all, it should not be an abstract work of pure movement. Most of the contestants are too young and too inexperienced to handle this kind of work. And the costume, another dangerous item in the second variation section, should be kept very simple. Feathers, capes, flowing drapes, or props are fine in performances, but when the work must be repeated again and again, they become the worse for wear.

You will be surrounded at contests and competitions with people who may give you misinformation of what is going on. Know what is expected of you and leave all gossip in the dressing room. Block out as many distractions as you can and stay focused on your task. There will be fear, hysterics or laughing jags, jealousy, and even hostility in these highly charged emotional situations that everyone takes too seriously. It is mostly a result of fatigue and tension, but you must keep your mind on performing well, not judging yourself or letting others except the judges evaluate you. Use your support system to tell you when you should get rest, food, or practice a bit more. Let everyone see what you can do in a courteous, joyful, and confident manner.

If you are eliminated, judges in this kind of contest will tell you where your training is lacking or if your variations suited your style.

If you reach the semifinals, don't overplay the audience or your role, as the last few trials are open to ticket holders. Don't let them distract your concentration—it's still a contest—but enjoy performing. That's infectious even to judges. If you make a mistake, go on; it's possible that no one noticed.

Winning or losing a contest, audition, or competition is just a way of evaluating where you are now, at this moment in time and at your level of accomplishment. It is no guarantee of future roles, success, or imminent failure. Many times a dancer with everything to offer technically will fail audition after audition. Usually it's because they have not reached that point of emotional maturity where they are willing to risk their inner self and perform as an individual. Their technique is a shield against rejection or judgment by others. But this kind of dancer is a bore to watch, and the dancer does not understand the role of dance as an art form, which is to communicate to others. The nod to tradition we all make is not to preserve stuffy, passé, and outmoded roles but to infuse them with newness, freshness, and energy, so that they may live as universal statements understood by us all. Auditions, like everything else, require practice. Keep taking them until they are less anxiety-causing, until they are profitable for you, and until they are fun.

3

Reactions to Stress in the Student

Young dancers experience the usual stress and anxiety of growing up while preparing themselves for a career at the same time. Like most youngsters who want to excel in what they choose to do in the future, they have self-doubts and fears about meeting the standards placed upon them to achieve their ambitions.

Along with a good education in academics and dance, young dancers need encouragement, love, and nurturing, and should be urged to communicate their feelings. They express themselves in dance—their silent art—but need to express their problems and find answers to their doubts. Unfortunately, feelings are not easy to define or express at an early age, and parents, relatives, and friends may not have the most healthy, safe, or mature advice to give.

Yet, how we relate to ourselves, our family, our friends and lovers, our work, community, the world, and our spiritual belief will determine our progress and happiness throughout our lives.

Many of our reactions to stress are inherited or are part of the conditioning of our society. But the more we examine our reactions and our relationships, the more we become aware of our own contribution to our progress and well-being, and the more we are able to employ different choices and solutions.

The signals that indicate stress and anxiety may be the same throughout our lives. They become familiar to us and manifest in symptoms and behavior patterns that represent conflict. Stress and anxiety in our lives are normal. They trigger a hormonal reaction that provokes our basic "flight or fight" reactions alerting us to danger. The chemical reaction influences the heart, nervous system, muscles, and other organs. Symptoms of anxiety are butterflies in the stomach, dizziness, headache, nausea, shortness of breath, excessive perspiration, weakness, spasms, or trembling muscles. One or more of these symptoms may be experienced in any situation you find stressful—for instance, when meeting new people, going onstage before a large or special audience, or before an important audition.

The symptoms of anxiety are a very positive force alerting us to danger, the possibility of failure, embarrassment, rejection, or being evaluated in a negative way. Without some stress, life would be boring, stagnant, and without challenges. Stress in itself is not bad. It's the way we react to it that matters.

A performance of any kind usually arouses some form of stress symptom before or after the appearance onstage. No matter how experienced, how "cool" the performer may seem, or how unimportant the occasion, anxiety in the form of nervousness, slight or excessive, is to be expected.

Many dancers who are expressive and interesting in class become rigid onstage. They might be feeling understandably nervous because of having to do a role beyond their known capacity, because of insufficient rehearsals, or because of poor stamina. That kind of performance anxiety can be controlled eventually. But if the nervousness reaches panic proportions inhibiting the performer in reaching his or her goal, it is time for professional help.

STAGE FRIGHT

Stagework requires role playing, something we do in everyday life. The performer, however, must have dissimilar roles available and be able to assume a number of them at will and on a regular basis. Beneath the role being played, the performer must control his personal feelings while remaining watchful and ready to correct any mishap in his own performance or that of another performer.

According to Donald F. Klein, M.D., of New York's Columbia Presbyterian Medical Center, " 'Classroom' dancers who are so self-concerned they are unable to use their talent and technique to perform onstage should face two possibilities: They are in an overall anxious state that requires help or they are simply unequal to the task of performing in public.

"The profile of this person would be of a capable, meticulous, and conscientious individual who is probably afraid of not living up to a self-set standard. That person would be hypercritical, prone to dwelling on real or imagined slips or errors instead of the good aspects of his or her performance. This person would be fearful of an unpremeditated impulse that would indicate a loss of control. He or she would be inordinately sensitive to disapproval.

"Psychiatrically speaking," Klein continues, "those who lose role distance easily—distance between themselves and the roles they are playing onstage or in everyday life—are very suggestible and histrionic. They are constantly throwing themselves into one act or another. That doesn't mean they are emotionally unstable. Suggestibility as a description means that the suggestion that they are clever with their hands, for instance, will result in their doing things with their hands they may have never tried to do before the suggestion was made. Those who lose role distance easily are the best performers. They can shut out the audience without difficulty.

This may be a learned technique or a natural bent. It's still a subject for study."

In the Performing Arts Center for Health (PACH) clinic headed by Judith R.F. Kupersmith, M.D. at NYU-Bellevue Hospital in New York City, actor/patients have a tendency to role play even during therapy sessions, thus distancing themselves from real feelings and the therapist.

Some performers totter on the brink of losing themselves to a role and become unable to determine the real from the unreal onstage. Others can "become" a role and be considered exceptionally gifted yet a normal person offstage. Many therapists feel that the talent of a disturbed person is a "safety valve" as long as the talent is able to function. Others feel that the disturbance is a precondition of talent.

"The cause of anxiety—situational, social, or performance— may be trauma," explains Klein, "based upon the usual theory that it has something to do with the way a person is raised. People who are afraid of being independent, as an example, are people who have had too much independence demanded of them. These people may never have learned *how* to be independent, which is the cause of the conflict."

Whatever the cause of the conflict, "My impression," Klein sums up, "is that avoiding things that frighten you is a sure way to get into bad habits. There is no substitute for the situation you have to face. There may be a tremendous relief in walking away, but that is only temporary. The incubation period away from the situation will just make it harder and harder to return. Unless we try our limits, we may never know if we are facing ghosts or real danger. Most of us prefer to avoid the test of our limits, but that way, we can never reach our full capacity."

EMPTY SOLUTIONS: DRUG ABUSE—THE STUDENT

While winning importance and recognition in our cultural life, while gaining larger audiences, better training, public funding, more opportunities to dance, and more income, dancers have at the same time been subjected to increasing amounts of physical and psychological stress.

The student, the professional performer, and the injured or retiring performer each have specific areas of stress. The young student is concerned about competition, auditions, physical appearance, discipline, friendships, the transition from junior high to high school, not "hanging out" with others, family, earning a living, the possibility of being homosexual, loneliness, sisters, and brothers.

Although dancers in the past have had stressful conditions (political unrest, poverty, poor training, lack of social acceptance), today's dancer, now in the mainstream of society, has been affected by three current conditions to regard the use of drugs as a solution to stress: availability, media indoctrination, and social acceptability.

The availability of drugs for instant solutions to fatigue, pain, and depression or for "fun"; the environment created by the media for an over-the-counter drug culture; and the social acceptability of using drugs in a society that overlooks or condones popping pills have burdened every age group.

No one ever intends to abuse the use of a drug. Everyone believes drug use is only temporary and can be stopped at any time. Unfortunately, athletes and dancers have become addicted to hard and soft drug abuse as a solution to stress.

The following are typical arguments given by young dance students to justify their drug use:

"My mother gave me some of her diet pills to help me keep my weight down. She says it's all 'baby fat' and will disappear. If it's okay for her to take them, it's okay for me."

It is never advisable for anyone to take any medication prescribed for another, even if purchased over the counter without a prescription. Since weight watching will always be part of a dancer's life, it would be wiser for young dancers to learn the rudiments of good nutrition and moderation. Amphetamines, originally used for weight reduction, narcolepsy (a condition characterized by brief attacks of deep sleep), or brain damage in children, have been overprescribed for obesity.

"There's a lot of competition out there and I don't know if I'm going to make it. If I don't make it by the time I'm sixteen, I've had it. So there's no harm in taking a 'toke' once in a while just before class to keep up my energy and my spirits."

The use of marijuana—"toke" in street talk—is still considered healthful by some since it is legalized in several states for treatment of terminal cancer patients. Marijuana grown today is no less than ten times stronger than what was available during its earlier prevalent use in the 60s. Some dancers mistake increased sharpness of vision, sound, and touch with energy. Actually, impairment of memory and the ability to think is the source of this "up."

Unlike alcohol, which is quickly excreted by the body, one month after smoking just one marijuana "toke," 20 percent of its active ingredient, THC, is still in the body in active form. It takes five to eight days for just half of the THC from a single "joint" to be eliminated.

"I get a terrific craving for sweets and I just have to have something. I work it all off, so my body must need that soda, or a cup of coffee, or a few chocolate bars."

Chances are, the craving is less for the sugar in cola drinks and chocolate than for the caffeine. The cocoa plant that produces chocolate is not the same plant that produces cocaine. Caffeine, which creates an emotional dependence, excites the cerebral cortex of the brain and *will* be worked off. One twelve-ounce cola drink contains two thirds the amount of caffeine in one cup of coffee. Tea contains slightly less caffeine, and cocoa contains as much as colas. Moderation in the use of caffeine is advised since this drug has some useful temporary benefits.

"My family, my relatives, and my friends give me a hard time about dancing. I hate baseball and sports, so I like to get away from it all by myself and snort. It makes me feel big for a little while and it only lasts a few minutes and doesn't cost much. It can't be harmful because I've been doing it for year."

This dancer is experimenting in the most dangerous category of this age group. Whether sniffing gasoline, glue, paint, or lighter fluid, the danger of seeking new highs may tempt him to try any of the

LSD or PCP drugs. Feeling "big" is based upon the euphoria caused by the scramble of internal stimuli and impaired perception that snorting can bring. PCP is a leading cause of psychiatric admission.

"I don't think my legs are long enough for me to be a dancer. I don't think I'll grow because my family is short and I'm just not the right physical style right now. It makes me feel helpless and nervous, so I calm myself down with a beer now and then. Beer is not going to turn me into an alcoholic."

Beer contains only 4 percent alcohol and calms the drinker by slowing the heartbeat, breathing, reasoning, and sensory areas. If a dancer drinks alone, try to persuade him or her to drink one glass of water for every glass of beer. Unfortunately, increased tolerance may eventually require hard liquor for the same mental and physical effect. Since drinkers consider themselves witty and smarter than others, he or she is probably an irritable and argumentative companion, suitable to only another irritable and argumentative companion.

"There's nothing wrong with taking anything approved by the government or advertised in a TV commercial. They wouldn't sell something strong that would be harmful. People take aspirins and cold tablets or sleeping pills all their lives and nothing happens. If it's legal, it's okay to take."

Unfortunately, side effects are more dangerous than the Food and Drug Administration can determine. Cigarettes, for instance, still legal, required long-range statistics to reveal their danger. Use of a drug that is nonaddictive is but a temporary solution to be used until the real cause of the distress is investigated.

"I'm sick of all the discipline. I'm never late, get good grades, toe the line, and give up a lot of fun. I resent it sometimes, but I don't let it show. My classes are expensive and I've given up a lot to have them. I work every day so my conscience won't bother me. I'll never be dependent on drugs."

This dancer is a likely candidate for drug abuse because a rigid routine, when it becomes boring, is frequently altered with drugs as a solution to changing feelings and experience. Anger with an inflexible schedule, for instance, when it is turned inward, has been given as a motive for addiction. This dancer needs to learn to change a schedule without feeling guilty, and to appreciate the importance of occasional release in the form of harmless fun. Drug abuse can be used as an excuse for wanting to stop a confining life instead of coping with discipline as a choice rather than an imposed burden.

For whatever reason, such as peer pressure or distress, if a young person becomes addicted, a place to start making a change is with an adviser, such as a coordinator with SPARK (School Prevention of Addiction through Rehabilitation and Knowledge). State funds provide this service in the public schools. Ask the principal of your school or write your board of education for information. All cases are kept confidential.

Symptoms of excessive drug use may vary but altered behavior is the first clue. Look for irritability, anger, antisocial behavior, bloodshot eyes, dilated pupils, and extreme fatigue.

DRUGS IN COMMON USE

Drug: CAFFEINE (in coffee, tea, cocoa, cola drinks)

Effect: *Excites the cerebral cortex of the brain for more sensory awareness. Effect lasts several hours.*

Consequences of Prolonged Use: Prolonged use creates emotional dependency and anxiety. Cola drinks are unsafe for children during period of growth and brain development. Diet colas, which contain fewer calories, contain the same amount of caffeine.

Drug: VOLATILE SUBSTANCES (lighter fluid, gasoline, glue, paint, lacquer thinners, nail polish removers, shoe polish, spray paints, nonstick coating substances, room deodorizers, deodorants, hair sprays, glass chillers, and substances that vaporize into gaseous forms at normal room temperature)

Effect: *Effect is excitation, loss of inhibitions culminating in depression. Lasts five to forty-five minutes.*

Consequences of Prolonged Use: Prolonged use damages the brain, leads to loss of memory, inability to concentrate, confusion, unsteady gait, cardiac stimulation, erratic heartbeats, increased pulse, harm to kidneys and liver, and may result in sudden death.

Drug: LSD (lysergic acid diethylamide-25, a synthetic hallucinogen)

Effect: *Effect is highly colored and exaggerated visions with flashback recurrences. Lasts ten to forty hours, with user in trancelike floating or exalted state, experiencing changes in time and space, unreal sensations, and "fireworks."*

Consequences of Prolonged Use: Prolonged use results in sweating, nausea, chills, increased heartbeat, tremors, flashbacks to LSD experiences days or months later, slowed creativity, difficulty with abstract thinking. Can result in injury to self, sudden death due to dangerous actions, panic, violence, suicide, or loss of sanity.

Drug: MARIJUANA (THC—Delta-1-tetrahydrocannabinol from cannabis dried flowers or marijuana plant, smoked or sniffed)

Effect: *Effect is dreamy state; may increase sharpness of vision, sound, and touch. Distorts time. Body fat retains THC, impelling user to seek higher highs with other drugs. Impairs memory, learning, speech, reading comprehension, arithmetic problem solving, and thinking ability. User loses interest in friends, activities, work. Biggest danger is in driving motor vehicles.*

Consequences of Prolonged Use: Prolonged use damages reproductive organs, menstrual cycles, and can affect fertility. Increased cultivation now produces marijuana higher in THC than several years ago.

Drug: NICOTINE (in cigarettes, cigars, pipe tobacco, inhaled and smoked)

Effect: *Effect stimulates heart and breathing, cuts appetite, lasts ten minutes.*

Consequences of Prolonged Use: Prolonged use linked to lung cancer, heart attack, and lung diseases. Results in shortness of breath, phlegm, rise in blood pressure, carbon monoxide in blood. Implicated in hypertension, chronic bronchitis, and emphysema. Greatest increase in statistical use among young girls. Wrinkled skin can be a symptom of constricted blood vessels which may serve to warn of damage to heart and lungs. Physical and psychological dependency.

Drug: PCP (*synthetic hallucinogen, snorted or ingested*)

Effect: *Effect is depressing and stimulating and/or hallucinogenic. Subject appears "spacy," apathetic, and experiences "flashing." Alternates between violent actions and euphoric, convivial states.*

Consequences of Prolonged Use: Prolonged use may result in brain damage, memory gaps, frequent disorientation, difficulty with speech, delirium, muscle rigidity, seizure, convulsions, and paranoia. Poisoning from PCP may be recycled into the body for up to two months. Leading cause of psychiatric admission, surpassing schizophrenia and alcoholism. Can result in death.

Drug: NONBARBITURATE TRANQUILIZERS (*Miltown, Equanil, Noludar, Noridan, Placidyl, Sopor, Valium, Librium, Xomnifac, Parest, Mandrax, Quaalude, and others*)

Effect: *Effect allays anxiety and tension, provides mild sedation. Quaalude creates effect of "drunkenness" without hangover and is purported to make one feel "sexy," although, like alcohol, it depresses sexual feelings.*

Consequences of Prolonged Use: Prolonged use leads to blood damage, nausea, convulsions, and coma. Important short-term use for relief from extreme anxiety, grief, or severe depression.

Drug: AMPHETAMINES (*dextroamphetamine, methamphetamine, and Methedrine*)

Effect: *Effect is stimulated nervous system, increased talkativeness, general hyperactivity, purposeless activity, false sense of energy leading to excessive use of body resulting in deep fatigue, danger of injury, and depressions. Appetite control is a debatable claim.*

Consequences of Prolonged Use: Prolonged use produces mood swings, panic, circulatory and cardiac disturbances, paranoid thoughts, convulsions, coma, brain damage, speech disturbance, acne skin resembling measles rash, trouble with teeth and nails, and dry lifeless hair. Can produce emaciation, frenetic and wild behavior and may reinforce homicidal tendencies.

4

Body Care for the Student Dancer

Your body is the only dance instrument you have. Learning how to care for it properly on a regular basis when you are young will permit you to use your body at its optimum health and energy for the greatest length of time.

When we are young, there is a tendency to think we are physically indestructible. And to a great extent, a young body mends itself quickly, restores its energy almost overnight, and remains in working order despite casual misuse. But eventually neglect, abuse, or ignored warning signs take a toll upon your stamina, your image, your career, as well as your sense of well-being and happiness.

There is no way to separate the instrument you use for dance from the personal use of your body. That doesn't mean that you must be ready to face a life of self-denial or be constantly self-concerned. Good nutritional habits, rest, and regular body care are all that is required. An occasional abuse can then be acknowledged without guilt but will require a repair as soon as possible.

Dressing room talk and legends passed along from company to company will not help you make the best decisions for the inner and outer care of your instrument. Today, there is no longer any need to avoid the family doctor who thinks a dancer is just too thin, or wants you to stop dancing because of a pulled muscle. Dance medicine, a spin-off of sports medicine, has brought new insights into the needs and use of the body as an instrument. Information about nutrition, body care, and knowing when to respond to physical and psychological warning signals are all you need to create good lifelong habits.

MINDING YOUR FOOTWORK

Nearly everyone experiences a blister, callus, or corn during a lifetime. Some dancers experience few of these painful irritations, while other dancers seem to be in constant pain. Soft shoes worn during class or onstage are not likely to cause as much hard friction on soft skin as boots or street shoes. Yet perspiration and hard floors add to the dancer's foot problems. The construction of the foot determines its suitability to pointe work; its correct use determines the likelihood of injury, but good foot care habits can help you solve small problems and avoid big ones.

Your feet, biological masterpieces that they are, contain one fourth of all the bones of your body—fifty-two—twenty-six in each foot, one more than in each miraculous hand.

While dance does not injure the feet, misuse does. In addition, a combination of heredity—genetic programming of certain muscle strengths and weaknesses—age, and environmental stress cause foot disorders. The slightest problem—a callus, corn, or blister—will be reflected in another area of the body. Lower back and neck pain, for example, are frequently associated with foot complaints. In dance, as in everyday walking, feet distribute and balance the body weight and act as the body's shock absorbers—sustaining a gravity-induced pressure of up to three times the body weight when walking and up to ten times when jumping.

At the bottom of it all, correct placement of the foot for perfect balance resembles a tripod of weight-bearing points of the heel, the base of the little toe, and the base of the big toe. The foot's job is to be a flexible adapter to a surface and a rigid lever to help you push off.

There are generally considered to be two types of feet: flat and high-arched. According to Louis Galli, D.P.M., "You can tell if your foot is flat or high-arched by observing its impression on sand or on your bathmat. If the inside of your arch is imprinted, your feet are more or less flat. Another test is to put two fingers underneath the arch. If your fingers don't fit, the foot is flexible and flat. If the arch does not touch the fingers, the foot is inflexible and high-arched.

"The flat foot is too mobile and remains flexible at the support portion of the gait," Galli tells us. "This type is associated with arch strain, shin splints, knee pain, bunions, heel spurs, and Achilles' tendon problems. High-arched feet are poor shock absorbers. They are prone to ankle sprains, outside knee and hip pain, stress fractures, and neuromas, the technical name for tumors formed of nerve tissues."

The best advice for prevention of injuries is the constant attention that should be paid to correct alignment or placement of the body. Remember that the bones of the feet are not completely ossified or formed until eighteen to twenty years of age. A foot injury can indicate misalignment of the knee, hip, spine, or head and those areas should be investigated as possible cause of the foot injury.

New High-Tech Aids

The familiar Polaroid X-ray in the podiatry office has been replaced by the lixiscope (low-intensity X-ray image), a small, hand-held X-ray gun developed originally by NASA to photograph celestial bodies. The lixiscope exposes the inner workings of the foot on a video screen instantly and with little or no radiation. It allows immediate diagnosis, and acts as a guideline during surgery for the insertion and positioning of pins, wires, and screws. It then provides an invaluable tool in checking the healing process.

The new electrodynogram (EDG) focuses on how the foot bears

body weight. The EDG device consists of a six-ounce recorder pack wrapped around the waist. Seven flat sensors placed on areas of the soles monitor every movement. In thirty seconds, the device gives a computerized printout of specific stresses showing areas most subjected to wear and tear. It is a breakthrough in locating vague pain, and priceless in providing information as a basis for prescribing corrective exercises.

The EDG also forms a basis for the creation of an orthotic, a custom-made foot support that slips into a street shoe, sneaker, or dance shoe. (Pavlova wore a steel half-orthotic in her right pointe shoe.) Orthotics restore correct alignment by retraining the muscular system of the foot. They enhance muscle action and redirect weight stress, without the jarring effect often created by conventional arch supports.

The insert, or orthotic, varies in size from a partial foot measurement to a full foot size. The material varies from leather and steel to plastic, foam rubber, or cork. Available by prescription only, the orthotic is frequently required because of pronation—flattening and inward rotation of the arch.

An initial visit in the making of an orthotic involves measuring the patient's foot for a cast, which is then sent to a laboratory with the diagnosis. The creativity involved in the development of orthotics in recent years has extended their use from the street shoe to the stage shoe, for use by the beginner or the injured dancer, and varies, as well, in price.

Most important to the dancer is another device of high-tech capacity, the CO_2 (carbon dioxide) laser, which emits a thin beam of high intensity light. Used in eye surgery at an earlier time, the laser is now correcting foot ailments such as warts, pinched nerves, and ingrown or thickened (through fungus infection) toenails. The laser beam vaporizes the affected tissue and cauterizes blood vessels so that bleeding and chances of infection are minimal. In the past, painful warts or soft corns between the toes were treated by acid, surgical incision, or cryotherapy (freezing). Scarring and swelling were the frequent result of this recurring condition. The CO_2 laser surgery, however, performed under local anesthesia, with its pinpoint precision, leaves adjacent healthy tissue unharmed.

Bunions

Do pointe shoes cause bunions? Not directly. But bunions caused by hereditary foot imbalance can be aggravated by friction of the shoe—a constricting street shoe or a hard, tight pointe shoe. If you experience pain in this area, wear the stiffening of the pointe shoe lower than joint level. Pointe shoes may also be softened at that point with alcohol or water.

Bunions are painful growths of bone that form along the joints of the toe. The correction of the problem is in fracturing the bone and sliding the bump deeper into the foot where it is eventually absorbed and remolded by being draped into the proper position.

"My first choice for this condition," Galli says, "is conservative

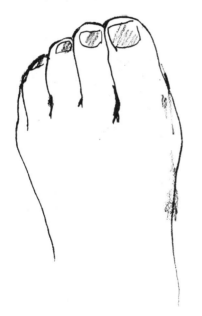

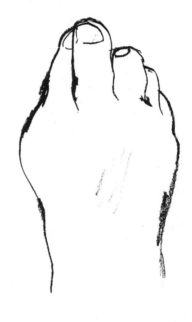

Corrected bunion

Bunion pushing large toe against second toe, making it longer

treatment involving specially constructed toe separators, realignment of the gait and feet in dance technique, and in suggesting more suitable footwear." *Minimal incision surgery, so popular that it has become practically a walk-in business, should be the last resort for a dancer.* "Because flexibility is important to the dancer, bunion surgery should be undertaken when a career has ended. In extreme cases, it should be considered if there is a gross deformity, considerable pain, and if the dancer cannot perform with the condition."

Minimal surgery, while it sounds quick and easy, is not the answer for dancing feet. However, it has a popular appeal to those who no longer require flexibility. After taking X-rays and a blood test, the area is anesthetized and an incision approximately four sixteenths of an inch is made. Using an electric bur, the bone enlargement is pulverized into a paste which mixes with blood and is squeezed out. One or two stitches may be necessary. No one can wear a regular shoe for three or four weeks afterward, no matter what may be claimed.

"Rarely is it just 'a bone problem,' " Galli adds. "Many times, minimal incision surgery will involve tightening up tendons or capsule, or replacing joints. The decision should be based upon how the foot is going to function not a few days or months from now, but in twenty or thirty years after surgery."

Injury to the Feet

Should you injure your foot, wait thirty or forty minutes before bearing weight on it. If it is extremely painful to do so, don't. Get to an emergency treatment center or doctor immediately. In the meantime, keep the foot elevated and packed in ice. The well-known RICE (rest, ice, compression, elevation) technique for injuries will serve you well until you see a doctor. If X-rays prove negative, don't bandage the area for the first twenty-four hours but keep placing ice packs on the area constantly.

Cold reduces the swelling and internal bleeding by constricting the blood vessels at the injured site, applying outside pressure prevents the accumulation of fluids, and elevation slows down the circulation to the damaged tissue.

Mild injuries may be managed at home, but if you have any of the following symptoms, see a doctor immediately:

- Severe pain, swelling, or discoloration
- Inability to move or put weight on injured area immediately or a few hours afterward
- Moderate pain that doesn't relent after a few days' rest

If X-rays indicate broken bones, they must be set immediately and then immobilized for three to six weeks. A sprained ankle should be softcast or taped by a professional.

Evaluate your movements as to the probable cause of the injury to correct your movements and prevent future injuries of a similar kind. Did you roll over, inward or outward? Land heavily instead of softly first through the toes, sole, and heel? Did you wear heels too high? Not break in your pointe shoes sufficiently?

Healthy Foot Care

Toes and fingers need to be groomed in much the same manner. Use a pumice stone on flaky patches, calluses, and corns. Be careful to remove only enough callused material to retain flexibility. Wash in warm water with plenty of soap, rinse alternately with hot and cold water, rinsing thoroughly especially between the toes.

For a foot odor problem caused by the one half pint of perspiration the 250,000 sweat glands of the foot give off daily, use an antibacterial soap, lotion, or Hibiclens; pHisoHex is also an excellent soap available without prescription.

If calluses are not too tough, soak the feet first for fifteen minutes in sudsy warm water to which two tablespoons of baking soda have been added. Then rinse with hot/cold water for quick relief from soreness.

Use a nail clipper for excess length, clipping from one edge to the other following the natural curve. Clipping straight across will sometimes result in an ingrown toenail. The length of the nail should be flush with the end of the toe, but not shorter. (Early ballerinas let their nails grow over the toes for protection in pointe shoes.)

Rub down the cuticle with a towel or use a cuticle remover and push the cuticle with a towel or with a cuticle knife (no orange sticks), lift the cuticle, and scrape the surface and undersides of the nails clean, working from the sides to the center. Clean under the tip of the nail and wipe with sudsy water. Nail enamel provides additional strength to the nails of the toes. (The nails of the hands are never painted except for colorless polish.)

Before applying polish, separate the toes with a tissue. First, apply a base coat, any color you like or colorless polish, and then apply a top coat or second coat of colored or colorless polish.

Never apply color on fingernails. It is never permitted onstage because the color red under stage lights makes the hands look like

Placement of tissue before applying polish

talons dripping blood. Do not use nail enamel in a bright color for an audition.

This procedure should be followed once a week or more frequently except for the applying of polish, which should last unchipped for at least one week. Apply softening lotion to the feet after bathing or more often. White spots or flaky or ridged nails indicate a lack of iron or calcium in the diet.

FIRST AID FOR FEET

Sore Feet: Alternate five-minute hot and cold water soaks. Wash, dry, dust with ZeaSORB powder. Treat yourself to a pedicure. Or massage feet with Barielle Total Foot Care Cream. Roll a tennis ball with your bare foot to massage the arches.

Bruises and Cuts: Apply a cold compress or Kold Pak, available at Pasteur's Drugstore, 10 Park Avenue, New York, NY 10016. Ice in a dishtowel or plastic bag is suitable.

Splinters: Gently open the skin with cauterized point and remove splinter with tweezers. Apply Betadine solution.

Blisters: Drain fluid with sterile needle, but *do not remove the blister cap.* Apply Neosporin or Betadine, loose bandage or moleskin. Air to heal faster.

Calluses: Rub with pumice stone, sea salt, or Hoffritz's motorized slough machine. Cut out adhesive pad around joint of big toe to remove pressure. A serious condition, sesamoiditis, may require surgical attention.

Soft Corns: Cut out adhesive pad to fit just over the corn to prevent pressure. Serious enlargements may require surgical procedures.

Hard Corns: Rub down with pumice or emery board until area is flexible, but keep protective covering. Never use caustic commercial products, razor, or knife.

Bunions: Inflammation and swelling of bursa with thickening of skin at base of big toe. Keep big toe flexible by making circular movements holding tightly with fingers. Wear larger-size shoes (or wider) or Dr. Scholl's latex toe jacket. A toe separator may also be worn. Check foot alignment.

Hammertoe: Deformity of toe in which there is a permanent angular inflection of second and third joints. If interfering with flexibility of foot, may require surgical procedure. Stuff pointe shoe with lamb's wool or cotton to keep pressure even in shoe.

Spur: Recurring hard mass on heel or ankle. Can be relieved by orthotics or hospital surgery as last resort.

Ganglionic Cyst: Tumor growing on tendon sheath. Best left alone unless it interferes with movement. May be surgically excised but frequently returns.

Plantar Warts: Transmissible virus infection. Requires professional care. Painful.

Athlete's Foot: Red, swollen, itchy fungus infection. Relieved by Desenex or Lotrimin solution.

Shoes: Be sure pointe shoes do not cause numbness or tingling sensation. Boots and street shoes should be one half inch longer than toes, with snug heel. Buy real leather. Sneakers are okay.

MINOR ACHES AND PAINS

It is natural to feel some fatigue and minor muscle aches as the body grows in size and strength. If the increase in physical activity is kept at an easy and gradual pace, there will be no undue strain or discomfort.

While each student's physical work load must be considered on an individual basis, there is a general pattern that has evolved over the 300 years of dance training that coincides with the growth of the child: weekly classes for the preballet and beginners (eight, nine, ten years of age); twice weekly for eleven- and twelve-year-olds; with classes increasing to six weekly, adding pointe and pas de deux classes.

Some of the classes may be less strenuous than technique classes, such as character class, historic dance (styles for past periods of dance), jazz, or tap dance. It is wiser to make a decision about the form of dance that most interests the young dancer after two or three years.

After the first two required years of ballet training, the modern dancer may begin serious modern dance classes and attend only one ballet class per week.

At this point, within two to four years of training, it is possible to see what weakness or malalignments, not due to incorrect teaching, are present. Body-conditioning therapy may be advised. The Pilates Method, for instance, used by early modern dance pioneers as well as more recently by members of the New York City Ballet, is available by Pilates-trained teachers throughout the United States. The practice of taking two or three classes per day, especially when the classes are in different locations, has resulted in students "marking" (not dancing full strength) or leaving classes before the strenuous jumps at the end of class. The excuse is to save oneself for the next class. The body, used this way, will never reach its full technical potential and strength. It also begins a habit of carelessness in execution of the work that, along with fatigue, sets the stage for injuries.

A professional dancer may often choose to do a full and strenuous barre, ease up on rehearsals, then use all available energy during a performance. But this is not the pattern for a student.

It may not be the pattern for some professionals. George Balanchine never permitted his dancers to mark any part of the class or rehearsal. He wanted stamina to be maintained and would not permit careless execution or an energyless approach at any time.

Basically, the body, if used correctly and with a gradual increase in physical activity, is amazingly strong and responsive. There is one exception for dancers—the shape of the toes may cause some young women extreme pain on pointe. The most comfortable shape is two or three toes of the same length to permit a stronger and slightly larger surface on which to stand. However, the strength of the legs and knees is more important in pointe work, since these support the body on pointe. Even toes are more comfortable but not essential to pointe work.

Male dancers who begin dance in their adolescent years may suffer discomfort in the turnout. It is best not to force the body but to work within its limitations.

According to Bertrand Agus, M.D., rheumatologist and assistant professor at New York University Hospital, "Incorrect training is the most frequent cause of arthritis in younger persons."

Arthritis is a disease for which one is never too young. It manifests itself in more than 100 varieties, and two forms, *fibrositis syndrome* and *osteoarthritis*, are frequently found in young and older dancers.

Arthritis, defined as a group of diseases in which heredity and biochemical factors are involved, causes joints and connecting tissue to become painful and, in some cases, inflamed. "A trauma," Agus explains, "the overuse of a joint area, or *stretching before proper warm-up* can be harmful and potentially hazardous. Fifteen minutes are needed to warm up the body before a stretch of any kind should be attempted, and thirty minutes are needed if the dancer is over thirty. Strains, sprains, tears, and rips in the groin area are the frequent results of excessive stretching with insufficient warm-up."

It is likely that the dancer anxious to acquire a high développé or grand battement does not realize that height, which cannot be maintained with stability in the center without the barre, has insufficient musculature to support that position. In an effort to speed up technical proficiency, the poorly taught or impressionable young or novice dancer will strive for flexibility without realizing that it interferes with stability if not *acquired at the same time.*

A "passive range" of motion implies a potential height as far as the anatomy is concerned, but if that height cannot be sustained without support, it cannot become part of the technical equipment of the dancer, only a stretching habit.

"Hypermobility," Agus tells us, "endangers the spine as a result of pushing a lax and hyperextended body. This mobility, an *entrapment syndrome,* belies ease and a special predilection for certain kinds of movement. It must be guided carefully by the teacher and understood by the dancer.

"Asymmetrical growth in young persons is a difficult assessment when diagnosing growing pains or training discomforts versus real pain and dangerous forcing. Adolescents do not grow at the same time in all parts of the body. They sometimes appear to be all legs, all back, or all arms. Here again, it's best not to force the body too much beyond the natural bent. There is no need to be discouraged. The body eventually will shape itself. We all have to accept our congenital limitations. If the dancer follows the normal principles of correct technique for dance, the result will be beautiful in the short, the tall, or even in the inharmoniously shaped dancer."

A fibrositis syndrome manifests itself in various parts of the body as stiffness or aching, with disturbed sleep—frequent waking up during the night in discomfort or pain—as the only physical symptom. Activity must be stopped when pain is involved. Endorphins released to the brain during physical activity mask and anesthetize pain. Do not permit this "high" during physical activity to obviate your knowledge of this condition. Seek correction for faulty habits from your teacher or therapist.

Most aches and pains will disappear after a few hours of rest or a good night's sleep. But arthritis, which typically begins gradually and tends to run a course of ups and downs, may be present. Aspirin, the most commonly used drug for arthritis or general pain, may upset the stomach. If it cannot be tolerated, aspirin substitutes or non-steroidal, anti-inflammatory drugs are available. While steroids have become popular because they provide initial relief, long-term oral use of these drugs usually produces dangerous side effects. For this reason, the condition should be treated by a doctor. While arthritis is not curable, it can be contained. Exercise is not excluded in the treatment.

There is no research to confirm an arthritis/food connection. Neither is there research to confirm massages, hot baths, ice packs, heating pads, alfalfa tablets, warm climates, acupuncture, cod-liver oil, copper bracelets, or wool socks—all magical cures. DMSO (dimethyl sulfoxide), an industrial solvent considered by some a miracle cure of injuries and pain, has a remarkable property of penetrating the skin and going directly to the bone, joint, or organ. It reduces swelling and inflammation, but if the solution is not pure, or used in unregulated amounts, it may have severe side effects and endanger vision.

Basically, a warm bath, the use of epsom salts in the bathwater, heat and massage, along with rest, are the best recommendations for aches and pains.

PMS (PREMENSTRUAL SYNDROME)

Premenstrual "blues" can range from a mild, achy feeling prior to the onset of the menstrual period, to heavy discomfort, twinges, pangs, tweaks, pulls or cramps, and mild depression or irritability.

What a young woman is told about the meaning of her first flow and how she is conditioned to feel physically and mentally set the pattern of her monthly reactions. Knowledge of the physiology of her body and maturity can change the "sick" pattern.

Alis Vasicka, M.D., a noted professor of gynecology and obstetrics, who is on the staff of Lenox Hill Hospital in New York City, says, "Too often, the period is used as a convenient excuse to resist responsibility. Of course, if there is real or persistent or recurring pain, it must be investigated. But nature's normal warning signals should not be misinterpreted as disabling."

Ethnic factors are included in the determination of when the cycle is expected to begin for the first time. Latins, for instance, start the cycle at eleven or twelve years of age, while Scandinavians usually begin the cycle at the age of fourteen. The genetic factor, however, is secondary to the environmental factor in the change of the cycle. Traveling can disrupt the cycle as can nutritional deficiencies.

American girls usually begin the cycle between the ages of twelve and thirteen. If the menarche (men-AR-kee) has not been reached by the age of sixteen, an examination for organic or hormonal causes should be given. The cycle recurs every twenty-three to twenty-eight days.

Studies indicate that each year of rigorous physical training before the menarche delays the beginning of the cycle by five months. It should not be assumed, however, that menstrual irregularity or disruption of the cycle once the menarche has been reached is due to exercise.

Low body fat has long been accused as the factor in delayed cycles or primary amenorrhea (amen-o-RHEE-a: absence of the cycle). Estrogen, an essential female reproductive hormone, may be in short supply when stores of body fat are low. Physically active women may have only 20 or even 10 percent body fat compared to the 25 to 28 percent body fat of the average woman. On the other hand, a normal cycle can exist in a woman with only 17 percent body fat. Illness or injury that stops exercise can often cause a cycle to begin or resume although no change in body weight or fat level has occurred.

No studies exist on the long-term effect of delayed menarche caused by exercise, but one theory suggests that the growth period may be prolonged. The release of reproductive hormones commonly stops bone growth once menstruation begins. For a tall girl, further growth may be undesirable.

"Bloating," Vasicka says, "or a feeling of heaviness, or feeling swollen, is the most frequently heard premenstrual complaint by dancers. Water retention can increase the body weight as much as five uncomfortable pounds. Although diuretic pills can alleviate the discomfort with increased urination, they are not recommended since loss of water can mean a loss of vital nutrients such as magnesium and potassium. Exhaustion can be a side effect as well. Lightheadedness, dizziness, loss of appetite, allergic skin rashes and hives, or sensitivity to sunlight, blurred vision, and nausea or diarrhea are other side effects to the use of diuretics. Excessive urination and loss of nutrients can lead to weakness, muscle aches, cramps and spasms, and, in extreme cases, death. The habit of some young dancers of using diuretics for weight loss is an extremely dangerous practice.

In 1981, a highly absorbent tampon, Rely, was implicated in cases of TSS (toxic shock syndrome), a bacterial infection caused by staph aureus, a staphylococcus organism. Although the incidence of TSS is now estimated to be only 10 cases per year per every 100,000 women, the symptoms should be noted: chills followed by high fever, vomiting, diarrhea, sunburnlike rash, peeling of the skin on fingers and toes, liver or kidney failure, rapid drop in blood pressure leading to shock and death. The American College of Obstetricians and Gynecologists now recommends that women avoid superabsorbent tampons, change tampons at least every six hours, and alternate tampons with pads. Dancers who wear tampons during class or performance may change to pads overnight.

Products that deodorize, spray perfume, rinse away, or otherwise disguise odor are useless. Air is the culprit when it and the discharge mix. Mild soap and water and general cleanliness solve the problem and should be preferred over highly advertised products that assure "feminine daintiness." No pad or tampon should be thrown into a plumbing system.

A warm bath, moderate exercise, a cup of tea (herbals may comfort although they contain some amount of caffeine), a heating pad, and a good night's sleep may be a smooth way to let nature take its course.

NUTRITION

Most Americans are aware of the danger of obesity, or even a few excess pounds. There is hardly anyone who is not at times "careful" or on a diet. Thin is "in," as in fashion and dance. Everyone wants high energy at low body weight, especially the dancers. Technique demands a quick, light, flexible body. And no one is more willing to sacrifice health and the enjoyment of food to meet the aesthetic and technical standard than a dancer.

The best way to maintain a stay-thin-yet-healthy diet is with the help of a nutritionist. Since nutritional needs are individual, consulting a professional nutritionist is a wise but expensive course. Finding a suitable nutritionist to assess your needs may be as elusive as pursuit of the "perfect body." Most doctors find dancers too thin and abusive to their body.

Starting young on a varied diet, eating small "meals" four to six times a day, drinking plenty of water, and avoiding binges will establish good nutritional habits. But dance mythology about food and vitamins is hard to avoid as time goes on. There are temptations to crash diet, use drugs, or otherwise abuse the body. Crash diets never work because the body loses only two pounds of fat per week. If the weight loss is greater, the loss is in precious minerals, water, and *muscle*. When dining becomes a social activity, food takes on new interest—a tour becomes boring and the main relaxation is dining out. Experiencing the cuisine of a new country is tempting and fun, and restraint is difficult. Binge/purge can become a dangerous habit. Eating excess amounts of a favorite food or a very heavy meal followed by induced vomiting is not an infrequent habit for an emotionally disturbed overeater. There are warning signals that all is not well, according to Dr. Harold Markus, a New York City orthomolecular physician and psychiatrist. "For instance," Markus explains, "an ache or pain that is more than fatigue, the discomfort during a menstrual cycle, the 'pins and needles' pain in an arm, the need for more than three cups of coffee or extra sugar, the drippy nose, the nondance-related cramp in a calf—these are all indicators of conditions reversible with proper nutrition.

"To begin with, the basic requirements for optimum health for a dancer begin with protein. Protein may range from 15 to 25 percent of the total diet and should consist of fish and chicken with the skin removed. A quick snack in the dressing room or during the day might be water-packed sardines.

"Complex carbohydrates should compose the major portion of the diet, as much as 60 percent. This group includes fresh vegetables, fruits, seeds, nuts, grains, and breads. With the exception of salads, vegetables are often the least appetizing items on a restaurant menu. Raw vegetables, washed and munched during the day, are one solution. Celery, carrots, seeds, and nuts (except pecans or Brazil nuts) are easy to carry anywhere.

"Twenty-five percent of the diet should include saturated or unsaturated fats, such as safflower or olive oil, with butter, whole milk, and cream representing only about 5 percent. Bone-structuring calcium may come from lowfat cheeses (cottage, feta, etc.) or yogurt.

"When traveling, take along one-serving-sized plastic bags of granola cereal, mixed at home with nuts and raisins, thus avoiding sugary cereals.

"While on the subject of travel, if constipation occurs, three bran tablets taken orally, that you can buy at a health food store, are a better choice than a commercial laxative. For flatulence, charcoal tablets available at any drugstore, taken orally, give quick relief.

"In general, roughage or fiber foods should be part of a diet. Popcorn, without butter or salt, is a fine fiber food. Women, in particular, should keep their urinary tracts cleaned out by drinking unsweetened cranberry juice, six ounces, every other day."

In a stress condition or when traveling, Markus recommends a multivitamin such as Solgar VM 75 once a day; vitamin C, 2000 micrograms; bioflavin, 1000 micrograms; E, 200 to 400 micrograms, increasing the amount as you grow older; and selenium, 90 milligrams. Psychological stress can call for vitamin B complex, 50 milligrams, in place of Valium or Librium. If you take birth-control pills, take extra vitamin C and B_6. (The Pill, however, is not recommended.) And smoking will reduce the effectiveness of all vitamin intake by one half.

Vitamin Supplements

Except for stress or unusual conditions, vitamins do not contribute significantly to body structure nor are they a direct source of body energy. They function primarily as regulators, governing the hundreds of biochemical reactions involved in organ function, growth, and energy metabolism. The typical American diet contains enough variety to provide an adequate supply of nearly all the vitamins, even if the caloric intake is low. No one food contains sufficient levels of all the vitamins needed, but a varied diet selection from the different food groups provides an adequate supply and eliminates the need for vitamin supplements, unless there is a specific disease-related health problem, or if the dancer has been deprived of an adequate diet for a prolonged period of time.

But myths die hard. Dancers persist in thinking a vitamin supplement is necessary for added energy. Although some doctors categorize dance as endurance activity, Jerald L. Cohen of the New Jersey Medical School, in cardiovascular testing of dancers, found ballet to fall within the range of nonendurance activity. Dance requires sprints of high energy activity with periods of rest between. The dancer needs calories to burn yet must remain lean and thin in order to move quickly. Best foods for this high energy activity are carbohydrates such as cereals and potatoes, fresh and dried fruits. Leafy vegetables like celery are high in cellulose, a large, complex carbohydrate, which represents roughage in the diet.

Animal protein in the form of meat, when added to a vegetable diet, contributes additional amino acid even though modest, and enhances the protein efficiency of the vegetable proteins in the diet.

Here are the food groups from which you should choose every day for a healthful diet. The amount of the necessary servings may be small and spread out over the day in five or six "meals."

MILK AND CHEESE

These calcium-rich foods also contain fat, cholesterol, and calories. Choose lowfat or skim milk, buttermilk, yogurt, ice milk, and hard cheeses over whole milk contents. *(Two servings.)*

FRUIT AND VEGETABLES

These fiber foods provide vitamins A and C, and carotene. Select dark green vegetables for riboflavin, folic acid, iron, and magnesium; citrus fruits, melons, berries, and tomatoes for vitamin C. Collard, kale, mustard, turnip, and dandelion greens provide calcium. This group is low in calories. *(Four servings.)*

MEAT, FISH, POULTRY, BEANS

These sources of protein contain phosphorus, vitamins B_6 and B_{12}. Select lean meat with fat trimmed off, beans, peas, soybeans, nuts, liver, and egg yolks. Haddock, cod, flounder, and halibut have somewhat lower amounts of cholesterol than shellfish. Choose chicken and fish over red meat but include red meat once a week in your diet. *(Two servings.)*

BREAD AND CEREAL

Grains are sources of the B vitamins, iron, protein, magnesium, folic acid, fiber, and vitamins A, C, and D. They contain no cholesterol. Check labels for added sugar, refined flour, fats, and preservatives. Choose bran and whole grain products. Pasta, recommended in this category for quick energy, may be too filling and uncomfortable for the dancer. But a small quantity can be substituted for rice or potato. *(Four servings.)*

FATS, SWEETS, AND ALCOHOL

Although high in calories, this category is rich in vitamin E and fatty acids. Select margarine over butter; lemon juice over mayonnaise or salad dressings; dried fruit over candy, jams, jellies, syrups, or other sweets; water or seltzer over soft drinks; white wine over beer or liquor. *(Moderation.)*

Foods made from healthful ingredients need not be dull or tasteless. Here are some easy and inexpensive recipes from the Fryer Research Center, 105 E. 22 Street, New York, NY 10010, where you may write for additional recipes.

Sesame Dip

> 1 cup sesame butter (tahini, in health food stores)
> ½ cup fresh lemon juice
> 3 cloves garlic
> 1 to 2 teaspoons soy sauce
> ½ cup cold water
> Process in blender, adding curry, onion, tomato paste, or herbs to taste.

Tofu Dip

> 1 lb. tofu (available in health food or Oriental greengrocers)
> 4 to 5 tablespoons diced fresh onion
> 1 teaspoon dill seed
> 1 tablespoon soy sauce
> 2 to 4 tablespoons safflower oil
> Juice of 1 or 2 lemons
> 2 tablespoons fresh parsley
> Process in blender.

Easy and Elegant Cheese Souffle

> 4 to 6 slices bread in oiled baking dish layered with:
> 3 cups grated sharp cheddar cheese
> Pour over this combination:
> 2 cups milk, or 1½ cups milk plus ½ cup vermouth or wine
> Mix separately and pour over ingredients in baking dish:
> 3 eggs, beaten
> 1 teaspoon salt
> ½ teaspoon Worcestershire sauce
> ½ teaspoon thyme
> ½ teaspoon dry mustard
> pepper
> Let stand for 30 minutes. Bake at 350° for one hour in a pan of hot water.

Serves 5.

Apple-Bran and Cinnamon Muffins

    1 cup whole wheat flour
    ½ teaspoon baking soda
    ½ teaspoon baking powder
    ¼ teaspoon cinnamon
    2 cups bran cereal
    1 cup milk
    1 egg, beaten
    ½ cup milk
    ½ cup honey
    2 tablespoons oil
    1 cup grated unpeeled apple

Mix dry ingredients. Soak bran cereal in 1 cup milk. Beat egg, add ½ cup milk, honey, and oil, and add to bran; stir in grated apple. Fold in dry ingredients just enough to moisten. Fill greased muffin tins ¾ full. Bake at 400° for 15 to 20 minutes.

Oatmeal Apricot Muffins

    1 cup dried apricots
    1 egg, beaten
    1 teaspoon vanilla
    1 cup milk
    ⅓ cup oil
    ½ cup honey
    1 cup whole wheat flour
    1 cup rolled oats
    ½ cup wheat germ
    3 teaspoons baking powder

Cup up apricots, cover with boiling water for 5 minutes, and drain. Mix wet ingredients into dry lightly. Fold in apricots. Fill greased muffin tin ¾ full and bake at 400° for 15 minutes.

Lentil Soup

    2 cups uncooked lentils
    8 cups water or vegetable stock
    ½ onion, chopped
    1 small carrot, chopped
    1 celery stalk, chopped
    1 small potato, chopped
    2 tablespoons oil
    2 bay leaves
    1½ to 2 teaspoons salt

Mix all ingredients in soup pot and cook until lentils are very soft, about 1 hour. Add 2 teaspoons vinegar at the end. Serve.

Apple Crisp

> 8 apples (green pippins are best)
> Juice of 1 lemon
> 1 teaspoon cinnamon
> 2 tablespoons whole wheat flour
> ¾ cup raisins
> Water or apple juice
>
> Optional topping:
> 1 cup rolled oats
> ⅓ cup toasted wheat germ
> ½ cup whole wheat flour
> ½ teaspoon salt
> 2 teaspoons cinnamon
> ½ cup brown sugar
> ½ cup margarine or butter

Preheat oven to 375°. Slice apples to fill greased 9″ x 13″ baking dish. Mix apples in bowl with lemon juice, cinnamon, flour, and raisins. Return to baking dish, adding water or apple juice to cover bottom. Mix topping in bowl and press onto top of apples. Bake 25 minutes or until apples are soft. (Cook same time without topping.)

The best rule is to avoid diet fads, fasting, diet pills, and to eat a little of everything.

According to a dietary and nutritional survey of female dance students attending the 1982 American Dance Festival in Durham, N.C., young dance students exhibit unusual dietary practices in a desire to be thin. Sixty-nine percent of the dancers attending the festival workshops used nutritional supplements—especially vitamin C and multivitamin tablets with iron. Twenty-one percent of the users were taking supplements of dosages exceeding the Recommended Dietary Allowance, a measurement established by the Food and Drug Administration. Few of these dancers consulted professional advice, and were most concerned about avoiding excessive sugar and calorie intake.

Excessive dosages of fat-soluble vitamins (A, D, E, and K) can be stored in the liver and accumulate to a potentially toxic level.

Water-soluble vitamins (C, thiamine, riboflavin, niacin, folic acid, B_6 and B_{12}, biotin, and pantothenic acid) are assumed to be relatively harmless because excessive amounts are excreted and not stored in the body. Water-soluble vitamins, however, ingested in large amounts, can affect the metabolism—the caloric rate of energy burning.

Iron was the most common mineral supplement used, probably because of heavy advertising suggesting its use and the belief that menstruation depletes iron. If the diet contains adequate levels of iron, supplementation is not required. Like fat-soluble vitamins, iron accumulates in the liver and may cause damage to that organ in excessive amounts.

In summary, a good diet is best recommended by a nutritionist on an individual basis. Information should not come from radio or television advertising, magazines, or from "a friend." If the diet contains whole grains, fresh vegetables, fruits and protein, milk (in lowfat form), and if the meals are eaten in small quantity throughout the day without overloading at any one time, the dancer will establish good habits and find no need for a crash/binge cycle. Drug use that purges the body of valuable minerals and vitamins along with excess food may become a psychological as well as a physical problem.

UNDEREATING AND OVEREATING AS PSYCHOLOGICAL DISORDERS

While axorexia nervosa is rare in the professional dancer, a borderline condition of the disease is far from rare among dancers on the student level.

Nervosa, an eating disorder of emotional basis, is an illness compounded by biological and psychological factors that result from food deprivation. It is now clearly defined, and the number of its sufferers is increasing according to *The New York Times*, 1984. Without proper treatment, up to 20 percent of these sufferers die from the irreversible effects of chronic starvation.

The illness hides in clever disguises. The sufferer usually comes from an upper socioeconomic family that puts a high value on achievement. She (for most anorexia sufferers are young women) is an intelligent, dependable, conscientious, compliant, hard-working young person who seems to be in control. She seems to be functioning on high energy, keeping a very active schedule, but she is slowly letting herself die. Male anorexics are usually found in contact sports, especially wrestling, where an effort to reduce and squeeze into a lower weight class may be encouraged by coaches.

Symptoms of Borderline or Full Anorexia Nervosa

- Weight loss over a period of time, not due to illness, amounting to 12 to 25 percent of the normal weight for height, age, and bone size.
- An odd diet begun in response to an *emotional crisis*.
- Extreme increase in physical activity or exercising in addition to regular dance classes.
- Concealed changes in eating habits and eating alone.
- Loss of muscle as well as fat, with lowered blood pressure and slowed heart rate.
- Loss of the menstrual cycle, overuse of laxatives and diuretics, and constantly feeling cold.

One of the difficulties in recognizing the disorder of eating too little is the seemingly logical and understandable reasons that disguise the condition.

Weight

While it is true that a balanced diet and physical activity produce a slender, muscular body, the anorexic or borderline case is forced into thinness that may not suit her body type because of trying to conform to a current aesthetic of thinness in dancers.

Muscle formation is a factor in the development of technique and in the creation of an aesthetic line that *cannot* be achieved by weight loss or water loss. Layered clothing worn in a heated studio, plastic garments, steambaths, laxatives, and diuretics only rid the body of water, not fat.

An Emotional Crisis

Reaching for the perfection and high level of achievement expected in the family, school, or from an authority figure can trigger an internal struggle that may result in a retreat into sickness. The crisis can be failure at an audition or competition, not reaching a higher level of technical accomplishment, or a scholastic challenge unmet.

In the home situation, a parent may be making all the decisions without expressing approval when the young person does something on her own. When it comes time to demonstrate independence during the adolescent period, an inner conflict may arise. It may be easier to be a "good girl"—compliant—and, by delaying the progress of maturity, gain more attention and continual care.

Inwardly, the future anorexic tries to be in control of everything, but does not believe she can be in control of anything except what she refuses to put into her mouth. She does not believe she can live up to her own expectations, doubts her looks, her talent, her abilities, and feels she is only in charge of her body weight.

Increased Activity

A particularly illusive disguise of this illness is the increased physical activity. This appears symptomatic in the average young dancer who seems to be following a natural pattern by increasing the number of rehearsals, classes, or other kinds of physical activity. But the energy expended in these activities is desperate and reflects *an extreme drive to excel.* The superachiever feels no fatigue, hunger, pain, or discomfort. She becomes inured to pain and dancing though an injury becomes frequent. The healing is slow because of her weakened condition.

The limbs of the anorexic frequently tingle, the upper lip grows numb, and a layer of soft hair appears on the body. These physical warnings are ignored because of her impaired mental functioning and constant agitation.

Eating Habits

It would seem that the increased physical activity would have a logical consequence in the disruption of eating patterns. But this disruption begins with a preference for certain foods without concern for a balanced or wholesome diet. Loss of control by eating forbidden food, a fattening item in the mind of the sufferer, results in guilt followed by self-punishment. A bizarre diet begins, and the discipline needed to maintain the body in perfect order disappears. To hide the changed pattern, eating in secret, on the run, or alone becomes the daily procedure.

But the victim, deprived of food, becomes obsessed with it as the brain rejects the idea of self-destruction. As an opposite reaction, and a far more clever disguise of a changed eating plan, the victim takes over the food shopping and prepares large and complicated family meals. Although no food is eaten by the cook, the camouflage successfully belies an elaborate preoccupation with temptation and denial.

Eventually, the stomach rejects certain foods, and the extremes of diet can lead to outright hallucinations, euphoria, or other mental changes, all by-products of malnutrition.

Despite these mental and physical changes, the borderline anorexic may continue to function for as long as ten years. Secondary or borderline symptoms have appeared in those as young as eleven or as old as fifty-five. Through bouts of severe depression and thoughts of wasting away, the borderline anorexic remains undecided about whether to live or die, to grow up or remain the good little girl forever. In cases of clearly diagnosed anorexia, sudden death may occur in 2 or 3 percent of the instances.

Breaking the Pattern of Anorexia

A teacher, company manager or friend, or special personal relationship can, with luck, persuade the dancer to do two things: Admit and accept that the condition exists and begin to correct the illness without self-hate. Loving concern should be expressed for the anorexic, who must be made to see that she is valued by those around her and that they will help her remove the condition.

At first, the establishment of eating meals in a social context with friends, in a relaxed and enjoyable atmosphere, can be attempted. *Force-feeding is definitely not recommended.* Food should be small in amounts and dietitian-recommended. This diet may be suggested by a physician after a medical checkup.

Weight gain is not the cure, just the beginning—the step before psychological therapy can begin to cope with the underlying emotional basis of the illness. Malnutrition impairs treatment, and it is only when the biochemical abuse begins to be reversed that the patient acquires the physical and emotional stamina to cope with the needed psychological therapy. Real progress is determined by the working out of the patient's personal relationships within the family and with authority figures. Including the family in the therapy is imperative.

Although the process of biochemical and psychological damage can be reversed, it may take years, but what will emerge is a better self-image based upon learning to love oneself. The dancer can then be herself without emulating any image but her own. The new self will have a more honest identity.

HOTLINE: ANAD (Anorexia Nervosa and Associated Disorders), 1-312-831-3438. Or write ANAD, Box 271, Highland Park, IL 60035 for information and a list of local treatment centers. Enclose $1 for postage and handling.

Bulimia: The Other Side of the Coin

While the anorectic hides and hoards food, but seldom eats, the bulimic hides and hoards in order to gorge, and will often resort to stealing when binging escalates.

Bulimia, the disorder of eating too much, was named in 1874 by a British physician, and is at the opposite end of the scale from anorexia nervosa. It is a disorder that is more difficult to discern since there are so many degrees of the binge/purge syndrome, and it is more frequently found in the general population than anorexia. But, like anorexia, it can result in death.

We've been admonished since childhood to spit out dangerous

objects and to purge or not to purge noxious substances swallowed inadvertently. We've watched puppies and kittens regurgitate inedibles naturally and without apparent aftereffects. The Egyptians considered a monthly purge a prophylactic against sickness, and the Romans invented a room to be used at banquets for the purification rite. In our century, the use of castor oil was a weekly nose-holding, quick-swallow ritual. Almost everyone has eaten too much at a festive occasion and run into the powder room, to the curb, or a back alley for relief. Regurgitating is familiar and, in some cases, desirable. But when the binge/purge cycle becomes a habit, the sufferer is a bulimic.

According to the University of Washington Psychiatric Clinic, bulimia is six times more common among young women than anorexia and ranges from frequent purging of high carbohydrate or starchy foods to purging as often as twenty times a day in extreme cases.

In the dance world, purging is considered by many a solution to occasionally overeating or a quick way to begin a weight loss diet, in addition to using diuretics and laxatives.

Like the anorectic, the bulimic woman is a perfectionist, highly demanding of herself, an achiever with a poor self-image and little self-esteem. For this reason, the former anorectic, who has not had enough therapy or time to recondition her body, will frequently become bulimic in secret.

Like the anorectic, the bulimic wants to stay slender because of a dread of becoming fat. Although they appear poised and confident, bulimics depend upon others for self-esteem and fear their purging habits, which they view with revulsion, will be exposed.

While the anorectic begins her self-torture in her teens, with reasons that include a retreat from sexual and emotional maturity, the bulimic, for the same reasons, may begin her self-torture at any age from teens into maturity.

The anorectic becomes visibly thinner or weaker, while the bulimic remains slender and functioning until medical or dental problems, financial and legal difficulties, or the deterioration of relationships with family or friends reveal the cycle. Undetected, and not even considered an illness by many in the medical profession, bulimia remains a hidden disorder, ill-defined and still questionably treated.

Death by starvation is the end result of the untreated anorectic, but the bulimic may live on, except for a heart attack, or she may strangle while disgorging. She may have disturbances in the body through the loss of body fluids because of low potassium concentration, neuromuscular problems ranging from weakness to paralysis, gastrointestinal disorders, and kidney disease. The bulimic has difficulty breathing and swallowing, has irregular periods (like the anorectic), stomach cramps, ulcers, is apathetic and frequently irritable. Her appearance shows broken blood vessels under the eyes and neck, blotched skin, and sores that do not heal. Tooth damage from sugar and fruit juices are obvious, as well as a change in the bite and lower jaw alignment.

Breaking the Pattern of Bulimia

Like the anorectic, loving concern from a friend can aid the bulimic to break the binge/purge pattern, big or small as that pattern may be. Because bulimia is a hidden pattern, it is difficult to know if there is a problem. The dentist, however, is more likely to be able to diagnose the disorder. Unfortunately, since dancers neglect *dental care more than any other medical treatment* (according to a Performing Arts Center for Health survey conducted in 1984), only the bulimic may know of the pattern.

Changing the pattern of eating is not easy for the bulimic since one can abstain from alcohol, drugs, or cigarettes, but not from food. In addition to sustaining the body, food defines our nationality, our religious beliefs, our notions of prestige, our rewards or punishments, and evokes delicious memories of special occasions. These same associations may be a clue to why some people become addicted to abusing food.

Another clue is the relationship of the bulimic to her father, unlike the anorectic, who is desperate to be mother's "good little girl." The bulimic usually sees her father as a distant and elusive figure who becomes stellar in concept—competent, dynamic, and dramatic. The bulimic's mother is usually solicitous and nonsupportive.

The bulimic must be taught to substitute less fattening foods like an apple or yogurt for the midnight binge and use an action, like washing one's face or brushing one's teeth, to delay the sleeplike state in which the binge usually takes place.

Methods of cure should be multidisciplinary and highly individualized in combination with therapy, nutritional counseling, and family therapy.

OVEREATERS ANONYMOUS, a not-for-profit, self-help group patterned after Alcoholics Anonymous, was founded in 1960. It relies heavily on spiritual guidance. Write World Services, 2190 West 190 St., Torrance, CA 90504.

SALT

Our hunger for salt is an instinct ingrained in us through thirty million years of evolution. While excessive salt may be a key factor in the diet of people who are genetically destined to risk high blood pressure, a daily amount of one tenth of a teaspoon is vital to life.

Our brain signals hunger when the body does not have enough salt to control the amount of water between the cells. Animals, too, have the same hunger and will chew bones for the salt they contain and will forage the pond bottom for plants that accumulate sodium. Common table salt is sodium chloride.

The salt-deficient person is likely to feel weak and lethargic. Muscle aches and cramps follow almost any physical exertion. Other effects are nausea, vomiting, and confusion. Another clue to salt-deficiency is loss of taste. It was thought at one time that salt tablets should be taken by those who perspire heavily, especially during the summer months. But that advice is no longer given (except in extreme cases) since the average American diet now contains more than *twenty times* the daily minimum need. According to the *Harvard*

Medical School Health Letter, there is no longer any need to reach for that salt shaker.

An increased salt intake builds up fluid in the heart and blood vessels, increasing blood pressure and forcing the heart to work harder. Prior to a menstrual period, water retention can make you feel waterlogged. Rather than taking a diuretic to release the extra water, go easy on salty foods about one week prior to the onset of the cycle.

Sodium is found naturally in almost all fresh food and dairy products. But preserved and processed foods contain excessive amounts of sodium. The most undesirable are canned soups, canned vegetables, many baked goods, flavor enhancers, baking powder, baking soda, catsup, relishes, pickles, mustard, horseradish, soy sauce, and garlic and onion salts.

Salt used as a preservative is found in large amounts in smoked products, bacon, sausage, luncheon meats, corned beef, canned fish, Parmesan cheese, some cereals, sauerkraut, and tomato juice.

Good substitutes for salt are pepper, herbs, spices, and sea kelp (available at health food stores). Nuts, popcorn, crackers, and other foods are available unsalted. Best choices on restaurant menus are low-sodium chicken or fish. Check the labels on diet sodas. Many have a high salt content.

WATER

Water is so important to the proper functioning of the body it must be considered a food. We can survive prolonged fasts, but several days without water would be fatal. Water carries nutrients, hormones, disease-fighting cells, antibodies, and waste products to and from the body organs. It lubricates the joints and mucous membranes and is the solvent that enables us to digest and absorb food and discharge waste. It also provides the body's cooling system.

According to Helen A. Guthries, M.D., of the University of Pennsylvania, reducing the body water by 4 or 5 percent will result in a decline of 20 to 30 percent of work performance. A loss of 10 percent of the body water would cause circulation failure, and a 15 or 20 percent loss can be fatal.

Normally, 2½ quarts replace the daily loss and are supplied by fruits and vegetables as well as liquids. Dancers may lose as much as four quarts a day, which can cause extreme thirst, giddiness, or a dangerous rise in body temperature.

To determine how much water you should drink, weigh yourself before you exercise and immediately afterward. Replace the water loss within the next few hours guided by your thirst in sipping liquids, eating fruits or vegetables, or drinking cool water—if cool or icy drinks do not give you stomach cramps. Weigh yourself again to determine if your thirst has guided you to the right replacement amount. Thirst may not be an accurate indication of need for fluid replacement, since it tends to shut off before sufficient consumption. By following this procedure a few times, you will be able to determine your own rate of loss, need for immediate or eventual replacement, and the kind of water loss replacement you prefer—water, liquids, or fruits and vegetables. Don't be dismayed by the increase in weight. Remember, it's only water, not fat.

At one time, performers ate large amounts of sugar or drank honey dissolved in water thinking it gave them an extra boost of energy. But it has been found that sugar or sugared drinks actually decrease endurance about 19 percent by raising blood sugar so high it triggers the release of extra insulin to process the sugar. In ridding the body of new sugar, the extra insulin also rids the body of the blood sugar that was there *before* the extra sugar intake. A quick sugar fix is soon depleted, creating a new low that feeds the habit of thinking more sugar is needed.

Caffeine drinks and alcohol act as diuretics and *increase* water loss through the urine, while sugared "athletic" drinks promoted as thirst quenchers or electrolyte replacements add calories. If you lose *over* three quarts in perspiration per day, add one half tablet of salt to your diet. Excessive perspiration may be caused by nervousness.

The weight you lose by layering rehearsal clothes on your body and by closing the studio windows to induce perspiration is only water loss—not loss of fat. Nor is perspiration an indication of hard work. You need oxygen to breathe and to function mentally while the working muscles give off carbon dioxide. There is no way to "sweat off" or spot reduce areas of the body with plastic clothing.

The usual recommendation that we consume six to eight glasses of water each day can be repugnant if your local water supply is unpleasant to taste and smell, and may be unsafe to drink. Although that amount of pure water is recommended for good health, it may be in any number of forms—juices, fruits, and vegetables. Plain tap water, if it is safe, is the most inexpensive, noncaloric, caffeine- and sugar-free drink to consume.

There may be any number of dangerous organic chemicals found in water—gasoline, photographic developer fluid, kerosene, herbicides, arsenic, asbestos, lead, industrial waste, seepage from septic tanks, and weed killers. Safe and good drinking water is odorless, clear, and clean tasting.

When traveling to another city or country, it might be wise to drink only bottled water, although the choices may be "enhanced" in a variety of ways. Basically, purchased water falls into three categories: sparkling mineral water (carbonated water, often from an underground spring); seltzer (carbonated tap water); and club soda (carbonated tap water to which mineral salts are usually added).

Mineral Waters

Copper, zinc, fluorides, radium, and magnesium are frequently added to mineral water. Minerals impart a distinctive taste and some believe they have health-giving benefits. Unfortunately, non-U.S. brands are not required to list the contents of the bottle on the label as American brands are required to do. Some non-U.S. mineral waters have as high as 135 milligrams of sodium per liter. The Food and Drug Administration gives a five-milligram limit to a label that says "salt-free." Clean-tasting, inexpensive mineral waters are: White Rock and Saratoga Naturally Sparkling Water.*

---

*Recommendations are according to a *New York Times* test, 1984.

Seltzer

Seltzer water in the famous siphon bottle has made a comeback. Cartridges of carbon dioxide and the bottle with the dispenser can be purchased to spark up tap water. Seltzers contain no or little sodium when purchased by brand, and are moderately effervescent. Recommended for low-sodium content: Krasdale, Manischewitz, White Rock, and Snapple Sparkling Water.*

Club Soda

Club soda is usually filtered and carbonated tap water flavored with minerals and mineral salts such as sodium bicarbonate and sodium citrate. It is a good drink to choose when your stomach feels queasy. Best brands are: No Cal, Krasdale, Hoffman, and Canada Dry.*

After you have read labels and selected your favorite drink, when and how you drink it is up to you. Some dancers prefer to "dry out" before a performance or class, while others can sip in the dressing room during a performance without discomfort. Still others, although it is not permitted in a good school, will drink during a class in the classroom. Still others prefer to replenish up to three cups of lost fluid within fifteen minutes after physical exertion. A few experience violent stomach cramps if they swallow iced drinks. Experiment until you find the best solution for you.

If you drink bottled water while traveling, remember not to brush your teeth with local water. Be mindful of water-washed salads or fruits. Order drinks without ice cubes. Yogurt, eaten daily for two weeks before departure, is said to compete favorably with disease-causing bacteria in the intestine and is especially effective in combination with antibiotic and antidiarrheal drugs. Avoid pasteurized varities of yogurt; you need live cultures for the best protection.

---

*Recommendations are according to a *New York Times* test, 1984.

SLEEP

Insomnia, difficulty falling asleep and staying asleep, as well as sleepiness and fatigue during the day, is a condition experienced by 59 percent of the professional dancers in the New York City area, according to a Performing Arts Center for Health survey.

Sleep, a natural function with a biological rhythm that should require no conscious effort, can be disturbed by daytime physical activity, psychological stress and interpersonal problems, physiological and organic disorders, and excessive worry.

How much sleep is normal varies from person to person, and the need for sleep seems to lessen as we grow older. Albert Einstein slept almost half the day while Thomas Edison, who resented the intrusion of sleep, slept only four hours a night with frequent short naps during the day. Alfred the Great preferred a pattern of eight hours for work, eight hours for play, and eight hours for sleep. But then, he didn't have to rehearse, perform, do homework, travel on planes, or experience jet lag.

Generally speaking, physical activity requires eight hours to recuperate from the day's work load. That time may be spent in repose or even in a mild state of dozing.

Extraordinary exercise, however, will require a significantly longer period of sleep to repair muscular strain and clear the mind. Rest relaxes the muscles and rids them of accumulated wastes called metabolites. Muscles, however, shorten with rest, making slow careful warm-ups necessary when you begin your class, rehearsal, or performance.

Extreme fatigue produces painful, stiff movements. Since tired muscles respond too quickly or too slowly, forcing the body to work in this condition leads to careless movements that can result in injury. No one can determine this point for you. You must know your own limit and become aware of your muscular condition and response time. Sleep may elude the exhausted dancer but quiet rest will gradually restore the body to a point of relaxation where sleep will come naturally. Being too tired to sleep is a warning that the mind and body are being overused. Complete physical and mental exhaustion requiring hospital care is not unusual for a performer but it is preventable.

Learn to Nap

Deep sleep, in the five-stage system describing brain activity during sleep, arrives after stages one and two of light sleep. The deep dream sleep of stages three and four involves rapid eye movement (REM). It is considered perfect sleep. Stage five is a light sleep before the wakeful end of the sleep period.

During the deep dream sleep the eyes dart about frantically, the brain works at full steam, and breathing becomes rapid, but the body is essentially unable to respond to the dreams—probably as a protection against acting out the dreams. During other stages of sleep, moving and shifting the body positions are frequent while the brain and heart relax.

Learning to nap might be one of your most useful accomplishments during a busy season. A good time to practice napping is during rehearsal breaks of one hour or more; while traveling on trains, planes, or long bus trips; during slow dress rehearsals or long days on the set. Naps that become sleep and more than a doze or snooze can range from five to thirty minutes. The procedure works on an inner alarm system and can be learned in the following way:

1. Lie in a comfortable position. Once you have mastered this technique, you will be able to nap in almost any position.
2. Close your eyes and visualize a clock with the hands of the dial in the position of the time *you want to wake up.*
3. Keep your eyes closed as you clear your mind of interfering thoughts, and obliterate colors by continually "seeing" the color black. Tune out noises as well.

Keep practicing, and soon you will wake up at the time you visualized. At first, you might set an alarm clock or a kitchen timer just to make sure you don't oversleep. Napping will not affect the nightly sleep pattern since its resorative powers are short-lived.

If sleeping becomes a problem, vary your preparatory procedures:

- Eat your lightest meal before your performance. If you snack at night after a performance, make it fruit or cereal.
- Have a firm mattress and keep a clean, comfortable, airy bedroom.
- Make sure your room remains dark in the early morning.
- Allow yourself a transition period including a warm or cool bath, a glass of skimmed milk (no alcohol or cola drinks), or an herbal tea brewed fresh each time. (Make sure it is not made from senna, buckthorn bark, dock roots, aloe leaves, catnip, juniper, hydrangea, jimson weed, lobelia, nutmeg, wormwood, or sassafras. These can be stimulating or produce side effects.)
- Develop slow-down rituals like personal grooming during this period.
- Avoid over-the-counter sedatives. The aftereffects are worse than sleeplessness.
- If you wake up during the night and cannot fall asleep within ten minutes, go into another room until you are sleepy once more. Avoid watching TV or raiding the refrigerator. If you awake worrying about something, write it down and face it in the morning. Return to bed when you become sleepy again.

Another sleep-inducing suggestion: Before getting into bed, try resting with your legs lying up the wall for five to ten minutes. Once in bed, do deep breathing exercises as you relax from toes to head, releasing the muscles and tension in each part of your body with deliberate effort.

If insomnia becomes chronic, let the body become so tired it will naturally fall into a sleep pattern. Don't use a sedative unless your doctor recommends one. Your body is trying to tell you it needs help, not a quick solution.

5

The Male Dancer: Starting Out

Statistically, male dancers in professional companies are almost equal in number to female dancers. Since the 1960s, dance has gained appreciation, a new audience, and steadier financial support. Male dancers may now consider a career in dance to provide reasonable financial stability, social acceptance, and a continuing career in dance past the performing years.

Dancers are considered athletes, to some extent, by today's audience and males have gained admiration by the comparison. Since gymnastics and sports are considered suitable for small boys, male dancers who have been active in sports and who begin their dance education at the age of ten, twelve, or even later bring some agility, strength, coordination, and quick reflexes to dance. What will be missing physically by starting dance classes at a later age than eight years will be in the turnout of the hips, although some bodies have a natural rotation in the pelvic area that can be gently encouraged into a good turnout.

Also missing will be the muscular development that accompanies the turned-out position. But turnout and muscular development may be induced with careful body conditioning to some degree.

A young sports-minded male also brings to dance a desire to excel through competitiveness, yet has a discipline to work with others as part of a team. Team sports also require communication with others during play. Male dancers incorporate team play seemingly with more spirit, verve, and sense of teamwork than do female dancers.

The American emphasis on sports and the need to excel in them works to the advantage of male dancers. No one type—musician, mathematician, bookworm—is as popular and visible, applauded and praised, as the sports star from the earliest years of school.

The young male expresses power, aggression, and control through the use of his body, and the family becomes proud of a young athlete. All this can be used to good advantage by the male dancer provided he has talent and learns that sports and the art of dance have different goals. Sports aim at optimum physical achievement, while dance aims at optimum communication and expression through the physical instrument.

In addition to the appreciation of the new audience for the dancer as athlete, the international stardom of dancers such as Edward Villella, Jacques d'Amboise, Rudolf Nureyev, and Mikhail Baryshnikov has given males new role models and inspiration. A male dancer, if he meets the mark, can now see fame and fortune in his future. And almost every major school in the country will search him out and give him scholarships to continue his training in dance.

Unfortunately, the young male dancer's journey toward a professional career may not be full of obstacles in gaining good training or opportunities, but in gaining acceptance as a dancer by his parents and family. Unlike other countries where dance has had social acceptance for a longer time and government support, Americans rarely place the male student in a dance class at an early age. The benefits of predance classes and serious study before puberty are not likely to be considered by American parents as suitable activities for their sons for some time to come. The average American, despite the male stars of dance and the new appreciation for the art, still associates homosexuality with male dancers—a fact dancers of the past would find hard to believe. Perhaps a quick outline of how dance came to other countries and then to our own will give the unfortunate association some historical perspective.

In general, men and women have danced together and separately at folk festivals, rituals, court, and social events. In America, the Shakers danced separately for religious reasons. North American settlers danced the square dances of their native England and Ireland and the clog dances from their Welsh and German heritage. Americans of African descent brought their dances, modified them because they were restricted in performing them, into our indigenous American dance—jazz and tap dancing.

During Revolutionary times, theater performances were forbidden for fear our frail revolution would be influenced by antirevolutionaries taking advantage of a gathering of people. President George Washington, who liked to attend the theater, attended "lectures"—afternoon performances where buck and wing dances, hornpipes, and other dances of the times were performed in "lecture halls." American society danced the minuet and gavotte but saw none of the great ballerinas or ballets of historical importance until the nineteenth century. We had talented dancers who were discovered in America but found their careers in Paris and throughout the Continent. Except for itinerant performers from Italy, Portugal, and France, America had no national theater, school, or even large theaters for visiting performers. The legendary Fanny Elssler performed in New York, Washington, and other cities, as well as in Havana, in 1842 and took us by storm. But she did not return, nor were we visited by the great performers of the nineteenth century.

When the Metropolitan Opera was formed in 1886 there were not enough trained dancers to form a corps de ballet of quality. Opera, the traditional spawning ground of ballets and ballet companies in Europe, did not spawn them in America. Despite the efforts by many talented directors and choreographers, including George Balanchine, the opera has never yielded a separate performing company of any note in America. So two opportunities to root dance in America, through an opera company or performers staying to create schools and companies, did not materialize.

The peripatetic Anna Pavlova danced at the Metropolitan Opera

House with her company at the turn of the twentieth century and Americans were again stirred by dance. Her company was followed by the sensation caused by Sergei Diaghilev's Ballet Russe and shocked by the onstage/offstage antics of the great but mentally unstable Waslaw Nijinsky.

Because he was the first male "star" Americans admired, perhaps his homosexuality became associated with male ballet dancers—an association that still persists if only as a reaction until common sense prevails.

While it has only been a little over fifty years since the first schools of dance associated with a company were established on the East and West Coasts, and only twenty years since dance has gained so much acceptance, it may still be difficult for a young male to overcome his parental objections to becoming a dancer. While it is true that there are homosexuals in all professions, sexual preference is not determined by the choice of a particular profession.

In some professions, life-style preferences are more likely to conform to generally accepted patterns or become hidden if the individual cannot conform. In the theater, however, where emphasis is placed upon talent and not social conformity, life-style becomes a personal choice.

Parental Support for the Male Dance Student

Entering any profession where there are a number of homosexuals can be a threat to gender identity and sexual orientation for a young person. Parents are justified in becoming concerned and need to confront the issue by examining their feelings and contribution to the gender identification of the child. Familial interaction, as well as the child's basic gender identity, should come under discussion.

It should not be assumed because a young boy decides he wants dance lessons or to become a professional dancer that he is a hidden or overt homosexual. If a young boy, however, in whatever subject he shows an interest, becomes confused, withdrawn, disturbed in his eating and sleeping patterns, worried, distressed, or fearful, the matter should be confronted by both parents. This is not to say that these are symptoms of homosexuality, but that early adolescence is a time of turmoil and sexual identity is part of the confusion.

It is normal for both boys and girls to admire and choose a role model of the same sex and then outgrow that choice. If it is discovered that the object of admiration is not heterosexual, there can be disillusionment and confusion if the youngster is at a stage of development where the sexuality may go either way.

At that point, the environment can be a large factor in the choices made, and the young person should decide upon a heterosexual or homosexual preference through an honest investigation of feelings and responses, rather than be permitted to fall easy prey to anyone because of a convenient life-style. *The sexual preference and life-style of a person should not be made a component in one's success or progress in any profession.* Talent, training, and emotional health are the determining factors.

At this point of sexual confusion in the adolescent, many males, because of disappointment with their encounters with the opposite sex, may choose a bisexual life-style finding dissatisfaction filling both roles.

Because the young male student needs understanding and support at this point, and it must be decided that he will receive acceptance in the family whatever his sexual preference may be, a confrontation between parents and child should be made. Since this confrontation may be charged with so many elements of moral and religious concern, disappointment with the youngster in choosing a profession that may not be in the family tradition, or any number of other highly emotional issues, it may not be able to be faced without professional counseling.

Should the confrontation reveal that the young student's preferred life-style will be homosexual and one or both parents cannot understand the basis for the choice, they will find that among counseling groups there are those that feel that the choice of a homosexual preference may be the result of maladapting to authoritative influences in early family life. For instance, the young child may have become confused about the role each parent played in his life as an example of male and female parent. Or there may have been unusual or disruptive incidents in childhood that forged the choice.

Other counselors believe the opposite, that homosexuality is the result of chemical patterns, while still others believe that everyone makes a free choice of sexuality based upon personal experiences with the same or opposite sex, such as a disappointment in a personal relationship that discourages sufficiently not to relate again with a person of the opposite sex. Whatever the basis of the belief of the counseling, *blame should not be placed upon anyone.* No matter how disturbing the confrontation, let the youngster know that he is loved, supported, and that his talent will be given a proper opportunity for development. The important factor is honesty in deciding how the youngster can live a comfortable, happy life. Then the choice should be admitted in order to achieve a more open, honest relationship with everyone, and in order for the youngster to develop into an emotionally mature person.

If the confrontation is not made early in the youngster's life, a confrontation at a later time will be more difficult and more painful.

Whether the male dancer begins study at the age of ten or twelve or later, the syllabus is basically the same as for girls, except that the execution of the vocabulary will be performed with more strength and at a slower tempo, will include a few steps that are not performed by women, there will be no pointe work, and partnering will be an important part of the training. Emphasis in the training will be placed upon using greater strength, in mastering typical male steps such as tours en l'air, big jumps, slow beats, and multiple pirouettes. In modern dance classes, large jumps, falls, and lifts should be given at a separate time. Character dance and jazz classes should be added. If the school is large and company affiliated, separate classes for male dancers are usually arranged, but if the school is small, separate time should be given in all technique classes for male dancers.

In pas de deux classes, usually begun at the age of fourteen for both male and female dancers, the first year should include promenades and balance exercise; the second year, lifts to the waist; the third year, lifts to the shoulder; and the final year, lifts overhead and excerpts from classical repertoires or impromptu choreography.

It is *vital,* however, that a male dancer perform male roles on stage with male characteristics, and that mannerisms that are not consistent with the role of a male character be removed. A good teacher will demand noble, simple, and courtly but courteous gestures in classical male balletic roles, and a freer, more informal, yet strong and aggressive characterization in more contemporary roles. *The personal preference of the performer has no place onstage.* If the male characterization on stage is homosexual, then, too, the male performer must enact a role and not play himself.

If mannerisms that suggest effeminacy are not removed from male roles that characterize accepted maleness, the performer will find his career and artistry limited. Today there are many roles with male/female characteristics incorporated into the role. But, again, they must become a part one is playing, as the performer keeps his private life private and not acted out on stage.

While the investigation of gender identity on the part of the student is necessary, it might not be difficult or unaccepted. In any case, the preference should be defined, admitted, and the support of an artistic, talented, motivated child should be given opportunity to be expressed. Whatever the outcome, socially, pyschologically, or academically, it is secondary to the happiness and right of talent to be developed. Usually, talent will find a way, with or without help. It's far better for that talent to receive good training, approval, and support than to never reach its potential.

The Dancer
as Performer

6

Image Making
and Remaking

There are times during your performing career when you will be turned down for a role because your physical appearance did not suit the role you wanted to play. To enlarge your scope of opportunities in role playing, you may want to consider making changes or corrections in your physical image.

Naturally, a complete makeover is not possible but a great deal of changing of face and body through corrective or cosmetic surgery is possible. Body conditioning can alter your muscular structure, as well as maintain your stamina and give you more energy.

Changes may not have been possible for you at an earlier age because of financial difficulties or because your body had not yet settled into its final image. Your goal should be a more harmoniously assembled face and body image that is individual yet not limiting. Some of these changes can be made with makeup and body conditioning, but advances in cosmetic surgery have been so remarkable in recent years, they warrant your consideration. One of the more recent procedures that has met with great success is suction surgery to remove fat on hips or thighs that will not diminish with diet or hard work.

And after you have made changes, you have to get the "new you" on the market for new opportunities. Yes, you are a commodity as well as a person. Promoting yourself can be done in a tasteful and objective way.

MAKEUP AND COSMETIC SURGERY

Makeup artists used to be part of every theater staff at one time. They attended to your face and hair while you, as a performer, mused over your role as they created the proper image for your role. Some individual artists and some theaters are fortunate enough to have these experts on hand.

However, most dancers prefer to apply their own makeup since it is usually a relatively simple matter with only occasional eccentric or exaggerated changes necessary.

Unfortunately, classes in makeup and period hair styling are not part of everyone's dance education. Many dancers simply enlarge their street makeup, which does not withstand bright lights and perspiration. Or they remember that someone, during a recital when they were a youngster, placed a large, bright red spot of rouge on their cheeks, and that habit is repeated with subtle changes forevermore. Then there is always dressing room information ready to mislead the inexperienced new performer. Your dressing room companions will be a help in reviewing your makeup under lights from the audience, but first, some basic information on the beautifying and traditional matter of stage makeup. Performing, from the first dirt-floor circle dance to today's stage, has required enlargement of the facial features to characterize and enhance expressiveness. Whether you require the East Indian dancer's four-hour preparation or just your scant half-hour call before showtime, those precious minutes are all you have to look your best. While you're thinking about your role and warming up, you'll want to be sure your makeup suits your part and is properly proportioned to your body.

Makeup is no longer harmful to the skin. The Food and Drug Administration now requires a listing of ingredients on all labels. It's more than 100 years since opera singer Ludwig Leichner, appalled by the effects of mercury on the skin, developed his own medal-winning and still available stage cosmetics.

Other traditional stage cosmetic houses have colorful pasts. Bob Kelly Cosmetics, first used on the Tony Pastor Girls at the turn of the century, offer a wide variety of colors and materials for creating new noses, beards, reconstructing the entire face, and wigs of every kind. Stein's, experts since 1883, created makeup for the Pickfords, the Gishes, the Barrymores, and the Mack Sennett girls in New York's Biograph Studios—the first motion picture location.

Today, with the exception of the foundation base which should always be a stage cosmetic, brand name cosmetics are suitable for stage or photographs.

Putting Your Best Face Forward

You can learn to put your makeup on quickly after you have given sufficient time for experimentation and received favorable comment on the way you look from the front of the house—the audience. Here are some basic rules for the basis of your experimentation:

1. Always start with a fresh face cleansed with Albolene, Pond's, or Nivea. Crisco or mineral oil are the least expensive cleaners. Or use a liquid or bar soap. Keep your dressing table, all surfaces, mirrors, brushes, and puffs clean with a mild soap or alcohol, and store makeup in covered containers. Keep your materials in your area of the dressing space and try not to borrow anyone's makeup.
2. Rinse the face profusely and remove excess oil or soap with alcohol if your skin is oily, or witch hazel if your skin is normal. A brand name cosmetic toner is expensive and contains some amount of alcohol or witch hazel.

   Apply a light moisturizer to the face, neck, and chest-to-costume area.

3. Use an underbase two or three times lighter than your foundation. Or use a white underbase if your foundation is very light—Kelly's Lady Fair is a good general choice as a foundation color.

   This very light underbase should be used to white out blemishes, undereye circles, "smile" or "frown" lines, or a dark beard. Smooth out the outlines of the applied underbase.

4. The foundation base is applied over the underbase to the entire face, neck (front and back), ears, chest-to-costume area, and, before putting on your costume, to the hands as well. Have someone check your color choice under stage lights from the house seats during a dress rehearsal. If you look too red, your foundation color is too dark; too yellow, you need more brown or pearl color. Muddiness on dark skin needs a copper, not a pink tone; sallowness needs a lighter color. Make your choice carefully—you might need to mix several colors to achieve a neutral, natural-looking base to match your skin. Don't be tempted to use street makeup as a base. Grease or pancake stage makeup provides depth, shape, and good consistency upon which to create larger-than-life features.

5. Contouring, with a darker color than the foundation base, corrects proportions. It can straighten, shorten, or lengthen the nose; give a hollow to the cheeks; and recede or disguise whatever you feel keeps your face from being three equal proportions horizontally and vertically.

6. Cream rouge is applied next, although you may prefer to use a dry rouge after the next step—powdering. This is the point at which most makeups go wrong. Your stage makeup should accurately reflect the time period of the production.

   If your role is a nineteenth-century character, a contemporary dark red slash across the cheek would be out of character. A pinkish color, blurred as a circle under the eye, would be correct for this period. Men and women performing contemporary characters are best off creating

*Correct proportioning of the
face in three horizontal sections*

*Correct proportioning of the
face in three vertical sections*

a triangular shape underneath the cheekbones in a rust or brown color for men or dark skins, and in nonblue reds or coral for women. (A blue-red often turns purple under stage lights.)

7. A neutral or translucent powder should be applied after rouge with the pat-and-press method. Be generous and powder all over. Then remove excess with a brush. A splash of cold water gently patted off will fix your base through a perspiring performance. Should your makeup become patchy from perspiration during a performance, pat it dry with a tissue, then reapply the foundation, make repairs, and repowder. Use your powder to soften outlines as you continue your makeup, especially for a photograph.

8. Eyes, the most expressive feature of the face, can become a dark hole, or can show your sparkle, sense of humor, or romantic intent. Basically, eye makeup requires a three-part

The triangular shape under the cheekbones is suitable for men and women in contemporary roles

application: a color line, a contour line, and a highlight line. Choose soft colors, brown or charcoal, not green, purple, or blue. Don't try to match the color of your eyes. You're too far from an audience.

Apply the color in a lighter tone than the contour line that is next applied, close to the lashes. Then the contour line, a darker shade of the same color, is applied *slightly* above the color line if the eyes protrude, a bit higher if the eyes are small, and midway between upper lid and brow if the eyes are deep set.

The highlight line may be the foundation base color and is applied above the contour line to brow. Overall, the effect must be a *gradual* and smooth shading from dark lashes lightening to the brow.

*Contour line for the
protruding eye*

*Contour line for the
deep set eye*

*Contour line for the
small eye*

*Brow line for droopy
or hairy brows, men or women*

9. Brows are made with short, soft strokes *above* the natural brow line. Block out droopy or hairy brows with dampened soap or foundation base.

   To decide upon the shape of the brow, line a pencil alongside the nose to the inside corner of eye to brow. Pivot the pencil from the nose to the outside corner of the eye plus one quarter or one half inch more. This defines the length of the brow line. The arch of the brow's high point (for women) is directly above the outer edge of the iris of the eye. Male dancers usually draw a slighter curve.

10. If your eyelashes are long, you might find a few applications of black mascara alternating with powder will give enough buildup to frame the eyes.

   If you prefer false eyelashes, place a smidge of Vaseline or cream along the upper lid, if your skin reacts negatively to liquid adhesive—Johnson & Johnson is the preferred surgical-type liquid adhesive. Cut the lashes to cover part

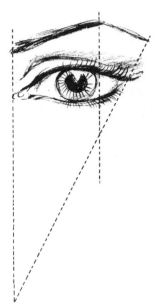

Measurements for the arch of the brow for women

of the upper lid, about one quarter inch from the inside corner to the outside corner of the eye—you may prefer to open the eye line by raising the outer corners upward.

11. The bottom line is applied *below* the natural lid and is most frequently just a straight line from the inside corner. If the eyes are very large and do not need to be "opened," the line may be placed directly on the lower lid to meet the outside corner.

12. Lipstick, in a "red red," terra-cotta, or coral color, should fill a darker pencil or brush outline. Outlining permits a change in shape, and enlarges or makes the lips smaller. Blot, repowder, and reapply lipstick. Lipgloss should not be used since it catches flying hair and smudges on costumes.

A good stage makeup requires experimentation and may eventually be applied in just a few minutes. Expert advice to help you make decisions is costly but worth it. There are a few books on stage makeup that help, but they are not the commercial ones selling off-stage beauty products.

It is unlikely that stage makeup, if properly removed and the face properly cleansed, will harm the skin. There are, however, a few procedures you might want to incorporate into your skin regime whether or not you use heavy stage makeup.

Since moisturizers do not add moisture to the skin, but prevent rapid evaporation, use a moisturizer immediately after rinsing and patting the skin dry after a shower, as well as a facewash.

Keep to a stage brand foundation base except for photos. Remove thoroughly with an oily remover before washing. If redness or irritation develops as a result of using foundation, change the brand name, not the use of a stage makeup. Perspiration leaves a high alkaline film on the epidermis, often blocking the pores and depriving the cells of vital moisture. That may cause blemishes. Remove perspiration as it accumulates during a performance.

Cosmetic Surgery

For the things makeup can't do, and because of the roles you may lose because you don't "look the part," plastic surgery should be considered.

Cosmetic or aesthetic surgery, once the privilege of celebrities and the very rich, has been sought in recent years by business and professional people of both sexes. In 1985, more than a half a million surgical procedures purely for purposes of improved looks were performed in the United States. In addition, some 609,000 reconstructive operations were done to correct deformities, rebuild body parts, and repair disfigurements, including restorative surgery of breasts.

Cosmetic surgery goes back to the turn of the twentieth century, while facial reconstruction such as nose rebuilding is said to date back thousands of years. Surgery to reduce the size of breasts has been done from the early 1900s. In the last decade, dramatic and profound changes in surgical techniques and approaches have evolved. The goals: finer, longer-lasting results and more natural, more individual designs. A list of board-certified plastic surgeons can be obtained from the American Society of Plastic and Reconstructive Surgeons, 1617 J.F. Kennedy Blvd, Philadelphia, PA 19103.

Teeth

One of the newest cosmetic procedures is bonding—an alternative to capping teeth. Resins and epoxy glues have been processed into a composite that can be shaped to correct a space between the teeth and damaged or crooked teeth—not as a substitute for capping but in some cases a suitable alternative. "If there is no dental reason to cap a tooth or teeth," Phillip Pierce, D.D.S., explains, "bonding is an inexpensive and quick solution. Although bonding may require glazing and polishing at a later date, or even require replacement after a period of time, it is a dramatic cosmetic solution for the performer."

Basically, the process requires that the composite of resins be shaped to correct the defect. An ultraviolet light binds the composite material to the existing tooth and it is then polished.

In a survey on dancers, Dr. Pierce found dental health to be the most neglected aspect of a performer's health. Along with proper care—using softer brushes, horizontal strokes at a forty-five-degree angle twice daily, and most importantly, using dental floss and fluoride toothpaste—Pierce urges performers to visit a dentist twice yearly. "Along with new cosmetic procedures, painless drilling and other modern advances have made a visit a far more pleasant prospect," he adds. Unfortunately, few health plans cover dental bills, so preventive care is important.

The effects of poor diet, bulimia, and anorexia can be devastating on teeth. A twice yearly visit to your dentist is imperative. When you are on tour in a strange country, go to a full-service (not private) hospital for emergency treatment. Call the U.S. consulate or embassy for a recommendation should you need help.

Chins

Man's evolution is resulting in smaller jaws, less sharp and prominent teeth, and practically no room for wisdom teeth at all. When a skeletal deformity or traumatic injury is the culprit, the combined effort of an orthodontist and plastic surgeon may be required. But in a vast majority of cases, a simple operation called a "chin augmentation," performed by a plastic surgeon and taking no more than twenty or thirty minutes to perform, can make a remarkable cosmetic difference. The process, described by Eli Milch, M.D., is "the insertion of a shaped, rubber silicone implant placed through a small incision in the mouth or under the chin. There are no scars after healing whatsoever. This silicone implant is not a liquid injected into the body, which can be dangerous, but a firm compound, in an enclosed package around which tissue grows, giving stability and permanence. It is an operation which can be done in a doctor's office under a local anesthetic and it can be performed from the patient's sixteenth birthday on since it will not be affected by any further growth of the body.

"Although this operation, as well as several other kinds of cos-

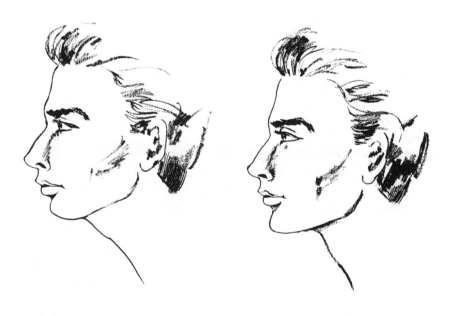

Undershot chin before augmentation

Chin line after augmentation to balance profile

metic procedures, can be performed in an office," Dr. Milch advises, "the patient should not consider surgery by a physician who does not have hospital privileges *as well as* board certification."

This operation may be a better choice than nose reconstruction to balance large features.

Ears

Ever since Goldilocks noticed those big ears on "Grandma," youngsters have been teased and taunted for ears that are not flat against the head. Pinning back your ears, surgically speaking, is an operation that goes back to the 1890s. It can be performed on a patient as young as five years old since the ear has by then reached 90 percent of its adult size. "This is," according to Dr. Eli Milch, "really two operations. They have been improved to produce a completely natural-looking result. Ears which stick out lack folds. We change the stress forces in the cartilage of the ear, its framework, to crease it back. This is also an operation which can be done in the office, but it takes about 1½ hours since both sides must be done at the same time so the matching can be carefully done.

"This operation requires a bulky dressing like a nightcap to be worn for a week. For the next six weeks, a ski-type headband is worn during the night."

Nose

By far, the most frequently performed operation is rhinoplasty, better known as a "nose job." The age group most involved in this alteration is fifteen- to twenty-five-year-olds. Performed under a local anesthetic and through the nostrils, the nose operation leaves no scars. The bone is broken and reshaped, and the nostrils are reduced in size. Although black-and-blue eyes and swelling may last up to three weeks, a small bandage is the only evidence of the operation. It takes almost a full year for final results to become apparent.

Eye- and Face-Lifts

"The excellent muscle tone of dancers," explains Barry H. Dolich, M.D., another well-known plastic surgeon, "puts them a step ahead of most people when it comes to keeping a vibrant, youthful ap-

Ears that spoil the image and head line

Ears after surgery maintain a clean head line

pearance. But while their trim, lithe bodies often seem to fool Mother Nature, inevitably time will make its mark and a young-looking body must live with an older face." The "face-lift," a catchall term that refers to the redraping and tightening of the skin of the neck, cheeks, temple, and chin, has been perfected to a remarkable degree. Similar problems of the forehead, eyelids, and eyebrows can be corrected at the same time. The eyelid lift is a frequent first facial operation for both men and women. Excess skin and bulging fat, or "bags" under the eyes, can be successfully removed, creating a rested and more youthful look. Barely noticeable incisions are made in the natural creases of the eye under the lashes. Most commonly performed on persons between the ages of thirty-five and forty-five, it is a procedure that takes about one hour and is done under sedation and a local anesthetic. Stitches are removed after three days, but full recuperation takes up to three weeks with some discoloration in evidence during that time.

The face-lift, incorporating an eye-lift as well, redrapes the folds beside the nose and mouth and erases some wrinkles, thereby setting the clock back about ten years. The incision begins at the hairline and comes down around the front of the ear. The skin is then redraped and resewn. The process takes two to three hours, with three to ten weeks for recuperation, when some discoloration and swelling are evident. Follow-up visits are required for about three to six months until the ultimate results become visible.

During all these procedures, Dr. Dolich advocates complete rapport with the surgeon. Be prepared to pay fees prior to surgery. Payment in advance assures the surgeon that the patient is not undertaking "elective" surgery that he is unable to afford, and the patient is assured that his fee is paid in full and no unexpected additional charges will follow.

Before you change your image with cosmetic surgery, consider the following advice:

- Consult your family physician or your local county medical society for the name of a plastic surgeon or write to the American Society of Plastic and Reconstructive Surgeons mentioned earlier. Although not every operation requires hospital treatment, choose a surgeon with hospital affiliations.
- Don't expect to be able to select the shape of a feature you desire to reconstruct. Your plastic surgeon will exercise his professional experience and skill to your greatest benefit. Remember, he is an artist too.
- A stable and realistic emotional attitude should exist before you contemplate aesthetic surgery. Social, sexual, or professional problems cannot be dispelled externally. Changing your internal image of yourself is required to go along with the new external image for best results.

Cosmetic changes can open career possibilities in areas not available before, or prolong an already existing career, or just provide the emotional boost we all need at times. There is no longer any secrecy or embarrassment attached to these procedures. It is simply a business, professional, or emotional necessity. And the cost is coming down.

Yes, breast reduction should be considered as a necessity if the bosom is large unless one performs Middle Eastern dance or belly dancing. Large bosoms don't bounce in time to music and place an unnecessary seductive connotation into roles. Seduction can be implied without being explicit in dance.

BODY IMAGES OF ANOTHER KIND

If your technique classes do not quite give you the stamina you need for today's demands, or if you had poor training or began to dance late in life, you should consider increasing your endurance through additional physical techniques and methodologies.

Devices and mechanisms to enhance the strength, flexibility, and alignment of the body are not new to dancers. In the last century, ballet dancers subjected themselves to a box into which they screwed their feet in first position to improve the turnout.

Male dancers in Russia wore weighted belts during the allegro portion of the class to provide resistance and improve their jump. Not only dancers but athletes and musicians have invented contraptions to increase their performance abilities—many to ruinous results.

From the turn of the century to the present, the dance profession in Europe and America has acknowledged and experimented with various therapies to enhance technique, relax and realign the body, rehabilitate an injury, and reshape the body.

Early therapists like Joseph Pilates and his followers have augmented the science and been recognized by such artists as George Balanchine and members of his New York City Ballet, Martha Graham, Hanya Holm, Ted Shawn, and Ruth St. Denis, to name only a few. Although the dance therapy movement started in New York City, there are many therapists throughout the United States who are qualified to rehabilitate and reshape the dancer's body.

Today's fitness craze has developed a terminology of its own:

exercise physiology and body conditioning taught by self-styled physical therapists or personal trainers. Naturally, cross-over therapists advertising remarkable results present a danger. One of the ways to protect yourself if you consider a body-conditioning studio (if a dance therapist is not near your area) is to ask questions. This will help you determine if the therapist, who may be qualified to practice in one discipline, is giving advice in another. You might ask: What are your credentials? Who are your clients? Do you work with the doctor of an injured client? What is your fee? Is your work mainly preventive? (Watch out for that one. There is no way to prevent an injury by manipulation except by dancing correctly.)

Licensed physical therapists, while suitable for the average person's recovery needs, are not always suitable for the dancer. Accustomed to hard physical work, their exercises often seem like child's play for a developed muscular system and do not maintain full strength to the areas surrounding an injury.

As a rule, the dancer is not interested in the "workout" sessions given in health clubs, gyms, or on videocassettes. These add nothing to technique, except to give some additional endurance if you have been neglecting the jumps in your daily class.

Enter the new world of equipment now available for the creation of a home fitness center through the purchase of machines—some similar to those used in body conditioning for dancers.

Is there any benefit in the purchase of a machine by the dancer? The decision and choices are individual, but generally speaking, exercise physiologists agree that the rowing machine gives the most complete workout, particularly in the stomach area.

A stationary bike is a good investment for increasing the power of the legs, as well as other parts of the body. Gadgets can increase the price to $20,000 for a Lifecycle complete with video to simulate various riding terrains.

For dancers who want to ski but do not dare risk injury, the PSI NordiTrack cross-country skiing machine provides a leg and aerobic workout to duplicate the winter sport at home.

Many dancers swim to release tension and to exercise against water as therapy for injured areas. Personal swimming pools, indoors or outdoors, cost from $4000 to $10,000. It would be less expensive to buy a season's ticket at the local "Y" pool.

Although there are machines to provide resistance to the body's weight, it is generally agreed that free weights such as dumbbells or hand and foot weights (2½ or 5 pounds) are more effective. With these, the body cannot favor working on the stronger side.

Then, too, with free weights you can increase strength without bulk by increasing repetitions of an exercise instead of increasing the machine weight to a dangerous level—adding bulk to the muscles. A sixteen-pound dumbbell set costs $30; ankle and wrist weights, $12 to $45; a tension band, $4; while pulley cords on racks can go for several hundred dollars.

Controversy still exists over the use of inversion boots that permit a person to hang by the ankles. People with back problems should avoid inversion since exercises in this position involve arching the back or pulling oneself up with knees straight. On the other hand, just hanging by the ankles for a few minutes without doing any exercises, with the feet in straps, can be a rejuvenating experience.

Despite the charts, detailed instructions, and pamphlets that accompany the purchase of equipment, there is no better safety measure in using machines than having a knowledge of the mechanics of the body. Insufficient warm-up before working at top-level performance does not give the body time to increase in temperature. Increased temperature is accomplished by the pumping of blood into the muscles and the stimulation of the release of synovial fluid (the body's lubricant) into the joints. Stretching before the necessary thirty-minute warm-up is an assault on the muscles, an invitation to injury, and the setting for an arthritic environment. Movements that arch the lower back instead of the upper back are as much a danger when using equipment as they are in the classroom. The body must work the machine, not the machine the body. You move it. It mustn't move you.

A beautiful body can be achieved with hard work if the talent warrants it and nature has not been entirely kind. But this kind of work has to be worth it to the student. Thighs can be reshaped, feet arched, and many aesthetic changes can be made, not to mention increasing stamina and flexibility with body conditioning work. But the therapist must adapt to the needs of the student, and the student must not decide upon the exercises to be incorporated into the regime.

Those dance therapists who work on a one-to-one basis with dancers, unlike the highly paid trainers or cross-over professionals, are not in business in the usual sense. They are dedicated toward overcoming the difficulties of technique to reach the art within.

GETTING PUBLIC ATTENTION

When you've worked hard to be part of a performance or to give one on your own, nothing is more frustrating than to perform for a small audience. No matter how loving your friends and relatives might be, you and your performers are a commodity. Modesty or a self-effacing attitude has no place here. You have to publicize yourself. Of course, you reason, if I'm good, people will know about me and come to see me perform. No. No one is keeping score, and good news doesn't really travel fast enough in the dance world.

Creating an image in the press and public eye is the province of a publicist or press agent, if you can afford one. If you cannot, you may consider doing your own research by listening to television, radio, or cable television interview shows and deciding which of the programs might be interested in your new role, new choreographic effort, or new company. Check the newspapers and magazines in your area for the same possibilities.

Then, have someone else, a friend, relative, or one of the concert press agents who charge less than unionized publicists, write the press outlet asking for an interview. Have this followed up by a phone call. It is far easier for an interviewer, program director, or newspaper editor to discuss your suitability to the outlet with someone other than you. Otherwise, it would become too personal a discussion and would cause embarrassment to both persons.

If you are asked to appear on a program or for an interview, be prompt for the date, have all your facts ready in writing for the interviewer to repeat at another time, and be cheerful, articulate, and nonjudgmental of the work of others. But sure to thank the interviewer at the time of the interview or later in writing.

If you are refused, remember to be courteous and not take the refusal personally. Each press outlet has its own policies and reasons for including or not including certain kinds of information. Just keep sending the same outlet regular information about your activities.

If you are a member of a large company, you should not consider promoting yourself. The company press agent decides which company members may be asked to do interviews or will receive talk show invitations. Should you be asked by a press person individually, get permission from your company press agent to appear on the show. He or she will give you the proper information about the company's activities and your role in that company.

Any photo in the repertoire of the company is property of the company and may be used for publicity purposes at any time without payment to you. You may ask for a press photo of yourself for your files, but may not send it out to press outlets. You may dislike the publicity photos taken of you, but that will not matter. Usually, the publicity photo taken by the company photographer will be far better than any other kind of publicity shot.

Most mentions of appearances do not appear in local papers or magazines for a very simple reason: The information does not reach the proper editor before deadline. Magazines require a two-month lead time before the event. In other words, your release or information must reach the magazine more than two months before the date of your event.

Local papers require at least two weeks notice, and Sunday papers a three- to four-week lead time notice.

Here are some good rules to follow if you want press for yourself, your company, or a series of performances:

- Check with your host theater to see if advance press material has been sent out. If it has, keep giving the press department details to continue the flow of information.
- If you are presenting your own work on a series, a single date, or in a new theater or city, issue a release before the deadline date of the press outlet even if you don't know all the details of the performance such as who will dance the roles, who is making your costumes, etc. The space must be reserved and a general mention of the performance is more important than the details of the performance. Phone each outlet to determine the right editor or desk to send the information to and to check the deadline dates for releases and photos.
- Good photos are a must. Costumes help gain you a place in print, but they must be simple and not blur your figure or face. Prints should be 8 × 10 glossy photos, in black and white, taken with a plain backdrop. They will probably not be returned so don't send your precious old photo of your first teacher.
- Learn to write a good release. It should be double-spaced and typewritten on one side of the paper. It should answer the questions who, where, what, when, and how. Sometimes why you are giving the performance will gain you extra attention, such as a twentieth anniversary.
- Before your radio or television interview, have someone rehearse with you. Don't wear anything black or white on television, ornate jewelry, or an outrageous hairdo unless that is part of your image. Keep your movements controlled and your voice more or less on an even level. Keep cool if the interviewer interjects a conflicting opinion in order to make the show more interesting or to present another view. Remember to give all the details of the upcoming performance or your subject such as where and when, and especially who will appear.

There are many management courses and many books on publicity available to the performer. There is no longer any conviction that "dancers don't talk" on media. Agnes de Mille, Margot Fonteyn, and Martha Graham have been superb talkers for their performers and their performances. Like everything else you do, you have to practice.

7

Body Care
for the Performer

Maintaining your health, beauty, and physical sense of well-being can become fairly routine, and be relatively inexpensive if you develop good and regular habits of body care.

A clean, tidy appearance shows you to your best advantage onstage and offstage and doesn't detract from your talent and ability—what you want everyone to notice. As you create an individual daily, weekly, and monthly routine, watch for indications of wear and tear and warnings that a change in your beauty or health routine is needed to prevent damage to your physical self. Eventually, if remedies are not found, your work will be affected.

YOUR EYES

Do you have trouble focusing on your "spot" during a series of turns? Find it easier to see your partner approach for a lift from one side of you than the other? Do you have to squint to see a combination given at an audition? Wait patiently for a stagehand with a flashlight to lead you to safety after a blackout?

The Council on Sports Vision believes there should be equal emphasis on physical and visual fitness because there is a direct connection between how well a dancer sees and how well he or she performs. In a pioneering research project initiated and directed by Donald S. Teig, O.D., the result of testing more than 275 major league baseball players indicates an unmistakable correlation between visual fitness and performance, visual training and expanded physical capacity.

According to the Performing Arts Center for Health (PACH) health survey conducted in conjunction with the New York City Department of Health, eye disorders were fourth on the list of ailments—an obvious area of a dancer's neglect.

Do you know which is your preferred eye? Teig describes this simple test to determine your preferred eye: "Extend both arms in front of you at eye level and make a triangular opening between your hands by touching thumbs and forefingers. With both eyes open, sight an object about fifteen feet away through the triangle. Close first one eye, then the other. If you are right-handed and the object disappears when you close your right eye, you are same-side dominant. If the object disappears when you close your left eye, you are cross-dominant."

While cross-dominance is ordinarily considered a defect, supposedly causing confusion in the brain, more people in the arts are cross-dominant and left-handed, thus activating to a greater degree the creativity center of the brain. While equal ability to turn to the left as well as the right is important to your training, if you are a "lefty" the vision experts believe you should turn to the left whenever possible. Most choreographers will accommodate on this matter. And it will be easier, as well, to see your partner coming toward you on your preferred eye side.

While the inner ear plays a large part in maintaining your balance and in preventing dizziness during a series of turns, correct "spotting" involves your ability to focus on one fixed point after each revolution. Teig suggests this exercise to improve the concentration on a fixed point: "In a darkened room, using a strobe light (available in electrical or hardware stores), practice turning in place while focusing on a fixed point. Do this for one or two minutes during a half-hour period seven times a week, varying the speed of the strobe."

Peripheral Vision

While seeing out of the corner of your eye has been part of your training, you may be slightly tilting or turning your head while dressing right or left. To improve your peripheral vision, Teig offers another home exercise: "In a darkened room using a flashlight on a near distant wall, block off the sight of one eye while following the light with the other. Keeping your head stationary, move the light to the outer corners of your vision as far as possible. Repeat with the other eye. Increase the distance of the circumference each day, side to side, up and down, diagonally and in circles. Do five minutes daily."

Ancient Chinese beauties watched goldfish swim in a large bowl for a few minutes each day to aid in smooth and effortless coordination of the eye muscles.

Depth Perception

In addition to the usual guides onstage (wings, front lights, illuminated stage marks), Teig gives an exercise to sharpen your awareness of distances: "In a well-lit rehearsal room, start counting distance from your partner by calling out the estimate in feet. This is good practice for the accurate placement of a lift from a jump. Gradually darken the area so your depth perception will improve on stage."

Slow recovery time after being in a spotlight or glaring lights indicates an eye examination is required. After a blackout, the transition from temporary blindness to normal vision should not take longer than one or two seconds. Ballerina Alicia Alonso, who is sight impaired, uses lights onstage as boundaries and has developed her perception to an astounding degree. "Strangely enough," Teig adds, "I find many performers have so adjusted to their visual limitations that they don't want to improve their vision because they are fearful of seeing the audience too clearly!"

Visualization

Although this exercise might seem more suitable in a drama classroom or a course in positive thinking, it is nonetheless important as an eye exercise. In the preparation of a role visualize the movement. "The neuromuscular system will respond to what you have 'seen' when you visualize your movements while sitting quietly and practicing mentally," says Teig. "Make your visualization positive, especially after an injury. See the movement over and over again in a positive way, never replaying your errors. See yourself always doing your best."

Sophisticated equipment and exercises have been developed to increase distance acuity, near-point acuity, convergence, and divergence (your range finder), depth perception, peripheral awareness, spatial awareness, and glare recovery.

Here are some questions to determine if you need an ophthalmologist (a diagnosing eye physician and surgeon) or an optometrist (a state-licensed professional who tests for defects and prescribes glasses or contact lenses):

- Do your eyes turn in or turn out at any time?
- Do you have frequent headaches, nausea, or dizziness?
- Do you thrust your head forward or backward to see a combination in class?
- Do you avoid close work, have a short attention span, or daydream a lot?
- Do you place your head close to your reading material?
- Do you frown, scowl, or have blurred vision when reading?
- Do you blink excessively or rub your eyes frequently?
- Do you confuse similar written words, become nervous or irritable after visual concentration?

Answering yes to any one of these questions indicates a consultation by an eye professional is necessary. The optometrist will refer you to an ophthalmologist if your condition needs more investigation. Often, both are in the same office.

Contact Lenses

Contact lenses for stage may be a suitable choice if you have an eye defect. Since 1508, when Leonardo da Vinci sketched his ideas for contact lenses, solutions have been sought for comfortable eye wear. The best solution for stage is the hydrophilic plastic lens that absorbs moisture. The cost is not inexpensive. Don't look for bargains when dealing with your eyes.

If you become a contact lens wearer, use your hair spray first when making up. Insert the lenses, then apply makeup as usual. Avoid lining the inside of the lower lid. Avoid eye whiteners. Remove lenses before removing makeup.

YOUR SKIN

Your skin, all 6 pounds and 17.2 square feet of it, works hard. It protects you from injury and disease, regulates body temperature, prevents excessive moisture loss, stores food and water, and disposes of waste. It contains a dark pigment called melanin which gives skin color and protects the cells below the surface from ultraviolet rays. A good skin is unblemished, uniform in color, firm, smooth, resilient, and responsive to the touch. It improves quickly with proper diet and regular care.

The epidermis or outer layer contains cellular debris created in the bottom layer which has risen to the surface and must be sloughed away. The dermis, or inner layer, contains lymph and blood vessels, oil and sweat glands, hair follicles, nerve endings, and collagen—the protein that gives your skin resilience. The subcutaneous tissue varies in thickness according to age, sex, and general health. The sebaceous glands keep your hair glossy while the sweat glands carry off waste through the pores.

Your Skin Type

The acid mantle on the surface of your skin is composed of secretions from the sebaceous glands and is mostly acid protein. The hydrogen level of this acid mantle, known as the pH balance (percentage of hydrogen ions), is rated on a scale of 0 to 14, from dry skin (acid) to oily skin (alkaline), with a normal skin reading about 5.6. Your skin pH balance can be determined in a blot test at a cosmetic counter of any department store. Bear in mind that your regime should be based upon long-range symptoms and frequent reassessment.

Dry skin (pH 0–4) is thin, delicate in texture, often scaly or flaky, and sometimes blotchy, feels itchy and tight, and wrinkles easily. Avoid strong soaps, harsh cosmetics, exposure to sun, wind, indoor heating, and air-conditioning. Dry skin requires mild cleansing, diluted toner (water mixed with witch hazel), rich moisturizer, eye cream, and a weekly masque and exfoliation.

Oily skin (pH 9–14) is thick, rough textured with large pores, shiny, greasy, and hard to keep made up. It probably has blackheads

Elements of human skin: Outer skin, epidermis, contains cellular debris; inner layer, dermis, contains lymph and blood vessels, oil and sweat glands, hair follicles, nerve endings, and collagen

or whiteheads, pimples, and dry eye and neck areas. Avoid dehydration from too-harsh soaps. Oily skin requires cleansing, an astringent (alcohol), light moisturizer, eye cream, and twice weekly masque and exfoliation.

Combination skin (pH 0–4 and 9–14) is dry around the eyes and neck but oily around the forehead, nose, and chin, with dilated pores, whiteheads, and coarse texture. It requires dry *and* oily skin care.

Sensitive skin (pH depends on whether oily or dry type) reacts allergically to certain oils and the elements, becomes irritated, congested, itchy, and red, and has broken capillaries. It requires dry skin care plus lubrication.

Black skin and its care are different only in that excessive irritation may cause increased pigmentation known as scarring. Dermaness has created Polished Ambers through Revlon, a complete program for oily, dry, or combination black skin.

Acne is not necessarily a teenage condition. Its pH depends upon the skin type. A new climate and unfamiliar food or water may cause a temporary condition. Most authorities agree that adolescence, hormonal imbalance, stress, and the assimilation of food are causes—but do not name nuts, chocolate, or sweets as the main culprits. Acne is not the result of any unclean habit and the condition should not cause any emotional embarrassment. Serious acne cannot be outgrown. Delaying treatment can result in permanent damage. Antibiotic or vitamin A treatments sometimes produce side effects. Consult a dermatologist.

Generally speaking, acne skin requires several washes daily using special soaps such as Fostex or Clearasil. Rinse profusely, pat dry, and use an astringent or a medicated lotion on face, chest, and back, and never, never squeeze or spread the infection by rubbing. Serious scarring can result from squeezing.

The Basics

After you have determined your skin type, choose your cosmetic products carefully and use them faithfully. It is not a question of price that determines the effectiveness of the product but your constant use. At the sign of any irritation or redness, discontinue use of the product.

Brands of color makeup for street wear, such as blusher or rouge, mascara, lipstick, or eye shadow, should be changed every six months in order to avoid a buildup of the contents in your skin that may eventually cause irritation. Products such as makeup base, liquid or solid soap, moisturizer, and night creams need not be changed once you have found the right ones for you unless irritation occurs.

Skin needs a cleanser (soap or liquid cleanser), rinsing as much as ten to twelve times with water, an astringent or toner to remove all traces of soap, a weekly masque—which might be homemade from kitchen products such as egg whites or commercial clay products— and exfoliation—removal of dead cells—through the use of a Buff Puff™, sea salt, or mechanized brush. Or you may consider a monthly thorough cleansing process done at a salon as well.

The number of times you wash, exfoliate, or have a facial in a salon depends upon your skin type, age, sex, and budget.

The Cleansing Procedure

1. Use an oily product (Nivea, mineral oil, apricot oil, Pond's, or Albolene) to remove all traces of makeup. Tissue off.
2. Rinse profusely with tepid water ten to twelve times. Pat dry.
3. Use a freshener, toner, or astringent commercial product. These range from strong to mild depending upon the alcohol content. Use with a cotton pad. (One part alcohol to three parts distilled water, witch hazel, or one teaspoon lemon in three teaspoons water will do for a normal skin. Straight alcohol is fine for oily skin, and witch hazel suitable for dry or combination skin.)
4. Apply a moisturizer before applying makeup base or use at night if your skin is dry.
5. Older skins may require a night cream that is highly nourishing. These are usually expensive and are given large advertising exposure. Avoid estrogen or hormone content in your night cream. Castor oil makes a good eye cream if that

is all you require. Because it is sticky, it is not comfortable if used over the entire face.

6. Masques and facials activate circulation, bring nutrients and oxygen to the surface, cool and soothe, deep cleanse, and purify. This step may be taken once a week after using a toner. (Avoid commercial mint masques or any with a prolonged tingling or cooling chemical effect. They may irritate the skin.)

   Apply the masque directly from the tube or jar with your fingers onto the face, avoiding the eye area. Leave on for twenty minutes, then rinse off. An egg yoke with three drops cider vinegar and one drop of olive, mineral, or castor oil plumps a dry skin. Warmed honey is antiseptic and stimulating. Yogurt, sour cream, or buttermilk will calm an inflamed or blemished skin. Moistened oatmeal will cleanse and brighten. A clay or mud pack—any commercial variety will do—is the oldest masque, mentioned on Egyptian papyrus 3,000 years ago. Chanel and Aida Grey make smoothing masques. Grey's come in fruit fragrances.

   A facial in a salon is expensive but relaxing and gives a temporary lift and plumpness to the skin. Once-a-month facials are ideal for both men and women. Be sure to choose a registered salon. Don't permit squeezing or removal of pimples except by a dermatologist.

7. Exfoliants. Any rough material used with or without a cleanser will remove the outer layer of dead cells. This step is important for older skin once a week or even daily if the skin feels rough and thick to the touch and whiteheads accumulate just below the surface. This cell-removal step may be taken after makeup has been wiped off but there is still a light film of oil on the skin. Sand, oatmeal, sea salt, or sugar rubbed gently over the skin then washed away with the cleanser is an ancient but effective exfoliant process. Don't be too rough on your skin.

Treatment for Troubled Skin

There are alternative procedures for less-than-perfect skin. Dermabrasion is a useful method of reducing the scars of acne, brown "age" spots, "smile" and "frown" lines, "purse string" wrinkles around the mouth, and the effects of too much sun—the skin's worst enemy no matter what protective sunscreen product you use.

Dermabrasion, a surgical procedure, is performed with a dermabrader, or planer, that looks like a dentist's drill. It sands off the top layer of the skin. After administering an anesthetic, the doctor uses the planer rapidly and lightly brushing the top layer of skin. The immediate results are swelling and a crust that temporarily gives a shocking appearance. But when the crust dries and becomes scab-like, it is removed and the skin below is smooth and new. Dermabrasion, which requires great skill on the part of the surgeon, may be chosen as an alternative to 5-Fluoracil (5-F.U.) treatments.

A chemical peel, the 5-F.U. creams and lotions for home use are becoming more popular for removal of small sun spots, lesions, and pigmentation. Like the dermabrasion process, the reaction of the skin is redness and scab formation. Unlike other chemical peels containing trichloroacetic acid (TCA) or phenol, 5-F.U. seeks out and destroys damaged cells without affecting healthy cells.

Another choice for treating deep lines or forehead wrinkles is collagen treatments. They are especially useful for raising scars, pits, cleft lips, or chin lines. Collagen, derived from the Greek word for glue, is naturally produced by the human body and accounts for one third of the body's protein. As fibers of protein, it is found in all skin, bones, tendons, ligaments, and dentin, the ivory-forming mass of the teeth.

The basic collagen fiber begins as a chain of about 1,000 amino acids. Three of these chains twist and link to form the collagen molecule. These molecules form fibers that weave with other collagen fibers to create a veritable latticework of tissue.

A test injection of bovine (cow) collagen is made on the arm, and if there is no adverse reaction, such as redness, soreness, or itchiness, for one month after the test injection, the treatment may begin. How collagen weaves itself into bone or ligaments is still a mystery, but when injected into the skin, it is tolerated by the body and not rejected as a foreign substance.

Pinprick injections of collagen are spaced in such a manner as to fill out the depression being treated, such as an acne scar or wrinkle. The collagen, carried in a saline solution, leaves some swelling that disappears in twenty-four hours as the saline dissolves and the collagen begins its cycle of molecular-fiber-scaffolding.

Bovine collagen, under the trade name Zyderm, is an injectable collagen that is manufactured in Palo Alto, California, and has been approved by the FDA for use by doctors trained in its use who are members of the American Society of Plastic and Reconstructive Surgeons.

YOUR HAIR

Your hair, crowning glory or disaster area, is a symbol of attractiveness, health, fashion, and beauty. Coifs can reflect a free-flowing, militaristic, celibate, or superficial society. For dancers, hair indicates a profession, costume, and, as it does for everyone, your degree of health, stress, grooming, and fashion sense.

You have about 140,000 hairs if blonde, 110,000 to 120,000 if brunette, and 80,000 or so if redheaded. Each contains a medula center, surrounded by a bulky cortex and a cuticle covering with melanin for color. It is composed of the protein keratin and grows six inches yearly. It has a life span of five years before falling out. Facial hair may be different from the hair on your head.

Oily hair is fine and limp, with very active oil and sweat glands, and possibly an odor. This kind of hair should be washed daily to avoid stringiness, but first use a conditioner for sixty seconds before washing with a mild shampoo—using half the amount of shampoo suggested. Rinse well, condition, and rinse again.

Dry hair is dull, tangles easily, is frizzy on the ends and coarsely textured. Shampoo after rinsing first. Condition full strength, using a warm olive oil pack weekly. Shampoo. Rinse. Towel wrap and comb with a wide-tooth, nonmetallic comb. Avoid direct sun and pool water. Bleached, permed, straightened, or damaged hair should be treated as dry hair.

Constant traction on the hair by pulling it back into a ponytail or knot can result in hairline hair loss in females.

Dandruff, from an inflamed or scaling scalp, a cousin to eczema and psoriasis, is of unknown but noncontagious origin. Massage rinsed head gently for thirty seconds with the pads of your fingers without using fingernails. Wash with a mild shampoo and rinse repeatedly. Use one part antiseptic such as Listerine, Seabreeze, or Scope to two parts water and with cotton pad apply inch by inch to the scalp. Change shampoos frequently. Avoid baby shampoos which are stingless but are harsh detergents, not soaps.

There are many fine hair products on the market. Any coloring at home, however, is a dangerous process. Have a good hairdresser make the first test and choice of color, then follow the choice with products bought in a beauty supply store. This is especially important on tour. Knowing your formula and having someone apply the color, activated with hydrogen peroxide that can be purchased in any drugstore anywhere in the world, will save you despair in strange salons.

Kitchen products work well as rinses for at-home shampoos. One part lemon or vinegar with forty parts distilled water removes the hard water you may have had to use for your shampoo.

Experts suggest you color and perm in separate sessions and never sleep in rollers or pins.

Hair loss in males can be traumatic. Early treatment should be considered although none are entirely successful. Nothing as yet can stop a programmed gene from balding a head, but abuse, neglect, or stress can take a staggering toll. Diet, work patterns, habits, illnesses, hormonal changes, shocks, and even one's sex life are reflected in the hair.

General Stage Hairdos

"Classical" hairdos for stage in ballet are based upon nineteenth-century fashion. It requires a center part and a bobby pin directly over the ears to begin the coif. Swirl the hair below the pins over the ears and secure with more pins. Draw the remaining hair into a large barrette center back. (Do not use a rubber band because it tears the hair.) Make a bun or attach a hairpiece with crisscrossed bobby pins or long hairpins with one end twisted outward.

If your hair is fine or only shoulder length, wrap the hair around

Crisscross bobby pins and twist hairpins for added security

tissue paper to make the bun look fuller. Cover the entire hairdo with an elasticized hairnet, tightening the net to make a neat covering. Remove and replace the bobby pins over the ears with hairpins that have a twisted end to prevent them from falling out. Keep everything smooth and tight. Spray or pomade stray hairs that may catch the light onstage and disrupt the trim and proper grooming of the hair. Give your head a good shake or two to discover loose pins. Repair.

Many dancers today prefer to have short hair and to wear a half wig for roles in this period. How often you perform roles in this era may determine your preference for your own long hair or a wig for this coif. Wigs are hot and get steamy. Part of your after-performance shower should include a shampoo.

"Semiclassical" hairdos are preferred for contemporary ballets. Center part or pull back the hair without a part to the top of the head and fasten with a barrette. Pull back the sides and back of the hair and fasten with barrettes. Make a bun of the remaining hair or attach tissue paper or hairpiece for more fullness. Place elasticized hairnet and fasten into smooth and tight cover. Spray or pomade stray hairs especially around the back of the neck.

This basic contemporary hairdo can also serve as a basis for period roles that require falls of curls, large hats, or headdresses. The bun makes an excellent anchor for hat pins.

It is also a basic hairdo for classwork and auditions. The hairnet can be omitted but the look must be neat and tidy. If you use colorful ribbons or clips, they must not fly about or distract as a fashion item.

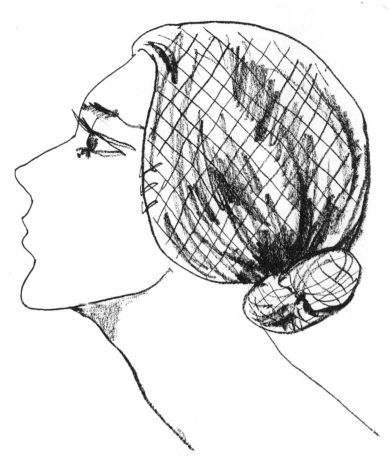

Basic classical hairdo for nineteenth-century ballets

Male ballet dancers prefer a coif with longer hair in back to avoid wearing a wig in period roles. The hair should be frequently trimmed to frame the face and clean and sprayed so it won't flop around during a variation.

Men and women modern dancers can be more currently fashionable in their choice of hairdos for stage, although "classical" modern ballets require the "semiclassical" hairdos of the ballet coif. Black male and female dancers prefer tight-to-the-head coifs and half wigs if the roles require them.

Whatever the coif, it must frame the face, remain fixed unless

Body Care for the Performer   133

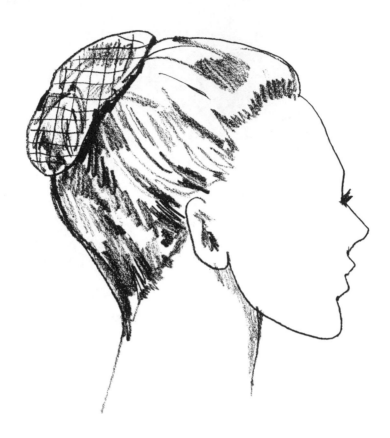

Semiclassical hairdo for contemporary ballets

the choreographer requires otherwise, and look clean. Like a good stage makeup, it's a question of experimenting to achieve a tidy yet attractive appearance onstage.

YOUR HANDS AND FEET

Hands are an expressive part of your body image from the time you are taught to round your fingers and connect your wrist to your forearm in your first class to the more articulate elongated fingers and arms used to express strong feelings. For the East Indian dancer,

Male ballet dancers prefer longer hair to suit roles in many eras

hands and fingers are an entire vocabulary of speech and part of his or her basic technique.

The lacquered and beringed fingers of the East tell the story as eloquently as the movements of the body. Western dancers, although not permitted jewelry or colored nails onstage, still require a well-groomed look.

Nails can indicate the state of your health. White spots, horizontal ridges, split or flaky nails can mean a lack of iron or calcium in the diet. There is no evidence, however, that gelatin added to food

Modern and contemporary female dance performers can be more currently fashionable in choice of stage hairdos

Male modern dancers may be more contemporary in the choice of stage hairdos

or drink is as good a source of protein for nail strengthening as a balanced diet that includes poultry, eggs, or cheese.

A weekly manicure can keep your nails trimmed enough not to scratch a partner, and a pedicure can keep your feet relatively soft and pain-free, or with the calluses in the right place with sufficient flexibility.

How to Give Yourself a Manicure and Pedicure

1. Remove old polish by saturating a small pad of cotton in polish remover. Place on nail once or twice to remove all color. Use emery board to shape nails using filing motion one way. Nails should not be longer than one quarter inch beyond tip of finger.

2. Rough spots on the feet—soles, heels, large toes—should be

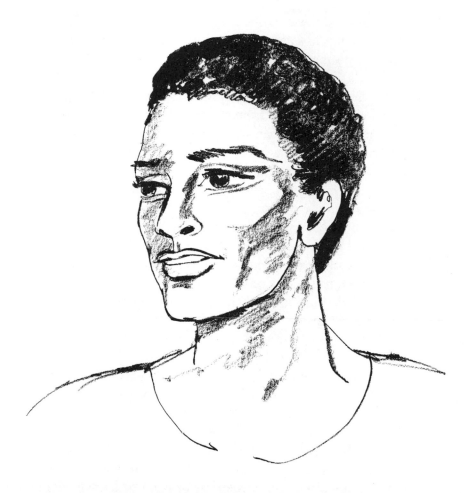

Male black dancers prefer tight-to-the-head coifs

rubbed off with sandpaper boards of a file. Keep calluses as protective to hard-used places on the feet, but reduce the dryness and hardness sufficiently to maintain flexibility. A nail clipper should be used to cut straight across the top of the toenails instead of a file. Length should be flush with the end of the toe, not shorter or rounded. Ballerinas in an earlier age used to let their nails grow over the toes before pointe shoes had sufficient stiffening.

3. Soak hands and feet in warm sudsy water for ten to fifteen

minutes and towel dry. Add two tablespoons of baking soda to the water to soften calluses and soothe aching feet, if you prefer this method for rubbing off hard spots from the soles or heels. Towel dry.

During the week, between manicures and pedicures, remove hard surfaces from hands and feet with a wet pumice stone after you shower or bathe. If calluses grow too hard to remove or lessen, and hurt, see a podiatrist.

4. Apply cuticle remover to each nail. During the week and between manicures, gently push back the cuticles when drying hands and feet.

5. With a cuticle knife—not an orange stick—lift the cuticle gently and scrape the surface and undersides of the cuticle clean, working from the sides to the center. Clean under the tip of the nail and wipe with sudsy water.

6. If needed, trim cuticles with a cuticle knife or scissors. Apply vitamin E, Crisco, or nail oil overnight to the cuticles once or twice a week to keep them from becoming ragged, dry, and developing into hangnails.

7. Massage feet and hands with Vaseline Intensive Care Lotion or a skin cream and rinse cream off each nail.

8. Separate toes with tissue and paint a base coat on each nail. Base coats smooth the surface and prevent discoloration of the nails by polish. You may color your toenails, if you are a female dancer, to strengthen the nails and to make the feet look more attractive. A colorless or plain pink color should be applied over the base coat and a top coat over the polish. Male dancers may use a base coat or may prefer to buff their nails to a shine.

Colorless nails are a tradition onstage because red color exaggerates the size of the hands and makes the nails look like dripping fangs.

Shoe Care

It goes without saying that a good fit of the shoe is required for comfort, safety, and happy feet. Experimentation with the vast number of manufacturers and custom possibilities will help you find the right shoe for ballet and for pointe classes.

Jazz and musical theater shoes come in high fashion colors and can be worn with street clothes, even when the street clothes are dancewear. Dancewear has developed into layered clothing that is so fashionable on the street, it is difficult to tell where someone bought the clothes and for what purpose. There are shoes to go with every outfit including boots for men and slightly heeled shoes for dance teachers in various colors.

All shoes for class or stage should look trim, neat, and be well-kept. Trim hanging threads on a pair you don't want to give up to age, and use a beige or peach foundation base on soiled pointe shoes. Powder and keep your ribbons washed and trimmed even for class shoes. Good habits take less grooming time in the long run. Because shoes are expensive, they should be properly folded if the shoes are soft, or wiped off after each use to protect the finish and remove spots before they harden and are more difficult to remove. If shoes are wet from perspiration, they should be stuffed with newspaper into the proper shape and permitted to dry thoroughly. Alternate wearing your pairs of shoes to permit them to harden between wearings. Some dancers alternate left and right pointe shoes and ballet shoes for longer wear.

When your pointe shoes become soft at the toe, use a plastic hardener on the inside of the box or bake them at 200 degrees, with the oven door kept open. While shoes worn by professional dancers seldom last longer than two performances, every now and then a pair will be so comfortable and durable that it can be worn for more performances. Because pointe shoes are handmade and fit to custom specifications, there is no guarantee that any pair will be like any other. But all will be expensive—the costliest part of a dancer's wardrobe for the company or the individual dancer.

Imported shoes are enjoying a well-deserved popularity. They are made with excellent leather, satin, good glue, and come in a great variety of beautiful colors.

Nearly everyone owns, even if they do not wear such shoes in their work, a pair of soft shoes—sometimes known as ballet shoes. These come in expensive leather or canvas and should fit less snugly than pointe shoes should fit, but should not be so tight as to numb the toes.

Dancers in the New York City Ballet never wear ballet shoes (considered men's ballet shoes) for rehearsals or class. The shank of a pointe shoe is removed by extricating five little nails after the shoe has served for performances. The box is strong enough to support the dancer should she decide to try a step on pointe during rehearsal or class. This custom strengthens the feet as well as providing a ready pointe shoe without going through the ritual of changing shoes every time the dancer wants to rehearse something on pointe. Nevertheless, a bagful of shoes to tote around throughout the day is the dancer's lot. Fortunately, a light one.

YOUR TEETH

Teeth should be cleaned as part of the stage makeup procedure. The purpose of brushing, as it is before bedtime, is to remove particles of food and to keep the teeth clean. Neglected removal of plaque, an odorless, invisible, transparent composite of bacteria, saliva, and food particles, turns into tartar, a hard substance which requires professional removal. Brush thoroughly at a forty-five degree angle to the juncture of tooth and gum tissue two or three times daily with a short *soft*-bristled brush. Use waxed or unwaxed floss as your nighttime final brushing. With a sawing motion, work up one side of the tooth to the gum line, then work the floss down the other side. Clean each tooth in this manner.

Toothpaste will not make teeth whiter; brushing does. Toothpastes containing fluorides are the best choice for the under-thirty-five group. Teeth sensitive to heat, cold, sweet or sour foods, even to touch, is a condition suffered by one in every four adults. Denquel is a brand of toothpaste especially formulated for sufferers of this painful sensation. Natural cleaners for the teeth are apples, celery, and carrots, but they are not substitutes for toothpaste.

Braces may not be noticeable from the stage. They are now bonded onto the teeth. Light-colored or transparent, they may be placed behind the teeth and/or be removable. Careful washing is required.

YOUR EARS

Prolonged exposure to disco music or long rehearsals with loud music can reduce physical and mental efficiency as well as produce high blood pressure, ulcers, and other problems of the circulatory, digestive, and nervous systems. The outer ear gathers sound waves from the air and passes them on to the eardrum membrane, which vibrates to sound. The middle ear, on the inner ear side of the eardrum, is a chamber about the size of a pea and contains the smallest bones of the body: the hammer, anvil, and stirrup. The eardrum's vibrations are conducted by these bones into the fluid-filled inner ear in the temporal lobe of the skull. The inner ear contains the cochlea, a small shell protecting the organ of Corti, with fine harplike hair that picks up high and low sound. Increased mechanization has increased hearing loss possibilities for each one of us. The louder the sound, the more vibration. These vibrations are changed into nerve impulses and conducted to the hearing center of the brain.

The fluid-filled ear is the mechanism that acts as a stabilizing gyroscope when you do multiple turns, keeping you from becoming dizzy. It is the reason we learn to "spot" when turning. Any rapid or irregular motion will upset the delicate balance and cause seasickness or airsickness. However, if you experience dizziness for any other reason, earache, buzzing, or noises, see your doctor at once. Ear discomfort when you travel can be prevented by keeping the eustachian tubes open. Stay awake while landing or taking off, and keep swallowing or chewing gum to equalize air pressure between the outer and middle ear. Try not to travel with a cold, but if you have to, use a nasal decongestant spray before takeoff.

As for those vibrations, it's the low frequency and high intensity sounds that can lower your energy and psychological reactions. Sound is measured in decibels. Decibels—named after Alexander

Graham Bell and abbreviated *dBA* when measured on the A scale audible to the human ear—increase logarithmically. Every ten dBAs the noise doubles. So ninety dBAs is twice as loud as eighty dBAs. Therefore, 10 dBAs is a barely audible sound while 140 dBAs is the pain threshold.

The safety zone is eighty dBAs to ninety dBAs. If you work or perform under disco-level conditions, take frequent fifteen-minute rest periods or use earplugs (for swimming too). Use a sound-level meter if you're not sure. The cost is nominal. Your hearing is priceless.

When cleaning the ears, around and behind the ear is sufficient. Never, never probe the ear with a cotton-tipped stick. Wax buildup can cause temporary deafness. Have a doctor remove the wax and clean the ear.

Piercing the lobes is a good way to keep from losing earrings onstage and off. Keep the lobes clean with peroxide.

HOW TO HANDLE JET LAG

Minimizing the effects of jet lag when you have a rehearsal schedule looming ahead is important. Not long ago, dancers traveled by bus and performed on an unfamiliar stage the same day. Union rules have all but eliminated that practice today. But there are exceptions.

Biographies of Anna Pavlova recount harrowing experiences of travel for her and her company in the early part of the century. There were storms during sea voyages, local wars, and dancing onstage by Model-T Ford headlights when electrical power failed. She never missed a performance and rotting stages did not deter her from her mission to bring ballet to the world.

But despite all the mishaps, travel was slower and there were days to rest between engagements. Today, airplane travel is so swift and comfortable, the performer is lulled into the general atmosphere on board of its being a social occasion only to find his or her biological clock ticking away in another time frame upon arrival. Hence the time hangover or, to give it a more glamorous name, jet lag. And because the performer can travel from one place to another so swiftly, engagements are frequently too tight to give much rest in between.

Some dancers feel no effects from travel and sleep, eat, or rest easily in any mode of travel. Others simply do not smoke or drink alcohol and eat lightly as a solution to jet lag. But for those with queasy stomachs during air travel, or those whose sleep habits are easily upset, NASA, our national space program, might have some solutions for you.

NASA has used the findings of the Division of Biological and Medical Research at Argonne National Laboratory in Illinois for space flights. The same division has created a transatlantic timetable for those of us who travel in a slower, lower atmosphere. Let us assume that your travel day is Wednesday at 9:30 P.M., eastbound and transatlantic. It is suggested that you begin adjusting to your new destination time frame on Sunday by eating your normal diet, eating lightly on Monday to encourage depletion of glycogen reserves, eating normally on Tuesday, and on Wednesday eating lightly avoiding carbohydrates, coffee, tea, colas, or alcohol. The findings for this flight also suggest you take heavy doses of caffeine at "tea time" on the transatlantic flight. They suggest you start your new day on "destination time," with a high protein breakfast, high protein lunch, and a low protein, high carbohydrate dinner. Westbound, the procedure is the same except on the light day before the flight and on the day of departure, caffeine is suggested before noon.

All this is to adjust to a six-hour difference in time on transatlantic flights. However, this is not a dancer's schedule since eating too lightly if there is a rehearsal or performance will deplete glycogen (energy) reserves too drastically. And it may be that the dancer does not take heavy doses of caffeine into his or her system at any time.

So you have to use common sense in the extent to which you use these findings. Eating lightly, avoiding heavy doses of alcohol, and resting in a darkened environment will reduce jet lag for everyone at any time during travel. But disturbing energy reserves when energy is what should be kept constant in a dancer might not be wise.

But there's light at the end of the jet lag dilemma. A hormone called melatonin, secreted by the pineal gland, a tiny gland near the brain, helps the body adjust to changes in light. In recent tests by biochemists from the University of Surrey in England, subjects who took melatonin for three days before and for four days after a transatlantic flight found the hormone alleviated jet lag. More testing is needed before the hormone is placed on the market.

But, again, we must weigh the consequences of taking drugs to alter our natural ability to adjust to changes in climate, time, and food. The best advice is to learn to rest if you can't sleep on your new destination time, to work carefully if fatigued until you adjust to your time schedule, and to know your own physical ability to adjust to changes. Large companies provide time for time changes. But smaller companies and individual artists must avoid pushing the biological clock to the point of injury or drug abuse.

8

The Stresses in a Dancer's Life

STRESSES IN PERFORMING

In the past two decades, dance in America has achieved tremendous popularity, accceptance as a viable career, and appreciation for its creativity and wide appeal.

Not too long ago, dancers faced economic deprivation, poor social acceptance, and struggled to find good instruction.

Although competition for jobs has increased, the number of opportunities to work in major companies and regional groups has also increased. "Today," as Robert Joffrey of the Joffrey Ballet puts it, "no good dancer need be without a job."

Yet dancers complain about the physical and mental demands of performing as never before.

Although technical demands on the body are greater than ever, instruction is begun at an earlier age and is generally on a comparatively high level throughout the country in almost all large cities. This permits technical demands to be met safely and on a higher level. Medical knowledge recognizes the need to treat physical ailments and injuries of both the athlete and dancer as specialized therapies.

Perhaps the complaints are based upon unrealistic concepts of achievement. Many dancers no longer see dance as a way of life, as they once did, but see dance only as a career. Without the stamina to remain in a profession because of love for it, unmet expectations can cause complaints.

In the findings of the Performing Arts Center for Health (PACH), the psychiatric clinic headed by Judith Kupersmith, M.D., at NYU-Bellevue Hospital in New York City, dancers tend to put physical problems before emotional distress. Although these dancers are able to handle professional responsibilities, in some cases, these professional achievements have been at the cost of emotional maturity. High professional achievement doesn't always give time for interaction with one's peers and frequently results in insufficient experience in dealing with emotional stress. Above all else dancers are people too. They are not exempt from society's demand for instant gratification and relief from all discomforts, physical and mental.

After breaking down the resistance to reveal underlying emotional complaints, the following arguments emerge as typical of performer/patients indicating stress:

"Now that I am a performer, and working with other dancers who are all more or less on the same level, how can I evaluate myself and my next goal?"

The issue for the individual who has successfully obtained a job or goal as a performer is adjusting to the changes that occur once that goal has been achieved. There might be a loss of interest and a general letdown physically and emotionally—especially for the dancer who has worked hard—once the goal is achieved.

The decisions you have to make at this point are very different from the ones needed to obtain that job. The "stars in the eyes" of the young student whose goal was to become a member of a company soon disappear if there is no realistic view of what that job entails. It is a new reality to find that going to classes, rehearsing, and hard work not only remain the same, but increase in amount. In addition, the pressure of performance, changes in hours, and the necessary change in life-style require changes in your personal, social, and economic life.

After you have given yourself a period to adjust to the changes and accept your new responsibilities, it is time to reevaluate your goals once more. The period of adjustment is not carved in stone; it will vary according to the difficulty of the job and each dancer's capacity to adjust to changes.

You can try to make do where you are and settle for that and enjoy that place for a long time. But if you become discontent or find that you clearly have another goal in mind, such as another company or another kind of dance experience, a conflict is definitely created.

Your responsibility is to your current job, and your other goals are secondary. It is not unusual for a performer who might be studying music, drama, or other subjects, while holding down a demanding performance schedule, to have other goals, but less time and effort should be spent on them than on his or her current job.

"Do I continue to compete with my peers? Are other professional dancers always my rivals?"

The sense of competing is still a part of your life. You are no longer the best one in your class or at an audition; you are working with others who were the best under those same conditions. Finally, working with equals and not being the best can be a shock, and can produce a defeatist attitude. Take your time adjusting to your new schedule. It will soon become apparent whether or not you are in a company where the dancers support one another. You will make friends and enemies, as happens in all situations, but you need not let your personal likes or dislikes enter into your competitiveness for new roles. Compete only with yourself.

"How do I handle the fact that every now and then someone seems to have all the luck, get all the parts, and with no apparent talent that is greater than that of anyone else?"

This luck—as you put it—is a "golden boy" or "golden girl"

situation where someone comes into a setting and, without striving or waiting for an opportunity to arise, automatically becomes the shining star. This person may not have worked any harder, may not possess any more obvious talent or personal charisma. But for some reason not clear to anyone else except the person making the choice, this individual becomes "perfect" for the part. That is a situation that produces a devastating and discouraging effect on everyone because it seems so unfair.

It is. But it happens in families too, in which one child is "perfect" and the others make all the mistakes. This child, like the "golden" person in any group, is the product of a fantasy on the part of the people who promote him or her. And this child develops according to the fantasy, for better or for worse. The outcome is never predictable because there is no one pattern to this situation.

The way to handle the matter is to isolate that person psychologically, not in a physical sense, but in your mind. The best way to deal with this would be to say to yourself, "All right, this has happened without explanation or apparent logic, just as things happen in the world that seem unfair and unjust. Do I fight the world? Or do I recognize that an individual is too small and that only with a concerted group approach can things be changed?"

The most constructive approach would be to consider these people exceptions and realize that most of us must function within the rules and regulations of progress and change. You must understand and accept the fact that we all have not been provided with the same fantasy and must earn our way ahead in another way through the usual course of action. Trying to operate on the pattern of "luck" that seems to surround someone else won't work for us.

"How should I handle that 'golden' opportunity if it should come my way?"

Success early on, before a maturing period within a person's emotional life, can create several upheavals. The first goal if you receive an unexpected reward is to maintain the work level without fear, panic, or sudden apathy. The component of guilt may be involved because the "lucky" person may *know* that his or her talent is only comparable to another person's talent. Just as in a sudden sickness, a sudden success can create a "why me?" question in the mind of the victim of unexpected success.

There has to be a certain acceptance on faith that the abilities seen in you by others are real and that you can live up to them. Here again, an early trusting relationship helps, but if that has not been your pattern in the past, you have some work to do on yourself and your capacity to meet new challenges.

"What should my course of action be if I am not one of those 'golden' performers?"

First of all, you have to have a feeling, an educated guess or an intuitive sense, that you can perform a certain role that you want. Moving ahead is frightening because you must convince someone else of your capabilities. It has to be done in a way that will not overpower, overwhelm, or take away from the person you are trying to convince, that it was *he* who thought you could do this role, not you. In other words, you don't want to protest his decisions, just to ask for a chance to learn or try out for new roles.

Some directors want you to walk into their office and, in an assertive and confident manner, tell them you are ready for great things. But usually the power and the control of the organization rest with him alone. A discussion has to be initiated that is not manipulative, but at the same time you have to present yourself as capable and worthy of the chance. You have to indicate that, if given the opportunity, you will be able to meet the demands. A positive approach can set up a dialogue in which you assert your possibilities.

If you are told that you are not ready, or are given a reason why you are not suitable, you can learn about your weaknesses in a way that you might not be able to see in your own assessment of your talents; you can then prepare to strengthen those weaknesses.

You have already asked indirectly if you are considered suitable to a role by having the conversation with your director. So the result can only be a constructive evaluation of your abilities. When you have given yourself a reasonable length of time to correct the weaknesses indicated by your director, you will be ready to try again for the next level.

Smoking

The house was full. The spotlight caught the ballerina as she made her entrance for her classical variation. There was something in her hand. She dropped it quickly and stomped on it with nervous bourrées. It was a lighted cigarette that she forgot she had in her hand.

An unlikely story. No. It actually happened in a major company with a leading ballerina. In those few seconds, the ballerina violated the fire rules of the theater, the characterization she presented to the audience, and her personal health.

Statistically, more young women smoke cigarettes today than ever before. The dancer, unfortunately, is no exception.

Nicotine, the poisonous alkaloid found in tobacco leaves and one of the most toxic and addictive of all drugs in the form of tobacco, is harder to overcome than addiction to heroin or alcohol. Although the average cigar contains enough nicotine to kill several people, its danger is largely destroyed while the cigar burns. But in smoking a cigarette, the nicotine content is still so strong that the body develops tolerance to protect itself in a matter of hours, compared to the days and weeks necessary to build tolerance to heroin or alcohol.

Tobacco addiction, in the form of smoking cigarettes, is still the most socially accepted form of self-abuse despite government-mandated warnings on the cigarette pack. Damage to lungs, heart, brain, and blood vessels from smoking has been common knowledge since the federal government demanded warnings on labels. Unfortunately, nearly everyone knows someone who has smoked for years without visible damage to the body. A confirmed or constant smoker is willing to play Russian roulette to be that someone who does not suffer damage from smoking.

Peer pressure, *everybody* smoking, is as much a reason to begin smoking as it is to begin anything else. The desire to grow up, yet to be part of a group, to be different, yet accepted, sophisticated, and "with it" provides the initial impetus. No matter how unattractive the dangling cigarette, the wincing mouth, the narrowed eyes, it doesn't matter if one looks grown-up.

While many have always considered men who smoke more attractive and sexier—flamenco male dancers even smoke onstage before performing to indicate their "macho" attitude—the attitude of and toward women who smoke has changed over the years. In the early part of the century, smoking indicated a kind of liberation for women. The use of a cigarette holder, the position of the hand, the posture of the head and upper body, the slow inhaling and exhaling, exuded daring, worldliness, and shocking behavior.

Today, the image is more "butch," tough, assertive, and may be largely defensive behavior. Cigarette advertising implies that smoking is now a woman's right and an indication of her sophistication. That's highly suggestive conditioning if you want to be considered mature beyond your years. But psychologically, cigarettes are adult pacifiers manifesting strong oral needs triggered by feelings of frustration, anxiety, boredom, or any feeling of deprivation in some part of your life. The mouth has to keep moving to comfort the apprehensiveness.

But the persistent habit of lighting up in the dressing room while putting on makeup or immediately after class indicates a physical dependency on nicotine that demands a smoke rather than the psychological need of the moderate or occasional smoker.

Although damage to internal organs and wrinkling of facial skin are the result of long-term addiction, the effect on vitamin intake and medication of any type is reduced immediately by half.

In long or short terms, smoking for the dancer reduces development of the breathing apparatus, which is necessary to increase endurance. If breathing is not comfortable while doing the allegro portion of class, or the jumping or other physically demanding sections, smoking may be taking a toll already. If you find yourself too tired, out of breath, or coughing during those portions of class, are you sure you're not leaving the room because of your smoking habit rather than real fatigue?

Other causes for discomfort may be smoke, insufficient oxygen, or general pollution in the room. The muscular system throws off carbon dioxide during activity and *more* oxygen is needed, not less, in the form of fresh air. Layered clothing will combat a chill but ventilation is a must.

Breath control, gaining a "second wind" during jumping portions after a few seconds of rest, is unfortunately not taught to the extent it once was. As a result, any discomfort in breathing causes the dancer who smokes to avoid the practice of that part of her or his dance vocabulary. For the male dancer, this avoidance is critical since large jumps are so vital to his technique.

Not caring becomes pervasive. The body is the dancer's only instrument. Not caring about it indicates not caring about your profession or dance life, and if you don't care about either, you don't care about yourself. If *you* don't care, no one else will or should be asked to care.

Techniques to Stop Smoking

As in any change, the first step is to admit the existence of the condition. The second step is to seek a technique to lose the addiction and the third is to take an active involvement in the addiction-ending technique. Hypnosis as a procedure works for the suggestible but not for the repressed, wary, rigid, or suspicious person. If you are a suitable candidate for hypnosis, be sure you choose a professional medical hypnotist, not an entertainer. Cassettes to aid in self-hypnosis work for some and are available through advertisements in a reputable medical journal.

Cold turkey, a total abstinence, has been the best method for some. For others, Mark Twain's comment applies. He, an incurable cigar smoker, said he could stop smoking at any time and had, several times. If you try this method, expect to suffer the effects of withdrawal: tremors, irritability, and restlessness.

The American Lung Association has devised a twenty-day program, a self-help procedure. It begins by congratulating the potential subject on deciding to "get rid of an ugly, unnatural habit that robs you of energy, blunts your sense of taste and smell, and costs a small fortune." Briefly the program encompasses: (1) Finding out why you smoke; (2) Learning about smoking triggers; (3) Seeking coping techniques that include deep breathing; (4) *Dispelling the myth about weight gain* if you stop smoking; (5) Choosing a partner to go through the program with you; (6) Brushing your teeth after each meal; (7) Coping with withdrawal symptoms; (8) Refusing offers of cigarettes from others; (9) Using substitutions for cigarettes; (10) Banking the savings of the cost of cigarettes.

The program is available from your local American Lung Association. Because of the discipline and concentration already instilled in the dancer, this program should work for you.

While some laws have provided protection to the nonsmoker in airplanes, trains, and elevators, there is still insufficient protection in restaurants, offices, backstage, and in studios. If you feel strongly about this, you might ask that smokers light up outside in the hallways away from the studio and dressing rooms, and see that a fresh supply of oxygen runs through the room before each class.

Asking someone to stop smoking in your area demands tact, courtesy, and sometimes assertiveness. Be prepared for a sharp and defensive retort. Remember, the smoker is addicted and not likely to consider your rights and feelings any more than he considers his health.

STRESS IN RELATIONSHIPS

"How can I make friends outside my profession?"
It is possible to have friends in the same company despite competitiveness. Relationships are important to progress and happiness. But the regimented life of a dancer can make friendships and relationships quite complicated. Friends outside the company can be a source of delight, relaxation, support, and inspiration—provided they understand the restrictions of your profession without becoming offended. People in other professions or arts would understand your limits. You can make your tours a wonderful way to expand your knowledge and friendships by obtaining the names of people to call wherever you go. Discovering a new city through friends of friends can fill your limited time with enjoyment. Maintaining friendships through letters is easy enough to accomplish between rehearsals. Keep the lines of communication open.

"How do I compete with the 'playgirl' image of our society?"

You don't have to compete. Beginning with the English model Twiggy a few years ago and with the general recognition that exercise is beneficial, the more slender silhouette is considered attractive. Young men today prefer active young women. If you feel unfeminine or unattractive with a typical dancer's figure, or if you are being "put down" for physical reasons, find a new beau.

"How do I compete with the 'great provider' image in our society?"

One of the biggest problems of the profession is projecting a financial picture into the future. Dance and theater make financial commitments very tenuous, and that must be clearly understood. It does not mean that dancers are irresponsible; it does mean that, despite all our progress in the past two decades, some sectors of society still hold the view that male dancers cannot provide sufficiently for others. Very often, money, respectability, and self-worth, which are separate considerations, become bound together erroneously. Males with a good attitude toward money will find the means to provide for the needs of others through the new opportunities provided within the profession. A sense of respectability requires that men and women follow a clear-cut code of ethics that they share with friends. Self-esteem grows with fulfillment, achievement, and creativity within your career. People who have put aside their dreams would place a high value on your pursuing what some would consider a risky business.

"How can I manage a career and a deeper relationship?"

Meeting someone who is attracted to you as a "glamorous" person may not be difficult at all. But meeting someone who can empathize with your emotional state after a performance, share the good times and the low feelings, acknowledge that your personality offstage may not be what it is onstage is another matter.

Sustaining a relationship that is not superficial or based solely on physical attraction is a bit easier for women today. Changing attitudes in our society have recognized the need for a personal creative life in order for both parties to expand and grow separately and together. Making choices of freedom in some aspects of your life, while you keep traditional values in other aspects, is what you have to work out between yourself and your partner.

While there are more couples involved in relationships in the same company or profession than ever before, a mutual understanding has to be reached when a career decision involves a separation, a change of geographical area, or a change in the work schedule. The most important factor here is to come to terms about what is important to you and then to give that information directly and honestly to your partner. Sometimes a partnership that is entirely one-sided seems to work, and the personalities do seem to mesh. But that is an exception and it does not work over a long period of time.

On the sexual level, women have become more demanding and outspoken. This has put a new pressure on the sexual performance of the adolescent and the older man. We have to realize that responses vary. Some men respond only physically, some emotionally at first, then physically, and some with a combination of both. Communication of a gentle, loving, and undemanding nature is required.

"What effect does a long separation have on a relationship?"

None, if the relationship is a strong one. However, we all know those sayings that go "Out of sight, out of mind" and "Absence strengthens love, weakens affection." You can look at it any way you want, but our feeling is that a lot of understanding is required during these separations. That means phone calls and letters to maintain communication are necessary. Being busy is no excuse for not keeping in touch. It is not a matter of a lack of trust, but of communication.

"How can one handle the possibility of a 'one-night stand' in a relationship?"

Every relationship is a form of contract. If there is a mutual agreement that during long separations, the "one-night stand" may come into the picture, that can be worked out. There is no formula. Many times, the more involved relationship will reveal its strength or weakness in this kind of circumstance more clearly than if that possibility became a secret or was not discussed at all.

The "one-night stand" is all right for certain people in certain settings; it is not something on which to pass moral judgment. In some instances, it adds to stress; in others, it relieves stress. Here again, if it is understood that it is a short-term contract, there will be no remorse or guilt. That kind of relationship may be the only extent to which someone can show caring. Trying to prove one's worth with promiscuous activity is rarely more than prefabricated excitement followed by the need to prove oneself again and again. Intimacy without closeness is not love.

There is a great difference between making love and loving. On the other hand, one occasionally finds someone so limited in relationships that no sexual involvement enters the picture at all. This kind of repression or fear of sex has more to do with developing trust and showing one cares than it has to do with sex itself.

"How does one balance a twosome in which one dancer seems to be able to handle progress when the other is not progressing?"

Elliot and Hilary lived together and were members of the same dance company. Elliot, while a good and successful performer, did not see himself leaving his career to become a teacher or choreographer. Elliot, older than Hilary, was beginning to think of developing more security, of marriage, and having a family. Hilary was still inspired by her profession and not ready to give up her career when all was going so well, and she was enjoying her rise in the ranks.

Elliot was considering a career change that would not take as long as it had to learn to perform—ten years. His ego, talent, and self-esteem were tied up in it. Rather than teach or choreograph, he wanted to do something completely different. That was his way of coping with loss. It takes a long time to reintegrate after a complete change. But with determination, will, and perseverance, a new career will emerge. He knows that if he breaks with his theatrical life, he will have to break with his girl friend as well. It would be too painful for him to see her continue and succeed while he does not. If Elliot can cope with the career loss in a short time by finding a theatrical outlet, he will have a new sense of security and direction. But if he finds, during the course of his therapy, that he must run far away into a completely new area because dance means too much to him, there will be a complete and final break with Hilary.

Both are in therapy separately. Elliot is working on his career and personal problems equally. Hilary seems not willing to give up her career. In the best of circumstances, a two-career theatrical twosome has a difficult time. To succeed, growth must be parallel, but not necessarily equal. The age difference between Elliot and Hilary is a factor. But the fact that Elliot was the star when they first met and now Hilary is the star is giving Elliot's ego a beating. Give and take are part of every relationship; how much each must give to find a balance requires flexibility, communication, and adaptation. There are some men who can thrive on the success of a wife. Some cannot. Society requires the male to be the protector and provider.

Elliot will eventually learn that his discipline, creativity, and former experience will not put him at the beginning of a career, but somewhere ahead of others.

Hilary will be happier with an intimate relationship in her life. That may be with Elliot or someone else at a later time. A painful course is ahead for both Elliot and Hilary, but at the end of it they will know themselves better and make choices they can live with and not be dictated to by other circumstances.

"How should one handle a homosexual relationship and can there be a protection for couples living together?"

The homosexual relationship is handled the same as a heterosexual relationship. Communication, emotional maturity, sharing, and caring are important to the growth and happiness of everyone. It would be wise for homosexual or heterosexual couples living together to devise a cohabitation contract. Although this may seem very impersonal, or a form of commitment, it provides for the protection of children, property, or personal effects that might be threatened by a dissolution of the cohabitation arrangement. It is an active, responsible, and aware stand to make, and it is important to every relationship.

"How does one handle a situation in which sex, drugs, or excessive drinking are involved in the progress of one's career?"

Peer pressure is around us from the time we are children and throughout our lives. It is of great significance to the adolescent to understand that it is not necessary to compromise in order to further his or her ambitions or to get along with a group. Ask yourself how you would be able to live with the knowledge that your career was based upon your social acceptance in a new group, rather than on your talents. If you can live with this, fine. If you cannot, without passing judgment on the life-style of others, simply make this fact known and limit your involvement to the activities you can enjoy without including the ones which might become self-destructive.

If your pattern has been self-destructive, you can always find a new opportunity to continue that pattern. Only you can judge to what extent you can reap the rewards of your career without harming yourself.

"I have what others consider a 'celebrity status' and have much to offer. But I find it difficult to make the person I'm closest to see that my career makes great demands on me."

Felice and Jason were married. Felice had a nontheatrical job and catered to her dazzling celebrity spouse in every way. She adored him and deferred to all his decisions, making her needs an afterthought. There was glamor and excitement in being attached to someone as famous, successful, and attractive as Jason, but Felice was beginning to become angry, stifled, and resentful. In a sudden move, Felice left Jason although he became violent and hostile to her when she threatened to leave him. He indicated bodily harm to her and himself and made passionate pleas.

But Felice left, went into hiding, and in a short time met someone older than Jason who was an exact opposite—established, settled, and who deferred to her. Felice then found herself struggling with her new freedom. Although she is bright and talented, she has to find a balance for her career in cooperation with her new partner.

Jason has not found a new "mother," or someone who is willing to bask in his glory and become the caretaker of a rebellious, immature man-child. Jason entered therapy and found that despite his success and talent, he is a shell of a person—there is no real person underneath.

For all the wonder and joy of spending one's life with an extremely talented person, the relationship is with the real person inside the shiny exterior. Each partner needs support whatever he or she does, however large or small the talent, no matter how that relationship is assessed by the outside world.

Some intimates survive with one partner accepting the role of servant because of a vicarious thrill, a spin-off reward of some kind, or a need to be needed even if it is in a dehumanizing or lowly station. But in a healthy relationship disparity is hurtful and unhappy.

An aspect of life with a celebrity is thrust upon a theatrical performer to a greater extent than in nontheatrical partnerships: false accusations that imply illicit intimacies in order to attract attention in the press. If a partnership can stand rumors and gossip, if the communication can be kept honest and open between the partners, the deliberate lies can be laughed off or seen as good for business. But that is rare.

It is far wiser for the famous partner to make it understood that press and interviews that involve rumors of on-the-set or backstage love affairs will not be tolerated, and if published will be investigated and journalists made to suffer the legal consequences of inflammatory statements. This is a hard rule to enforce, and the ultimate stance may be to give no interviews at all, while letting popularity rest on accomplishments instead of image-building tactics.

Of course, triangles do occur in the lives of theatrical and nontheatrical people. These should be treated the same: investigated, discussed, and the participants arriving at the terms for continuing their relationship or dispelling it.

THE STRESS OF LOSS

While traumatic events are common to us all, the three most difficult for dancers to handle are loss of a relationship through separation or death, injury to one's body, and career change to another profession or job.

While all of us find loss a stressful condition, performers who travel a great deal, change their life-style frequently, and whose talent can take them from "rags to riches" in a short time are more often subjected to loss.

Loss of Love

Love, not as poetic as songwriters or screenwriters would have us believe, is a complex emotion. Below the surface of the idyllic relationship is the nitty-gritty of living together and facing changes. The first essential to achieving harmony and smooth transitions is to acquire the habit of being in touch with your feelings. If you are fully honest with yourself, you will be able to make meaningful changes.

Friends who have successfully made similar changes are a good source of information. If you can't express yourself directly in a relationship, you should try to persuade your partner to have a qualified consultant present while you talk. Qualified consultants may be found through your local American Psychiatric Association, through your county medical society, or through marriage and family counseling groups.

If you can't make changes, you leave behind opportunities and emotional growth. For some, the idea of any kind of change may be so anxiety-provoking that they choose to remain in unsuitable situations. However, if there are conditions you cannot accept and you have explored all the options, try to overcome the fear of change. Risking is necessary for growth.

When a loss of any kind is inevitable accept a period of mourning. Expect mixed emotions of anger, hurt, guilt, despair, and anxiety. Being stoic or denying the hurt of loss delays the process of recovery. Do not be surprised if this period lasts six to eight weeks. Should the period extend over three months and include symptoms of insomnia, weight loss, change in personal image for the worse, the mourning contains too much self-deprecation and requires therapy.

You might find—if the relationship was based upon immaturity or a set of conditions that no longer exists—that your reaction may be one of relief and a sense of freedom.

Loss of Capacity to Perform

We carry memories and feelings of past injuries with us that may cloud our evaluation of a present injury. Some of those feelings are loss of self-esteem, power, control, or fear of deformity. Denial of injury is a normal defense mechanism. Because discomfort in a dancer's body is frequently attributed to fatigue, real injury is often met with shock and disbelief. Pain is frequently ignored, overridden with absorption in the work and a strong sense of responsibility to others in the group. There is a difference between a sense of responsibility and the cliché "the show must go on." "Going on" in some cases makes for martyrdom and risks severe injury. Sacrifice can be self-destructive. Fear of losing your place in the group must be faced in an open confrontation with your director. Admit the injury is real and that you want to return to dance as soon as possible. Both you and your director want your best work onstage.

Severe pain warrants some medication and, in some cases, the injured part may be used. But if pain persists and the use of pain-killers is long-range, reevaluate the injury and see another doctor.

Immediate reaction to an injury should be RICE (rest, ice, compression, elevation). If pain persists longer than three days, see a doctor. Today a number of doctors specialize in caring for dancers. Call the nearest professional company for a recommendation or go to a sports clinic. Be wary of a doctor who says you will no longer be able to dance as a result of your injury, or who tells you to rest more than three days. These doctors have not had sufficient experience in handling dancers in their need to maintain some amount of muscle tone while resting an injured area. The muscle tone should be maintained in rehabilitation work, body conditioning, or healing massage, as the situation warrants.

Of course, this advice does not apply if your injury is acute and you have had more than one opinion concerning your condition.

Research has placed the dancer into the "sprint" and "endurance" category in comparison to athletes who are in one or the other. A piece of choreography, a rehearsal day, or even a vigorous class will require endurance with sprint moments. There are a few avant-garde choreographers who push athleticism and endurance to the point of permitting no moments of release from muscular tension or adequate rest to restore normal breathing and lower the heart rate.

Many dancers, dedicated and persevering, drive themselves physically without sufficient attention to the development of the emotional content of their work—the artistic quality that distinguishes one dancer from another. It's easier to withdraw into the physicality of dance than to develop all its components—emotion, musicality, dynamics, phrasing, and that special individuality and versatility that makes for a long and interesting career.

Anna put a tremendous emphasis on her endurance capability, worked her strong, healthy body with joy, and took no interest in developing any sense of beauty or other qualities. The school in which she received her education was a good one, and they were proud of her physical prowess and energy. No one stopped her long enough to place a challenge in her way in another direction. "The artistry," her teachers told her, "will come later," as if artistic qualities are pasted on technique—as a veneer, thin-skinned, glossy, and fragile.

Anna at seventeen seemed to possess all the qualities of dedication, but she was actually obsessed, "high," and "out of it" when she took her three or more classes per day. Obsession works very well—provided its clockwork regularity is not disturbed. As soon as something in the routine goes out of "sync," the unexpected action can distort and shatter the obsessed. Wanting to work hard every day is a procedure that can accept a change now and then, but having to work hard every day because one feels that something terrible will happen if one doesn't is the basis of obsession.

Anna was made a member of a major company and was immediately given many new roles. Her willingness to learn and her energy seemed boundless. Unfortunately, the guidance in the company was such that dancers were not nurtured and cultivated but exploited and used up rapidly. Anna was not instructed in her training to know when to rest, stop, or ask for more time to conquer a role. She also did not realize that her drive was based upon the fear that if she were to rest, stop, or ask for more time, something terrible would happen to her. It did. A knee injury due to the stress of touring, imperfect stages for dance, and the pressure of learning new roles brought her to knee surgery and the end of her promising career almost before it had really begun.

Anna's immaturity, her fear that if she said "no" to a new role she would never be given another chance, was a significant contribution to the end of her career. She did not have sufficient warning from her teachers that she must learn to listen to her body or suffer the consequences. Adolescents feel indestructible physically. Yet their bodies are growing and need proper rest, and their minds must not be pushed to the point of inattention to signals of distress. Anna may have wanted to stop being on a merry-go-round and may have permitted the accident to happen. But she did not receive any guidance to warn her, if injury is what she did indeed permit to happen. A warning signal for others is in the serene appearance, the glazed look, and the lack of release in laughter, complaints, or anger that someone going beyond the edge of endurance exhibits as a release. Sleep disturbances are also a warning of something amiss. A mild tranquilizer may be suggested, but certainly not a stronger drug to increase energy or a heavy sedative, or prolonged use of any of these. It is not easy for an inexperienced young person to go to a director to ask for time off. There is always the fear that they will lose everything they have worked for. But there has to be a point of reasonableness reached between performer and employer. If the dancer is pushed into too many roles and does not refuse to learn new parts because he or she is afraid to appear unappreciative of the opportunity to do so, the dancer must learn to ask for more time to learn those roles and must not expect perfection in every performance.

An exception to injuries that are the result of hard, fast physicality is the congenital deficiency that is overlooked, misunderstood, or ignored, only to cause trouble at a later date.

Dance history is full of examples of well-known performers who overcame handicaps such as hearing loss, a clubfoot, and heart and lung problems. Nancy had a congenital hip deformity that became increasingly painful during her ten-year professional career. Her physical vulnerability in the hip area was exacerbated by the stress of performing and created a severe arthritic condition at a far younger age than this inevitable worsening condition usually appears. Fortunately, Nancy's training was good and did not cause added stress so she was able to enjoy a professional life—a decision she made despite medical warnings that it would be a short career. Surgery in her youthful years would not have corrected her hip condition, just alleviated pain at the price of her career. Nancy never considered that an alternative to pain. Her choice of a career may have been based upon knowing the facts of the medical prognosis, or it could have been a denial of the prognosis to some extent.

But whatever the price—career now, pain and crippling results later—Nancy made the choice. No one can judge for her if it was a right or wrong decision.

What is in the psychological makeup of a Nancy or anyone who overcomes physical handicaps to perform, play, or prove a victory over fate? For some people, tolerating pain is a joy. A martyr component can enter into such suffering. The martyr feels smarter, more powerful, and stronger than others, and is able to gain sympathy and attention. If there has been an early conditioning to see life as a series of trials to be endured and overcome, there can be a strong denial of the severity of the illness and a dismissal of consequences. The sufferer feels better for having triumphed over adversity and for having been able to tolerate what others would have rejected.

Another element that enters into tolerance for hurt or pain on the physical or psychological level is guilt. If the person has felt "lucky" or privileged in some way, an oppressive handicap seems a way fate has evened the score with others. Somewhere, during the developmental stage, this person was told to appreciate what he or she had been given because others were not given the same opportunities or advantages. That load of guilt will accept the burdens of just about anything. This dancer will probably not be able to discern the wrongful or rightful cost of anything.

Some people turn a handicap to their advantage and use it as a battering ram to gain sympathy, additional consideration, or to place guilt upon others for their disabilities. One would expect a greater manifestation of this kind of use of a handicap in dance, but it, like less manifestation of outer physical pain because of psychic trouble, is found in lesser frequency than in the general population. The benefits of physical activity in increased blood circulation and the release of endorphins—the brain's natural opiate—obscures discomfort. But should physical symptoms caused by psychic disturbances appear, they should be treated physiologically and psychologically as usual.

Developing a physical injury or becoming accidentprone is not unusual as an excuse to stop dancing. It appears preferable to facing changes in one's needs, one's motivation, or to cover career disappointments. It is a less-than-honest but common way out. Injuries occur when there is insufficient warm-up for the task at hand, when the adult or professional dancer becomes fatigued or bored with the repertoire, or when the discipline of renewing preparedness through daily rehearsals palls. A touch of self-destructiveness is present in conditions that lead to physical injury—the acceptable and unquestioned "accident." Younger dancers tend to suffer physical injury because of poor training, a misunderstanding of underlying principles of technique, or because they have ignored body cues.

Without doubt, a long tour or discontent with one's level of achievement can leave an empty feeling inside that signals psychological fatigue. This condition sets the stage for carelessness. Inner resources are the key to renewing oneself from boredom. Reading a favorite author, practicing a musical instrument, drawing, painting, or becoming engrossed in art-related activities can replenish dwindling energy and stave off loneliness, deprivation, discontent, or fatigue. You are an important person to yourself and others, but the show can go on without you if you need to rest or are on the brink of severe anxiety.

Loss of Career

It is unrealistic to expect a young performer to think about changing a career when everything should be devoted to being the best performer you can be. Yet remaining open to other skills, developing them to a certain degree, is important. This backup of resources can be called upon at a later date and serve as a kind of preparation for the future. When a dancer reaches the mid-thirties in age, thought should be given to the future.

Although most of us would not be convinced that anything else can be as creative, meaningful, or important to us, this is really not the case. There is no real loss here since dance does not leave you even when you leave dance. The appreciation, response, and effect of dance on you and hopefully your good habits of exercise and diet will remain yours.

One of the inner battles to be faced by a dancer in a career transition is recovery from the loss of a familiar and hard-won image. There is a sense of loss of one's body image, beauty, and attractiveness. The enchantment of distance from stage to audience, enhanced by costume, makeup, and lights, is no longer there to create the specialness of the dancer, all part of role playing in a career. Offstage, the performer is not quite sure that he or she can compete on any level with others.

A career might have been won at the cost of being serious about anything else—a spouse or lover, a home or children. Those costs may be recovered after a career ends, provided emotional intimacy can be achieved.

According to findings at the Performing Arts Center for Health (PACH) at NYU-Bellevue Hospital, a clinic for performers, early concentration on career training during adolescence takes its toll. At a time when social interaction usually takes place in the teens, the young performer, by substituting rehearsal time for social time, may be postponing experience in relationships and in achieving emotional intimacy.

A counselor of students at the Royal Ballet School in London reports that the majority of students she sees are immature and underdeveloped as people. Identity is formed by each of them as a dancer, not as a person. She feels that current training encourages instability by its narrow focus in not allowing students sufficient time to explore who they are and what they want to be as people.

Stanley E. Greben, M.D., who is part of a team easing the problems of career transition for Canadian dancers at the Dancer Transition Centre in Toronto, says: "On the matter of immaturity, it is my belief that one can learn to achieve emotional intimacy at any age. It may not be the same since the normal time for interaction was postponed, but it is not an end to the possibility. How do you learn? If you are not in too much trouble with yourself, you must get out and meet new people and take some chances. Of course, that's not easy. But that is the best way out—on your own.

"If you are in too much trouble with that prospect, the way to break down barriers is with the help of a good therapist. Good therapy is an emotional experience, one that is a trusting relationship and will permit you to let down some protective devices. It may not be that you do not know what to do or how to do it, but that the barriers against hurt are best let down in the company of someone who is safe and well-meaning."

One of the startling discoveries dancers make when they begin a second career is that their discipline in giving a good performance every time is not a general rule in others. An "off" day at work is tolerated more easily than an "off" performance. Dancers are also surprised to find that it will not take another ten years of training to master another job as it did to perform onstage. That discipline from a career in dance has two positive implications for the therapist when patients are dancers. They work hard at the therapy, are willing to take guidance or direction, and they are willing to try something different to see if it works, however painful or uncomfortable that may be. Even young students come to therapy expecting to "take correction"!

Another implication in the dancer/patient is that when freed by therapy from fear, anxiety, doubts, or neuroses, he or she has a much higher rate of success at whatever the second career may be.

It is important to recognize the invaluable qualities dance has given you: self-reliance, initiative, capacity to play several roles, health, intelligence, musical and visual talents, independence, and on and on.

The growth of dance in the past two decades has opened many new fields requiring your dance experience. You might be asked to fill a job for which you have no training. Accept the challenge. Your experience is half the qualification for the job. The other half requires your willingness to learn, to accept your mistakes as part of the process. It does not matter how many times you may have to make changes. Maintain your motivation throughout life, and retirement can be a state you will never have to face. Many states, such as Pennsylvania, give career transition grants or provide retraining. Actors Equity Association is a good place to start exploring possibilities for career continuity in New York City. Consult your union for information on grants and opportunities.

EMPTY SOLUTIONS: DRUG ABUSE—THE PERFORMER

The performer turns most frequently to drugs for relief from stress, for a mistaken feeling of heightened performance, and for recreation.

Like the student, the performer rationalizes the use of drugs to compensate for specific problems:

"Being creative," explains one performer, *"means experiencing new sensations, going beyond your imagination. Drugs have been used since the beginning of time to stimulate inspiration. An artist has to be willing to expose himself to new ideas and sensations. If drugs are part of our culture, in order to reflect that culture in my work, I have to experience drugs."*

The conditions are not the same as in the past when opium dens of the last century were popular and involved controlled amounts. The conditions were controlled as well. The same was true for religious experiences—controlled amounts and conditions of exclusion for the users. The stimulation from amphetamines, for instance, soon becomes despondency, fatigue, and sadness.

There are no statistics on the direct artistic results of hallucinogens or any other drug. The habit is more likely to be an avoidance position than one of stimulation.

Another performer complains, *"I hate auditions, the waiting, all the people, not knowing the outcome for days afterward. I have too much riding on every call. I need something to balance me out just during those auditions."*

High performance need has sounded the death knell for rock stars, athletes, and dancers. Cocaine is the popular favorite since it has no particular withdrawal symptoms and is not thought by its users to be particularly physically addictive. It is the most costly because of its popularity. The purchaser can never be sure of the "purity" of the cocaine and therefore can never truly govern the amount of tolerance. The "down" side of cocaine use in the form of sniffing (more popular than injection) is fatigue, despondency, or suicidal tendencies.

"Becoming successful has meant leaving behind good friends, whom I consider just as talented but not as lucky as I have been. That separation has been painful and embarrassing. I haven't made any close friends with my competition as yet. I feel alone, without time for myself or knowing where my new status will take me. When I get over being scared, I'll stop taking something for my nerves."

No one can know his or her own tolerance level when taking drugs. That's part of the danger. Some people become addicted immediately to a drug, others have greater tolerance. That tolerance, however, lessens as more and more of a drug is needed for the desired effect.

Valium and Librium, along with Dalmane for relief from anxiety and agitation, were the most frequently prescribed drugs a short time ago. Findings indicate long-use side effects. Whatever the stress, it is far safer to work through the psychological discomforts and attack the cause. Prescribed beta-blockers may also have unknown side effects.

"I'm on the forever tour! Same old role. I don't seem to be making any progress. I have to keep 'up' for every performance but I'm so tired and bored. All I have to look forward to is unwinding after the show. You name it, I've tried it. It's all in knowing your limit."

Limitations can be imposed upon oneself such as keeping alcohol consumption to a predetermined amount. For someone searching for the ultimate "high," it might be reached in physical abuse. High-dose users of Quaaludes, for instance, have been known to fall down stairs and never realize it. Combining drugs, such as Quaaludes with alcohol, can result in coma. Death by heart failure and poisoning may become a less boring solution to playing the same role every night.

The Stresses in a Dancer's Life   169

"There have been changes in artistic direction in my company. I don't know if the new director likes me or not. Some dancers have already been fired. I haven't been sleeping too well as a result, so I'm just taking a few sleeping tablets until this crisis is over. Then I'll be able to relax."

This dancer does not want to calm down or unwind but to sleep, which will come as a natural consequence of fatigue if the internal clock is not disturbed. A barbiturate user runs the risk of not remembering how many barbiturate pills were taken since the drug interferes with memory. Many suicides are accidentally caused by barbiturate users. For deep depression, a physician may prescribe a sedative or antidepressant, but no one should buy over-the-counter drugs for sleep or depression.

"I usually have a tremendous thirst after a performance and water or soft drinks do not satisfy me. I know when to stop and my drinking has never interfered with my work."

Next to cocaine, alcohol is the most abused substance. Although this dancer does not believe he or she has not suffered professionally from the use of alcohol, some of the characteristics of alcohol use are thinking one is vivacious, intellectually superior, and the winner of every argument. The opposite is often true.

"I never wanted a career. I was just lucky and everything went my way. There was money and attention and my family wanted me to dance. But when I was injured, I had to take painkillers. Now, it would be harder for me to get off drugs than to stay on."

Painkillers, like barbiturates, are difficult drugs from which to withdraw. They create powerful physical and psychological dependency. First the physical problems must be relieved. Then a suitable psychological therapy needs to be found to provide a structure upon which to maintain the withdrawal decision.

"All of a sudden I have too much work, roles, partners, new apartment, traveling between seasons with the company. I haven't seen

any friends or relatives for a long time. I never have time to rest since I should always be practicing or doing something. I never feel really good, so I need to keep my energy up by taking 'uppers.' "

Pep pills or any of the amphetamines stimulate the nervous system to purposeless activity. More and more is needed as time goes on to achieve the same effect. Prolonged use will overwork the body, exacerbate an injury, and eventually lead to emaciation or an anorectic condition.

"My boyfriend gets 'high' sometimes and has encouraged me to 'get with it' for 'togetherness.' "

Shared "fun" drugs will result in neither person remembering the "fun." Like alcohol, recreational drugs act as a depressant and the user quickly falls asleep. A relationship involving a compliant, submissive person with a dominant, possessive partner is considered a suitable pyschological condition for addiction.

"I'm in pain much of the time since my injury. But I have to perform so I take something to kill the pain. As soon as I'm healed, I'll stop."

The root of the problem in our society, according to Donald B. Louria, M.D., professor of public health at the College of Medicine of New Jersey, is "the assumption in our society that no amount of physical or mental discomfort should be tolerated even for a short period of time." Pain is a warning that the discomfort should be admitted, accepted, treated, and the cause investigated followed by a restructuring of the physical and emotional habits. Replacement therapy for hips, knees, and other joints has returned many dancers to the stage. Foot and ankle surgery have made remarkable advances in the past decade. No performer need settle for a deteriorating condition. Experiments and new options are emerging in this country and abroad."

Symptoms for recognizing drug use may vary, but altered behavior is the first clue. Look for irritability, anger, antisocial behavior, bloodshot eyes, dilated pupils, and extreme fatigue.

DRUGS IN COMMON USE

Drug: COCAINE (oldest and most addictive drug known to humanity, currently most popularly abused drug, especially in the derivative form known as crack)

Effect: *Effect is euphoria, raised confidence and heartbeat, relief from fatigue, excitation, makes introverts feel charming and witty. Cost can be $2500 or more per ounce. Effect lasts ten minutes followed by depression. It is most often snorted or used topically during sex for heightened response. Can cause nose damage. It's physically damaging and psychologically addictive.*

Drug: OPIUM DERIVATIVES (morphine, heroin, and opium)

Effect: *Effect at first is unpleasant, producing fear, nausea, vomiting, craving for sweets, yawning, muscular twittering. Eventually gives sense of well-being for one or two hours. Reduces sex drive although it produces sexual feelings in oneself.*

Consequences of Prolonged Use: Prolonged use damages liver, blood, and brain. Insidious reactions and odd behavior frequent. Withdrawal is long and difficult, with chills, nausea, cramps, and jitters. If injected with unclean needle, may cause serum hepatitis, skin abscesses, and adds to possibility of acquiring AIDS (Acquired Immune Deficiency Syndrome).

Drug: BARBITURATES (secobarbital, pentobarbital, phenobarbital, amobarbital, butabarbital, known as Seconal, Nembutal, Amytal, and Butisol and eighty different manufactured combinations)

Effect: *Effect reduces restlessness and emotional tension if used in small, daytime doses. Can induce sleep in moderate doses but in large doses can depress the user and produce a hangover.*

Consequences of Prolonged Use: Prolonged use dulls the memory, slurs speech, impairs muscular control and perception. Creates physical and psychological dependency, mental confusion, slowness, forgetfulness, and giddiness. Because of impaired memory, the user may forget how many pills have been taken and in combination with alcohol or antihistamines may ingest a fatal dosage. Withdrawal can be as—or more—difficult than alcohol or heroin withdrawal. Abrupt reduction in use can result in coma and death.

Drug: ALCOHOL (wine, beer, and hard liquor)

Effect: *Effect reduces anxiety and the sense of unknown fears. Slows breathing, heartbeat, reasoning, and sensory power. User thinks himself clever and charming. Is argumentative.*

Consequences of Prolonged Use: Prolonged use usually begins with social pressure. If continued beyond enjoyment, alcohol may become addictive as more liquor is needed for the same mental and physical effect. Life span is lessened; respiratory, heart, kidney, or liver failure or delirium tremens can result in death. Malnutrition is a factor in user's sustained use of sugar content of alcohol. Users lose control of physical actions, memory, and often become aggressive, abusive, and capable of sexual molestation.

9

Relationships

PROFESSIONAL RELATIONSHIPS

The two most important areas of relationship when you perform or study are with your director, who may be your choreographer, artistic director, or teacher, and with your friend, lover, or spouse.

Generally speaking, as we have mentioned earlier, your relationship to your parents and family—those who represented earlier authority figures—will form the basis of your future relationships at work. Many of those reactions you may wish to change. But any disturbance is bound to have a basis in your reaction to your past. Reexamination of that portion of your past and your reactions by whatever means or therapies you choose will clarify the issue for you.

Directors and other authority figures are not made from a single mold. Some are pleasant, considerate, and helpful; others are mean, spiteful, and petty. The talent that created the position is separate from their personality, although some characteristics are common:

perseverance, discipline at work, and dedication. The most important thing to remember in a relationship with a director or choreographer is that you are relating to the position and the talent of the person rather than to his or her nonwork persona. Keep your reactions objective and a good work relationship will ensue. *Always remember, it is not necessary for you to like your authority figure.* It makes everything easier if you do, but the prime objective in working together is to produce a work, or production, or to develop your talent to its capacity. Taking corrections or comments personally, no matter how they are given or meant, can create a monstrous work condition—one that has, through gossip and jealousies, ruined many careers. If you dislike your authority figure, don't show it. We know this is easier said than done. But if this is not possible for you to accomplish, it would be wiser to find another position—unless you are moving too often for the same reason. Then you must examine your reactions more closely. It is not being deceitful to keep your personal reaction to an authority figure to yourself. It is a professional accomplishment to master a pleasant and cooperative attitude at work even when you dislike the authority figure.

There are some directors who seem to need personal relationships within their cast. This can mean anything from occasional cheerful group shared meals to a private talk in a dressing room, office, or classroom—occurring more frequently on a tour when personal life is strained. Meeting at any other time but work hours puts another value on the situation and should be evaluated before it becomes an unwanted burden or trauma. Respect is what you should offer your director, teacher, or choreographer for what he or she knows and offers in talent. If respect is not there, it is an almost intolerable condition. There is no way to change personality traits in others; you can only change them in yourself. If you can't work with many kinds of personalities, you limit the span of your career. Before you reach the breaking point, talk about the situation with friends or those whose values you trust *outside your workplace.*

As we suggested earlier, there might come a time when you feel that a conversation about your future is necessary, to ask if you may understudy a bigger role, or audition for another part, for instance. Again, make it an impersonal, honest, and direct conversation in the theater or school without referring to any personal events of the past or arguing about your director's implied feelings about you. This kind of a talk takes courage particularly when you might be the newest, youngest, or lowliest performer and the authority figure is famous. But it's worth a try. Whatever the outcome, you will have learned something new about yourself and where you want to go in your next move. Or it will "clear the air" for both of you.

PERSONAL RELATIONSHIPS

People who focus fully on developing a skill, art, or career at an early age have advantages and disadvantages in finding a balance between social, academic, and professional matters. While talent in the arts requires commitment at an early age to learn discipline, establish good work habits, and to progress at a self-imposed pace, finding a balanced life at the same time doesn't mean that all parts should be equal. The ideal balance is different for each person, and should be based upon personal motivation in devoting time to a personal life and social interaction—not the motivation or urgings of others.

The cost in later years of missing the emotional interaction typical at adolescence, however, may be in feeling ill at ease in social situations (something the public never understands in a performer) and emotional immaturity in personal relationships. While others were busy during adolescence evaluating themselves, their needs, and their capacity to give and take, there you were, dancing away your intertwining years.

You are not alone, according to the U.S. Census Bureau. Three fourths of all American men and half of the American women under twenty-five years of age are doing the same thing—postponing coupling until a career is established. Most of them, however, did not do without the practice during their adolescent years.

Can matters of the heart be postponed? Not for long. Some enchanted evening when someone comes backstage with a bunch of roses or a box of candy, you will wonder if the gift is for you or the role you played onstage. Or you could meet someone at a party or on tour who seems interested in you.

Many times, a talented person feels different from the group, left out, and sometimes more mature than his or her peers. The challenge is to find a social group that recognizes differentness as a necessary dedication at a crucial time. Athletes have the same difficulty but more understanding in public situations than artists. Dancers, however, are more inclined to be reticent about themselves and their dedication. Nevertheless, at some point you will meet someone irresistible and venture out into the other world. If you are a typical compliant and obedient dancer, you will submit to the choice of a disco evening (even if your feet can't dance another step), going to an ethnic restaurant (with a cuisine that always makes you sick), or watching a wrestling match or football game (with primitive choreography).

Of course your date should have asked where you would like to go, but if he doesn't, it's up to you to realize that continual compliant or submissive behavior is going to result in an unworkable situation. There is always the chance that a new experience will turn out to be fun, but there are times when it isn't. *The skills you develop in your authority or work relationship do not apply to your personal relationship.* That pleasant, cooperative attitude no matter what will eventually create a bigger problem in your personal relationships than a confrontation on a matter that needs immediate discussion.

Love, infatuation, fascination—or whatever has entered your life—for the flawless object of your affection will eventually need expression. Determining how far your demonstration of affection will go depends upon several factors.

Our society, especially through the media, is so sexually permissive it is difficult for young people not to respond. While pressure may not be valid, sexual feelings are present from the earliest years and surface with curiosity and experimentation during adolescence. The relationship may be comfortable for a time, but if a sexual drive is not met and needs to be fulfilled, then perpetuation of this relationship to the exclusion of any other indicates a lack of concern or sensitivity to the needs of one or both of the partners. It is not an honest relationship, a real friendship, or a real caring relationship but a self-serving fantasy. You should permit no one, however, to compel you to engage in a sexual activity unless you feel the same way. If you do care deeply about someone, and the feeling is mutual, be ready to assume the responsibility for your own use of contraceptive methods. (The choice is yours, but there is a strong leaning among most dancers away from the Pill because of its bloating tendency. Discuss your options with a physician.)

Since sex is so available in our society, many couples never learn to communicate with each other in any other way. Physical closeness is often confused with intimacy; sexual freedom with being open, free, and uninhibited; physical excitement with affection. *There is a difference between loving and making love.* Ask yourself questions and sort out the difference in your relationship.

You may have decided to rotate your relationships so there are no smoldering embers, or because of repeated disappointments prefer companionship over intimacy. If there is no romantic sexual fantasy attached to the relationship on your part, no deep desire to move a cool friendship into a hot affair, there is no harm in a platonic affair. However, if there is a romantic sexual fantasy involved that is kept repressed or hidden because there is a fear of normal adult sexual interaction, that can be detrimental.

Take another look at your excuses that keep you from normal sexual interaction to see if you might be waiting for your partner to develop an intimate interest in you. A sexual drive is evident in all people, no matter what happens to it—sublimation, repression, distortion, frustration, or perversion—it still exists. The direction it takes depends upon many factors.

If your partner never develops an intimate interest in you, are you to assume he or she is homosexual? Perhaps. Chances are if he or she is homosexual, you will be told so. As we previously discussed, homosexuality is not misbehavior; it is a discovery and a choice. If you are both mature and honest, and truly friends, the relationship can remain rewarding, valuable, important, close, and supportive without physical intimacy.

If you suspect your partner is homosexual but does not reveal it, or has not yet subjectively admitted these feelings, don't ask. He or she may have a separate life from the one you know that is not of your concern. Even if hope springs eternal, facts have to be faced. There may be so little self-esteem left in a young woman in a situation like this that she feels she cannot compete with other women for the affection of "normal" men.

The bottom line in all this turmoil is: Self-love should not be endangered by a relationship but enhanced by it. Most experts agree that love is not demanding but gives freedom to each partner to grow.

When the Relationship Is Sexual— What to Watch Out For

Shoud you decide to engage in sexual intimacies, there are some physical dangers to consider, not as a deterrent, but as a precaution for both partners. While it is never easy to ask your partner outright if he or she has a contagious venereal disease, it need not be a blunt question destroying the mood of the intimacy. If possible, it should be determined in a private but more casual conversation at an earlier time.

Not all partners are honest, caring, or even aware, in some cases, that they are able to transmit disease. For this reason, the responsibility lies with you to be informed concerning symptoms, and to know when and where to go for help should you need it.

The danger of contracting hepatitis, for instance, has increased. In its Virus A form, hepatitis infection can be transmitted through feces-infected water, through food contamination (raw shellfish from infested waters, for instance), or by personal contact.

According to Dr. Kenneth Ratzan, chief of infectious diseases at Mount Sinai Medical Center of Greater Miami, there has been an increase in Virus A transmission among people who engage in anal-oral sex. Hepatitis Virus B organism, however, is found in body fluids such as semen, or can be transmitted through contaminated blood in transfusions, as well as by unclean needle injections.

Symptoms of hepatitis are sudden anorexia, nausea, malaise, vomiting, fever, or flulike symptoms. Untreated, hepatitis can result in severe brain and liver damage.

The most frequently asked questions by young adults under twenty-four years of age of the medical professional concern herpes. Herpes viruses include chicken pox, shingles, mononucleosis, and herpes encephalitis. While one form of the herpes simplex virus causes cold sores, a second results in general sores that are a major form of venereal disease.

Herpes II is five times as prevalent as syphilis and rivals gonorrhea for the number one spot among venereal diseases. Like Herpes I, once the virus has infected someone, it stays forever. Herpes I used to be described as occurring above the belly button, while Herpes II occurs below. But since the sexual revolution, the two types often appear in upside-down locations.

Since herpes is a virus, and since few antiviral drugs are available, there is no cure as yet, but there is some alleviation for the flare-ups of this painful condition.

Genital herpes begins with red, blisterlike structures, or a group of blisters or sores that ulcerate within hours. Symptoms are fever, lethargy, disorientation, and swollen lymph nodes. Although some of these symptoms resemble those that indicate the possibility of AIDS (Acquired Immune Deficiency Syndrome), symptoms of herpes disappear and reappear at regular intervals.

Herpes is now so rampant, it is advisable to investigate all recurring cold sores around the mouth and elsewhere, and for men and women to check out any unusual discharges with their doctor.

Some of the reasons for the alarming increase in venereal diseases have been given as changes in sexual behavior, the widespread use of contraceptive pills and intrauterine devices, the emergence of strains of organisms less sensitive to antibiotics, and the fact that women are frequently asymptomatic carriers of infections.

But the most significant factor in the spread of disease is the sexual freedom allowed by use of the Pill. In addition to having long-term and side effects, the Pill, while allowing greater sexual freedom, *does not* protect against venereal disease. Condoms offer the only known effective prophylactic against the transmission of disease— including AIDS.

Delaying treatment is no longer necessary due to a lack of information or funds. Free clinics have been established throughout the United States for diagnosis and treatment, and it is not necessary for people under legal age to obtain parental permission for treatment; all information is kept in strict confidence.

The phone numbers to call are your local Board of Health or the toll-free national VD HOTLINE 1-800-227-8922 for a listing of treatment centers. And be sure to tell your partner, no matter how difficult that will be. He or she has a right to know.

When the Personal Relationship Ends

Relationships, like human beings, are seldom perfect. Your prince or princess out of the spotlight is just another human being. And perhaps a bit too human for you to handle.

Any partnership is in trouble when little telltale signs begin to show that your partner does not care to the same degree by a lack of response to words, telephone calls, or letters. Or there can be a lessening of support and of meeting previously shared responsibilities. Moodiness, grumbling, and indifference, if not signs of physical illness, are signs of discontent.

Although dancers usually find it difficult to express themselves in words, this is an important time to communicate. While you don't really know people until you live with them—as the saying goes—the phrase applies to roommates or dressing room confreres as well. If you lived in a family with harmony, one that was loving, supportive, and complete, there will probably be no problems in expecting the same from your relationship. But if you lived in a family with absent role models, deprivation, or emotional disturbances of one kind or another, this emotional baggage of your past has to be assessed, considered, resolved, forgiven, and not carried over into your present life. That's not an easy task.

Physical desire, lust, and sex are part of living and loving, but problems in this area are a little more difficult to sort out. Talking with a friend of the same sex about a fear, doubt, or question is a reasonable way to begin to arrive at a solution. We all need a sounding board at one time or another. If the purpose is not gossip, or a vicarious thrill for one of the participants, or a discussion of your partner's role in your sex life, the conversation, when it remains on how *you* feel, can be beneficial. Sharing is the key—expressing mutual feelings with someone of the same age group is a normal, natural, and understandable need. But there is a fine line between sharing and giving too much information—information that should be shared only between the persons involved. If the problem is deeper, consult a therapist or doctor for a more objective opinion and advice. If your conversation is with a friend or relative, be sure he or she is a good listener, one who is not going to try to influence you, to assign blame, or to use the information against you or against another person.

When the signs of breaking up increase and lead you to realize that it's time to risk the entire relationship, it's scary. It doesn't matter if the relationship is an infatuation, a serious affair of the heart, a commitment, or a marriage, the differences have to be faced. If you just walk away and drop the whole affair or remain hurt without coming to an understanding of what happened, you might be setting a pattern you're likely to repeat over and over again. If you want the best kind of relationship, you have to risk losing it, and keep risking it in order to keep it alive.

Take the time to examine the elements from your family pattern that you want to retain and those you do not want. Rejecting unsuitable examples is not an unloving attitude to members of your family. No one can live the same life or career as another. Remember that repeated patterns of rejection, self-destructive actions, and/or poor relationships wear many clever disguises. Consider if you are repeating a pattern every time you change partners. A repeated pattern may underlie a "poor little me" pose that always brings you sympathy and consolation.

Contrary to current manuals and books on the needs and wants of men and women, and their differentness, there is really no difference in what they want in a relationship. Both want understanding, support, emotional intimacy, and commitment. But the extent to which both are on the *same level and possess the same capacity* in the understanding, the support, and the giving may be very different. While society gives us more options, it requires more decisions. It is a question of working out the solution in an honest, open way to see just how far each partner is willing to balance the other. It is a fluid state, ever changing, and always needing reinforcement and read-justment.

Your Exit May Be More Important Than Your Entrance

In a love relationship, how you end it may be more important than how it began. This action may not be one of your more graceful exits, but it will gain you new roles. There is a last scene to play if the misunderstanding is a small one, a serious confrontation, or a final curtain. It is important to go into a confrontation without a set idea about the outcome. Keep an open mind about what might happen, but express your hurts and discuss your feelings. It might be possible to make repairs.

There is always the possibility that the other person will not communicate and does not know what his or her feelings really are. If there is a willingness to adjust to your attitude or conditions, don't try to turn yourself into a pretzel to accommodate because of fear of losing your partner. In the case of an uncompromising partner, you don't really have a partner, you have a dependent. Remember, too, that you cannot change anyone but yourself. Don't bother making judgments, hurling abuse, or seeking revenge. You'll only hurt yourself. If you have been honest, open, and forthright about your disappointments, then it's time to let them go.

After you've decided to make a clean break (that may take some time and several confrontations), expect a sense of loss, sorrow, rejection, and depression. Go ahead, cry. You may feel that you will never find anyone as suitable, as wonderful, and that you will never love or be loved again. And you won't if you don't get over it in a short time and start all over again.

Stay lovable—caring, responsive, trusting—and it will all be soon forgotten. You've had a good lesson in relationships, and if you've cleared away all the bitter memories, hurts, and the anger, you've made way for a new and better entrance.

How to Clear the Air
Some people clear the air with drama, some with a quiet talk, some with letters, notes left in conspicuous places, or even with phone

calls. Whenever a confrontation is necessary, learn to be fair. Whatever your style, big scenes, angry words, or arguments, here are some guidelines for a fair fight.

1. Ask your partner for a quiet time and privacy to talk about a *current* disagreement, hurt, or disappointment. Don't dredge up dead issues.

2. Keep the confrontation a *dialogue.* Monologues are good for stage, bad for partnerships.

3. If you feel a great deal of anger, wait until you can express yourself without becoming irrational. If your partner is angry with you, wait until he or she expresses the anger, and then talk about the issues calmly. Don't "catch a ball of fire," as the saying goes; tossing angry words back and forth just increases the flames.

4. Say you're sorry if the misunderstanding occurred through your fault or deed, and mean it. What you have to say or hear may hurt, but if it is said with care and concern, it can be handled.

5. Never make a comparison of your present partner to an old love, imagined ideal, or past relationship. Deal with the situation and person on hand and where you both are in that relationship at the moment.

6. Set some rules for similar situations, based on your new insights into your partner's feelings, so there is no further misunderstanding on the same issue.

7. Now forget the entire matter except for what you have learned, and don't bring up the matter that caused the difficulty again.

All this takes practice. But like everything else, it gets easier each time you do it.

10

Not All That Meets the Eye: Internal Cues That All Is Not Going Well

CONFLICT AND STRESS IN TODAY'S PERFORMER

Must artists be strange, odd, "crazy," or "temperamental"? Freedom to be oneself, whatever that self may be, may result in what appears to be odd behavior to the rest of society. It *is* odd behavior if the differentness is not the healthy expression of someone who is capable of handling his talent and the stresses of his profession and is able to cope with life in general. In that case, the talent will not reach full expression and there will be little success and little happiness— just as there would be for anyone else.

At one time, people talked about being strong-minded in order to succeed in a career that provided no guarantees, little security, and a constantly changing work pattern. Today, mental health is what we mean by being strong-minded.

The definition of success at one time was the capacity to achieve a victory over one's personal and professional storms. Now, we talk about coping mechanisms and defense mechanisms. Here, again, the terms are different, but the idea is the same. To achieve happiness and success, you have to rely upon more than talent. The underlying personality, the family experience, and your assessment of all these things, as well as your capacity to understand and change whatever has to be changed in your thought pattern and behavior, are the things that really determine how far your talent, big or small, will take you. You will rarely find, if you really look, someone who is successful but unstable. Stability is a prerequisite for success.

Some creators or performers may adopt an eccentric mode of dress or look. That may be the indication of unusual vision, high imagery, or unusual creativeness. But if the eccentricity is based upon a serious mental disorder, is tasteless, damaging, extreme, that is a sign that something is amiss and there will be difficulties later. An example of a small eccentricity was Balanchine's preference for Western string ties. He wore them for formal and informal occasions. They were his stamp, his mark of dress. But if he had appeared at rehearsals in a complete Western outfit, adopted a drawl, and attracted attention to himself in all social situations and professional encounters with this "Western" behavior, he would have been acting out some need to attract attention because of insecurity, or been able to express only one facet of his talent, or been insensitive and unable to adapt to a variety of needs, moods, and considerations for himself and others. None of this was true in his preference for string ties. He simply preferred them. And, yes, he knew he could always be recognized for it. And there was nothing wrong in that.

It is not comfortable to think that an artist-in-the-making or one that is in psychological trouble has an ordinary garden variety of neurosis. That doesn't seem quite right. With all the differentness that talent offers, why isn't the "sickness" different too? Simply because creativity has an individual means of expressing itself in each one of us. But each one of us uses that creativity subject to our family relationships, our individual assessment of our capacity and needs, and our accumulation of life experience. As human beings, we are all alike. As artists, everyone is different. Wonderful. So there is no mystery. The paths are well known to freeing one's personal uniqueness to function and blossom even if the therapy to do so is a standard method.

What we have learned in the PACH clinic is that we can minimize that time to freedom because of our understanding of and experience with the performing professions. We did not know, but can now be almost assured, that the performer in therapy will give the same discipline, cooperation, and sensitivity to therapy that he or she gave to performing.

Simply put, when therapy is needed, it is because of being in trouble in one's personal or professional life, but the profession did not cause the trouble. There is an inability to cope with stress because of a breakdown in the supportive environment (family, friends, close relationships), or there is a breakdown in the psychic functioning.

One cannot always hope that support will be available in a family situation since, as every performer knows, there is often envy present for the fact that one is sacrificing traditional rewards and values for something one wants passionately to do. Not everyone is capable of following what seems a dream for a profession with so many variables for success. Should the pleasures of the real world come to an artist who rejects them, that also doesn't make the artist odd, strange, or "crazy," unless success is too hard to handle for some reason and the struggle is more satisfying or gains more sympathy than success and rewards.

Every generation thinks they have more stress in their lives than the last generation. It is easy to point to competition, higher standards, or the speed of daily life as undue stress. Today's stress on the dancer is not more, just different. Because there are more opportunities and more choices, there is more confusion in making decisions, but clear thinking on motives, goals, and procedures will narrow the choices to the right one for everyone who takes the time to evaluate, and reevaluate again and again on a regular basis, what road to follow. If the motives for an art are based upon love for that art and not upon pressures from any outside person, school, or condition, there is every possibility that any stress may be overcome and the inner strength of the performer developed and made secure. Everyone feels the stress of living. We all feel "blue" at times, somewhat depressed, or disappointed at our performance. The feeling usually lasts a short time if we understand the basis of our feelings. Some action is taken such as a rest from the task, a talk with a friend or relative, or a self-evaluating reexamination of events and our reactions to them.

If, however, the feeling of depression lasts for a prolonged period of time and attempts to shake off the heaviness are to no avail, it's time to consider a deeper investigation of the feelings.

Preparations to meet a daily task such as a class, rehearsal, or performance supply a small sense of security. This involves a proper warm-up of sufficient duration; a quick onstage rehearsal if necessary before a performance; a check of props and quick-change items just to make sure you have a smooth performance; an inspection of makeup, costume, and shoes for safety, comfort, and suitability to the task at hand.

Part of the learning process and the performing process is a visualization of the fulfilled task—the result of imagination and imagery incorporated into the physical repetition. It is a mental choice made for work at hand. If there has been an error or accident in any part of a previous attempt, it is important not to "play" the error over in the mind, but to reinforce the correction and visualize a perfect performance.

Just before going onstage, many performers will take a deep breath, center themselves, or do or say something extra to guide and protect themselves from unforeseen calamities.

That "something extra" is a call upon something supernatural. It may be a silent or visual expression of hope for a little magic that will protect us from distraction that would cause a loss of concentration or control. It is a transfer of power from one's own control into the hands of another force to make one feel secure and protected.

The "something extra" may be based upon religious belief, superstition, or ritual—like the rubbing of a rabbit's foot that was a theatrical tradition years ago. The "extra" is the underpinning of the feeling of being protected. The belief is usually so strong that, should something go wrong, the belief is not challenged and another reason is found for the mishap.

This is not to say that "magic" is a bad habit, but that it is a valid part of preparation unless so much time is spent in useless or nonsensical behavior that necessary preparations are avoided and the time misused. At this point, the performer never feels ready, at ease, or confident, but always anxious that not enough ritual has been done to see him or her through. It all becomes an excuse for delaying the moment of truth.

Physiological changes take place whenever one faces a crucial moment. There are "butterflies" in the stomach, weakness, shakiness, or even nausea as one realizes that there is no turning back from the moment. But these symptoms should subside as the execution of the task begins. If there is insufficient concentration on the task at hand, the anxiety will continue.

The Olympic contestant differs from the dancer. Athletes practice every day but do not compete nightly during a season with matinees added. The soloist, star, and superstar in particular are required to please an audience that has paid a good deal of money to see a performer and expects that performer to excel. Some may never attend another of his performances if he fails to live up to their expectations and bad reviews can damage a hard-won image.

Fortunately, both athlete and dancer can make up for a wobbly performance the next time if they possess emotional and physical stability and face the next trial with confidence and the ability to forget the past and concentrate on the moment.

While an athlete has a clear-cut goal—winning—the dancer has a wider range of objectives on the emotional as well as physical level. But both should experience results that provide a sense of accomplishment and are pleasurable.

Warning signals that something has gone awry are in the absence of pleasure or the continual lessening of pleasure in the performance or afterward. This includes occasional displeasure with oneself, or even a feeling of not yet being equal to the demands of a role. But those feelings do not exclude the desire to perform again or continue in a career.

Too often, because of the newfound popularity of dance, press, public relations experts, and publishers have encouraged dancers to emphasize the difficulties of the profession in the media. Authors and performers have blamed the profession for pain or disillusionment when the cause has been within themselves. All professions have difficulties and stress. Not all personalities or temperaments are suited to the professions they choose. That is more likely the problem than the difficulties of the chosen profession. Unrealistic goals and early misinformation can set the stage for unhappiness. But if the performer, despite setbacks, disappointments, and sacrifices, still enjoys dancing, that is reason enough to continue.

Pleasure, however, is obscured when fear and anxiety take over and one begins to lean heavily on ritual, or uses the preparation time for unusual or bizarre activities, and depends upon others for advice to the exclusion of one's own judgment.

The use of stimulants or other harmful drugs on a regular basis, based upon the excuse that there is too much stress or personal pressure or the circumstances too unusual, puts the performer on the road to self-destruction.

What is needed is the reaffirmation of self-worth in knowing that one has done one's best every time, and that doing one's best every time creates a solid support system that is important to dwindling confidence.

If the self-esteem of a performer is damaged beyond the repair of a teacher, friends, and peers, then it's time to reevaluate some earlier conclusions about one's work.

In work with performers in the first psychiatric clinic devoted to the arts, Performing Arts Center for Health (PACH) in New York's NYU-Bellevue Hospital, it was found that depression was described as the most frequently experienced emotion. Clinically speaking, depression is not sadness alone but a complex mix of symptoms rather than a temporary sadness or depression.

Some depressions are endogenous—based upon internal biochemical causes—and seem to come from nowhere. Other depressions are exogenous—based upon external stress from real-life loss, trauma, or exaggerated grief reactions. While occasional depression is normal, when things reach a personally painful point, the condition can impair functioning.

While it should be kept in mind that the performers answering the questionnaire for a survey of the mental health clinic at NYU-Bellevue were admittedly in need of psychiatric help, the findings reveal the areas of stress for all performers.

The mean age of the patients in the clinic was twenty-six years. Females numbered 64 percent; males 36 percent; and 98 percent were Caucasian. The survey showed depression was experienced by 84 percent of the ninety-three participants in the survey; loneliness (72 percent); severe anxiety (62 percent); sleep problems (52 percent); family problems (48 percent); employment problems (40 percent); divorce/breakup (40 percent); difficulty getting along with others (26 percent); death of a significant other (14 percent).

It was not too surprising to find that dancers do not verbalize their complaints since they express themselves in movement, not words. They find difficulty in describing their feelings and tend to hide their emotions. This may be a developmental condition of early childhood, or just an ability grown dusty from disuse. But the psychiatric staff finds that dancers talk openly about an injury or eating disorder before mentioning an emotional distress.

Musicians tend to intellectualize their feelings, and actors, to dramatize and role play, according to the findings.

Because most dancers are stoic in the face of pain from an injury, they tend to ignore chronic pain—untraceable, nonorganic, recurring pain that seems to have no physical basis—until a physician suggests counseling to seek the source. Some dancers discover through intuition the pain/emotional distress connection. But even then they will mention the pain first and their feelings at a later time.

The vegetative signs of depression mentioned by the patients are anorexia, sleeplessness, early morning rising, and constipation. Eating disorders and use of drugs exacerbated the depression physically and psychologically. Among dancers under thirty years of age, another symptom of emotional disturbance was in the form of extreme dieting—starvation, frequent use of laxatives, and induced vomiting. Two thirds of the dancers felt their diet to be inadequate even though the cause was not a lack of funds.

The explanation being formulated on the second most frequent complaint—loneliness—as described by the dancer indicates ambivalence. While dancers know they have accomplished more than others in their age group, and that they are sometimes admired for their talent, they feel cut off from the mainstream of society. Their being artists is part of the rationalization for a sense of feeling separated from the rest of society even though society has now come to accept dancers as respected members.

Do dancers feel unlike others from the beginning, which motivates their desire to escape in dance? That is another one of those questions raised by the survey that will be included in subsequent questionnaires. Is the denial of relationships in the adolescent years that all young performers experience a factor in the feeling of being apart from others? Is being left out of social activities coupled with nonverbal habits the basis for their loneliness?

Since the PACH clinic is the first of its kind, it uncovers as many questions as it asks. But it is nonetheless the first attempt to understand the creative and performing artist—an area where past psychiatrists have trod with little experience, little research material, and even less personal knowledge. The PACH NYU-Bellevue clinic opens a new door on creativity in psychiatry.

What has positively been determined since the inception of the clinic in 1981 is that the kind of illnesses experienced by performers is no different from that of the general population. But the performer has an inordinate fear that his or her differentness is the cause and source of talent and that any interference will damage creativity and performing ability. Most artists believe they should suffer in some way or another, when in fact distress can immobilize the talent, inhibit growth emotionally and physically, cause unnecessary unhappiness, and limit the career. A free, joyful, unlimited creativity evolved without fear, in confidence, and with calculated risks to the full potential of the individual artist is the goal.

Dealing with Conflict Within the Dancer

Here are some examples of hidden conflicts experienced by performers in the clinic. Sifting away all the seeming difficulties requires work. Then the real problems are exposed. Not all the cases mentioned here have reached positive solutions. Some take more time than others. But you will see how typical problems of the performer can begin to reach a solution through therapy.

Lauren was nineteen, a professional dancer in a major company, one of those chosen especially by the artistic director from the ranks of a regional company. Everything seemed to be going Lauren's way except on the day the management took her aside to talk with her about her "puffiness." They felt that, although she was by no means "fat," just "slightly overweight," she did not look the way she looked when she was selected by their artistic director to join the company. According to her union contract, Lauren must remain in the same technical level and in the same physical condition as at the signing of the contract. Her management could have fired her on the spot, but since they believed in her talent, they agreed to have a "talk" with her.

There is, of course, a need to maintain a strengthening yet slenderizing diet. Food, however, to Lauren was an overriding passion and she was a hidden bulimic—a secret binge/purge eater who disgorges her food after loading up on sweets or starches—or whatever her particular temptation.

Psychologically, bulimia indicates a starving emotional condition for which food has become a substitute and the gorging/disgorging practice a habit. Within a short period of time, in an almost nonstop outburst of desire for large amounts of food, the bulimic eats in secret, and often. Almost immediately, guilt sets in and induced vomiting follows, or the overuse of laxatives. While there is no apparent weight gain, the body looks puffy due to physiological imbalances such as a disrupted digestive system, and there are severe dental problems because of the passage of partially digested food. There is frequent discomfort of the body's disgorging mechanism and other problems. Although this is a condition usually found in older patients, Lauren could not conceive of giving up food in large amounts and she used the fact that she must not gain weight as an *excuse* for her binge/purge habit—a habit she would have had even if she were not a dancer.

The bulimic eventually has as much difficulty in maintaining stability in a career as in personal life. The conditions may change, but unresolved conflicts find a way of repeating their symptoms, and in Lauren's case, difficulty with a previous employer for the same reasons had occurred in her hometown. The pressure to function on every level as a mature professional when Lauren was so young, alone, and troubled had to result in difficulties. Although she appeared to her peers to be in perfect control of a "charmed" life, meeting the demands of her artistic director, several choreographers, teachers, and peers, as well as competing to maintain a body image when food was her weakness, placed too much stress on her. She thought she could handle anything. So much had come her way, and she had overcome each hurdle. Her expectations of herself were very high. There was no room for failure or not meeting the level she set for herself. Refusing to recognize that every human being has weaknesses, she expected herself to be perfect in every way.

What triggered Lauren's return to the binge/purge habit was the prospect of an upcoming tour. She was sure everyone would be able to handle that better than she. She was afraid she would lose control and not live up to expectations.

The problems she had in her previous company she attributed to her home environment. She was sure that when she left home all would be well. And it was, until the news of the tour. But Lauren had brought her home environment with her. The problem was not external, but internal. The stresses were twofold: those of her profession and those demands of her inner, unresolved conflicts. The family conflicts were in her early relationships. She began her secret habit at an early age as well.

Lauren feared that everyone would see her changed body image, her dissipated look. She began missing classes and rehearsals to avoid comments and being found out. Her "talk" with management was a blow to her self-esteem. She had always had the outward indication of control, but now her management knew about her loss of control, and the deterioration began to escalate.

Why, one might wonder, didn't Lauren pop amphetamines to control her weight, or take one of the many diet pills so readily available on the market? She had some control over herself but not enough. Rather than seek quick gratification by using drugs to suppress her appetite and risking the aftereffects, Lauren bypassed the quick "fix" for the comfort of food believing food is love. And that's what she needed. Binging seemed less dangerous than drugs. Getting rid of food quickly because of guilt for overeating produces an immediate solution. Lauren's personality type prefers the comfort/discomfort punishment procedure over an appetite suppressant. The feeling described by bulimics is that of being out of control. Once the binging starts, it's unstoppable. Depression, which is present all along, sets in and the inability to function up to standard. Anger with oneself compounds the problem.

She saw the repeated pattern from her first company and indicated that she wanted help. She didn't want to repeat her pattern and lose her best chances with her new company.

The first step for Lauren, as it is for everyone, is to acknowledge the problem and set about learning more about one's habits and oneself. Lauren entered the PACH clinic and, because of a busy schedule, worked with a behavioral therapist on nutritional and diet information and procedure.

It was a long procedure. Time was also needed to work on her psychological problems with her family. Early deprivation and her perfectionistic personality were the basis of her need to maintain control. Because of her unmet needs, control became an overriding factor.

With time, Lauren will solve her problems. But the binge/purge habit, a frequent solution for dancers who feel constantly fearful of weight gain, will not resolve itself without help. What has to be realized is that good nutrition does not make one feel deprived. It's not how much or how little you eat, but the balance of choices. Naturally, everyone indulges in a favorite food now and then. But small damage requires only small repair.

Mythology frequently enters the picture: "The family runs to fat," "Exercise will burn off calories," "Exercise increases my appetite," "The only thing to look forward to after a performance is a good meal" all are worthless excuses.

Fear and Loneliness the Performer Faces

Loneliness is a frequent companion to performers on a long or continual tour such as members of a national road company. Some find travel stimulating. Others have few interests and no inner resources. Rather than use the time to develop a second career interest or learn something new to enlarge their professional talents, they become increasingly withdrawn and isolated.

Young dancers coming to New York City for the first time often feel loneliness. They require time for adjustment to the high professional standards of the classes, the fast pace of the city, and the pain of leaving friends and family behind. Although the excitement of new experiences in dance can provide the day with plenty to do, the nights frequently end all social interaction.

Instead of using the facilities of the city to enjoy cultural activities such as "free" night at a museum or "free" performances, the young dancer may develop symptoms of extreme loneliness in sleep disturbances, excessive phone calling back home, in acting childish and immature to gain attention, and even in becoming reluctant to go to auditions—the main reason for coming to New York in addition to advanced classes in technique.

An extreme case of fear and loneliness that required therapy was Megan, a twenty-two-year-old dancer who auditioned from New York for a regional company. She had just learned to handle the pace of the city, to make friends, and to begin to enjoy classes. Separation and loneliness were not unknown to Megan. She had moved several times at an early age to gain her success and made the big move from the Midwest successfully. Now, she was faced with another move and separation for an offer from a regional company that was too good to turn down.

Megan was undecided about the career move. To compound the problem, she had a boyfriend about whom she had to make a decision. Was the relationship meaningful enough for her to give up the opportunity for which she had worked so hard if he refused to move with her? In a short time, Megan realized that her relationship was not strong enough to be part of her decision to take her new job. Breaking up was not an indication of her not wanting a close relationship with another person, nor did she reject the idea of marriage.

What Megan realized in her therapy was that she didn't want to experience the loneliness of separation once again, nor to adjust to another new place. But since she had managed so well in her last move, she was assured that she would again be able to make friends, probably find a new intimate relationship, and take full advantage of her new professional opportunity as well.

Megan agreed that should she feel any heaviness of despair or sense of isolation for any length of time in her new environment, she would seek help. She now knew her own personal signals that tell her it's time to work out her difficulties with professional assistance.

Dan, a successful performer in his late 30s, suffered from extreme loneliness despite the fact that he had had many girl friends and led an active social life.

Initially, he thought the basis of his loneliness was concern about career change. But in fact he was unable to establish a long-term satisfying relationship that made him feel less alone. Much of this was due to the nature of his work—traveling, working long hours with little time off—but he ended relationships with his girl friends for reasons he did not understand. When he broke off a long-term relationship with someone with whom he lived and who had become pregnant, he realized that the breaking off was no longer a matter of career demands. This was a situation in which career demands did not interfere with the relationship. In despair after breaking off the relationship, he considered career change and experienced depression, unhappiness, and great discontent. He knew that there was something in him, despite his love for his partner, that would not permit him to be sharing, loving, and giving to a child.

After a period in therapy, what emerged was an early family life that revealed difficulty in identifying with his father. His parents were still together and the family intact, but he had endured an attitude of ridicule and disdain from his father because of his choice of dance as a career. Dan adopted the same attitude toward his father.

Despite all Dan's success, the recognition of his talents by the public, the winning of awards and grants, Dan was not accepted at home. With Dan's poor image of his father, he rejected his own decision about becoming a father—a role he identified as painful.

Dan learned that until he came to an understanding of his relationship with his father and confronted it, he would not be ready to accept the responsibility for any other person, even a child, in his life. Because the parents were accessible, Dan was able to examine his reactions, understand his fears, lessen the anger toward his father, and gain new confidence in his ability to be himself without needing the approval of his parents. He is on the way toward self-understanding and forgiveness for the lack of understanding in others.

It is entirely possible that his father will never accept Dan's profession nor give him approval. But then, it may be that his father would have not been the kind of person to give him approval and acceptance no matter what Dan chose to do. That is something his father will have to work out. But eventually, Dan will be able to assume the role of a father in his own way. It may be that when he does once again achieve a loving and lasting relationship and becomes a parent, his own father will begin to relate to him in a different way. Regardless, Dan now knows that he has a right to create his own life without fear of disapproval. His future life-style will not be like his own past environment. Whatever he chooses to do in the future as a profession is a viable choice for him.

Sandy waited until she graduated from high school before she came to pursue her career in New York City. Although her teachers were supportive and encouraging, Sandy knew that she would be on her own in every way since her parents did not approve of her decision to become a professional dancer. Although she had done well in a local company, Sandy knew that at nineteen years of age she would have to make a break from her hometown and family immediately in order to polish her technique, take auditions for larger and more challenging companies, and fulfill her dream.

She got a scholarship in a school with a major company but had no means to support herself. The pressure to do well on a scholarship program was not as upsetting as the pressure to earn a living to support her stay.

Sandy's brothers and sisters felt that she should do what they were doing—staying home and going to college to eventually earn a living in a more traditional way. A lack of support from them, as well as from her parents, did not deter her from trying to go it alone. Her desire to succeed was stronger.

She was told she needed a year of hard study to come up to the level of competition for auditions. So she found a part-time job and dug into a confining and demanding schedule. She was lucky enough to find an apartment that she could share inexpensively in exchange for light housekeeping for an older woman. Although Sandy was now doing what she wanted to, after six months, she found herself in the same situation she had left at home—a heavy class schedule, outside work to earn living expenses, a home situation in which she received no support or encouragement. She gave cooperation and help to others, but received none herself. The result was extreme depression.

When Sandy came into therapy, she talked endlessly about the girls in her class who arrived in cheerful moods, full of energy because they had none of the demands she had to fulfill.

A clue to her depression was in her past when, in order to avoid the strife between her parents at home, she would find escape by going to her room to practice music, read, and avoid hearing the arguments and difficulties around her. She never got really close to her friends at home or in New York, and because of a sexual experience with one of her teachers at home, was always suspicious that a social situation would lead to another seduction.

All of Sandy's authority figures—her parents, the male teacher who had seduced her, the demanding new people in her professional life, and even her therapist—were too much for her. She cooperated for a few sessions, but became so fearful of closeness shown by a caring, warm, or supportive attitude, she would miss her sessions and avoid coming to grips with her problems.

Sadly, had Sandy been able to get closer to her teachers at home and in New York to accept their help, she would have been a better dancer and had an easier time of it. But unable to make a complete commitment to dance or to therapy, Sandy decided to become the "good little girl" that her family would accept and returned home.

Although Sandy had to face heavy and frightening troubles for a young person alone, they were only temporary and could have been solved. It is not easy to go it alone, but it has been done. None of the difficulties in a classroom are ever as hard as the difficulties in one's mind that interfere with the flow, development, and expansion of one's talent, progress, and happiness. Sandy was in the right place at the right time in her life, and although help was everywhere, she went back to the same situation she had left at home, but now with a feeling of failure, and without the strength and maturity to assert herself to meet her own needs.

Perhaps Sandy will learn that what transpires between two people can be worthy of trust, and that risk is part of trusting. Despite her disappointment in others in her past, in order to grow and overcome her fear, she will have to keep trying to give and find trust so her relationships may grow into a mutually nurturing and rewarding friendship—first with a therapist and then with others. She cannot blame her opportunities, the stress of living in a vital and active city, or the demands of her chosen profession. She will find the same problems everywhere, whatever she does, unless she comes to a resolution. Suppose that Sandy had had more talent and was given a "golden" opportunity to reach her ambitions. She would, at some point, as many others have done, thrown it all away for no obvious reason. Although it may appear to others that there is little reason to be self-destructive when all signs point to success, a self-destructive tendency is always present, waiting for the victim to be convinced that he or she is not worthy of the good fortune or the talent. They are convinced that they can never please the people who have made the strongest impression on them, so they destroy opportunities by not meeting their responsibilities, and this in turn plunges them into depression.

Sandy and others like her must learn that early unhappiness is not a contribution nor a necessary element for success, but something to be overcome. At some point, Sandy will have to start over, leaving the past authority figures behind and relating to new ones in a different way. Unfortunately, she may never do so. The pattern of avoidance may be repeated so often in the future, she will never reach her potential.

Oliver's family, in sharp contrast to Sandy's, was one that traditionally included the arts in its life-style and encouraged participation at an early age. Oliver took lessons in music and dance as part of his education and moved from his hometown to New York, where he quickly found jobs in small companies. He led a bisexual personal life. By the time he was in his 30s, Oliver gave up his bisexual life for a homosexual preference and lived with a male lover. Oliver's family, despite the support they gave him for his activity in the arts, were disappointed that he did not go to college and into his father's business. His family knew about Oliver's earlier girl friends, but not about his male friend.

Oliver was beginning to tire of putting on a front for the sake of his family. His work problems were growing. Despite his intelligence and experience in the arts, his inability to communicate with others was disguised and his communications were often hostile. Just as he had a "closet" approach about his homosexuality in front of his family, he had a "hidden" approach in his work which manifested itself in too frequent career moves. Finally, Oliver entered therapy where he learned he must stop blaming others for his job problems and grew strong enough to confront his parents' religious objections to his preference with its consequent reactions of shame, failure, and disappointment in themselves.

As expected, the confrontation involved disbelief, anger, and resentment on the part of the parents, but Oliver felt better that everything was out in the open. Fortunately, the family eventually accepted him and his lover and Oliver realized that he had lost many years of a good and free relationship with his family by remaining hidden, guarded, and by hiding in every aspect of his life. Oliver was fortunate that he had understanding parents.

Brett, on the other hand, was a homosexual with an inordinate fear of contracting AIDS (Acquired Immune Deficiency Syndrome). Although he was right to follow precautions, every cough, sneeze, every unusual symptom, such as a mark or swelling, set him off into a panic.

Short-term therapy revealed that his fear of AIDS and its consequences was making him miserable and boring his friends. He was morbid, difficult to work with, and his personality changed from a charming, cheerful, and cooperative performer into a hypochondriacal personality.

What was really in the back of his mind, however, was his

mother's recent death—an event that was never resolved in his mind, a loss never properly mourned and let go, and the terror of death and its sadness never given its due and released.

Brett kept this inexplicable fact of life close to him on a daily basis by his fear of AIDS. It submerged his capacity to work, play, love, or enjoy his life. When he came to terms with his loss and was able to talk about it, he could come to terms with the fact that disease and death come into one's life, and that life is not governed by them, but by the affirmation of life.

Rejection

One of the early traumas of rejection is brought about by the professional schools who evaluate a dancer on the basis of appearance—never a reliable yardstick. Granted, well-trained dancers have a certain "look," created in part by early correct alignment of the body, slow development of technique, and careful adjustment to changing body conditions.

Being told by a professional school when a child is eight years of age that he or she is not suitable to a career in dance is traumatic for the parents. But being told at the age of fourteen or fifteen that one is not going to become a professional because of one's image, or because one's talent has reached a peak, is particularly devastating to the student.

Cathy was asked to leave a major professional school in New York at the age of fifteen after having studied in that school for eight years. The school's policy was to make an evaluation at that age to save time, money, and sure heartbreak. But the option of remaining in the school was left open.

The school's evaluation of Cathy was that she was not sufficiently motivated in her studies and that her body had changed—thickened and did not develop harmoniously. Cathy and her parents were shocked and desolate.

She did not want to give up dance. She studied in other studios, and because of her previous training, was the best dancer in practically every class. She auditioned but was often told, "We'll take you the next time when there's an opening."

With the support of her mother, who suggested therapy, Cathy discovered new talents that resulted in auditioning for commercials and dramatic shows. She never knew she possessed talents other than dance and gained new confidence, looked energetic, and did not, in this new world, look thick and changed or anything but beautiful.

Some acknowledgment must be made of the fact that dance has become accepted by society as a profession in the past two decades and dancers have therefore not been out of the stream of society's ills and temptations as they once were. Drugs, for instance, have become available to every strata of society, and are a temptation for the performing professions as well. That is the "down side" of societal acceptance. But drugs have to be rejected by all levels and are no more peril to one group than another. The dependency, whether physiological or physical, is the same problem for all and requires the same resistance. And, to bring us back to our initial premise, the basis for therapy is the same for everyone. It takes effort. And since we have fostered a narcissistic society that will cope with little discomfort and wants instant gratification and relief, the conditioning of today's life-style will have to be overcome without placing blame on a profession when the triumph should be a personal one.

CHECKPOINTS TO INTERNAL CUES THAT ALL IS NOT GOING WELL

- Do you require more time to prepare for a performance, class, or rehearsal than ever before?
- Do you have to have that cigarette, cup of black coffee, caffeine soda, candy, or sniff to face any of the above?
- Do you feel insecure without your favorite talisman on your person or on your dressing table?
- Do you feel yourself in such good form that you can skip a warm-up or class and do just as well with a massage, a spinal manipulation, a handful of vitamins, or a few minutes in your inversion boots?
- Are you so fatigued, bored, or disenchanted with your work that you wait until the last minute to prepare for it?

If you have answered "yes" to any of the preceding, it's time to investigate your need for "crutches" and get some professional help.

CHECKPOINTS TO INTERNAL CUES THAT IT'S TIME TO SEEK HELP

- Have you been depressed for a longer period than two or three months?
- Do you feel that your unemployment or failure at auditions is because of politics? Bad luck? Your body image?
- Do you feel the loss of someone in your life (parent, friend, lover, teacher) is so devastating that you cannot go on as before?
- Do you feel that your body is so different from those of other dancers that you cannot be taught the technique of dance according to any methodology or syllabus?
- Do you feel that your nutritional needs are so unusual you cannot eat what is called a "normal" diet?
- Are you stricken silent when someone asks you how you feel—except to report on your physical condition?
- Do you find it difficult to express anger, frustration, distress?
- Do you feel that the healthy are born to health and that happiness is a matter of karmic luck?

If you answered "yes" to any of the preceding, you might do well to take yourself to the nearest shaman, guru, or mental health center to seek help in unfolding your potential in a happier, healthier way.

LIST OF TRAITS THAT INDICATE ILLNESS AND HEALTH

The following list of traits and attitudes by no means indicates the cause of illness or happiness. It is just a list of symptoms that reveal happiness or unhappiness, health or illness, in yourself or others. We all have some of these traits some of the time.

These Character Traits Indicate Illness:	These Indicate Health:
Self-pity	Self-forgiveness
Resentment	Self-forgetfulness
Anger	Love
Defiance	Understanding
Intolerance	Acceptance of reality

**These Character Traits
Indicate Illness:**

False pride
Greed
Blaming others
Indifference
Dissatisfaction
Impatience
Fear
Self-hate
Envy
Depression
Anxiety
Guilt
Remorse
Psychosomatic illness
Insomnia
Irritability
Tension
Suicidal and homicidal tendencies
Misuse of loved ones
Loneliness
Withdrawal

These Indicate Health:

Tolerance
Humility
Service
Generosity
Compassion
Satisfaction
Patience
Faith
Not judging
Concern for others
Gratitude
Happiness
Rich, full life
Joy in living
Lack of emotional pain
Laughter
Responsiveness
Warmth
Peace of mind
Usefulness
Adjustment
Purpose

11

The Vague Discomforts Faced by Today's Performer

Everyone shares one or two vague discomforts such as continual competition, rivalry, and uncertainty about our progress. Sometimes the competition is close to home. And sometimes the competition is so far away we can't decide with whom or with what we are competing.

How does one handle a rivalry when two or more dancers are in the same family, for instance? More and more dance companies include brothers and sisters, couples, and parents and offspring. We wish our sibling rivals well, but they are competitors nonetheless.

All our lives, we try to meet standards imposed by ourselves, our family, authority figures, friends, lovers, and society. Acceptable patterns of behavior change as society conditions us, as we mature, and as our talents, opportunities, and awareness grow. Some patterns must be rejected—such as the use of drugs because members of our peer group find it acceptable. Other patterns must be rejected at the risk of losing the friendship or esteem of others. These demands become easier to reject or accept as we grow in experience and consciousness.

But some are so subtle, intimidating, seemingly innocuous, they gnaw away in secret because they make us too guilty to reveal them. A frequent stab of rivalry, envy, jealousy, or competition between best friends, sisters, brothers, or lovers is not uncommon when two people are striving to do their best.

We know from child development studies that a newborn is influenced by the fantasy of the parents. How a child is touched, treated, given or withheld from love or approval, all are influenced by the parents' image of what they desire that child to be. If siblings are born close together, or are of the same sex when the wish of the parents was for opposites, children who have not lived up to that wish will sense and know, on a conscious or unconscious level, that "something" is wrong with them. At an early age, they set out to compensate in some manner for the disappointment or hurt they think they have caused. There is a feeling of inadequacy in fulfilling the wish of the parents for a beautful, brilliant, talented, or famous child, or a replica of themselves—if they have any one or all of those qualities. Remember, it's all a fantasy. The parents may not realize that they are fantasizing and think their expectations perfectly reasonable. The message is sent to the child, who doesn't know what to do with it, and feels confused and uncomfortable, and that feeling forms a basis for vague discontent, if not for a more self-destructive pattern.

Having an older brother or sister who studies the same subjects as you can set an example and be a positive component in a sibling relationship. But there are negative aspects as well. Children will often wish a sibling dead. "Dead," that is, within the understanding of that child that the "death" will soon be over and everything set aright once more. Such a wish in an adult becomes horrendous, repressed, and frequently unresolved. We wish students who perform better than we do would just disappear, go away, so we can be forever the best, most talented, luckiest, and forever the youngest.

Returning to the early environment and the part parents and relatives play, very often a natural occurrence among active siblings such as quarreling is considered "cute" or "something to be worked out by themselves," instead of a situation to be handled by the parents. It can even be vicariously enjoyed by observers, thus making a rivalry between the siblings a substitute for disagreements not expressed or resolved between parents.

In the developmental years of siblings, physicality between brothers or young males in the form of wrestling, tumbling, or showing affection for each other is a normal, acceptable expression of aggression, affection, and wanting to be the other person. Looking up to an older peer is in good perspective when the peer is seen as human, subject to mistakes, and having faults. Trying to *be* the other person changes admiration from a healthy influence to a substitute for self-development. These differences are subtle and require constant, honest evaluation. The perspective may swing back and forth between being positive and healthy, or charged with rivalrous and disruptive overtones.

Imitation of an older sibling's accomplishments without sufficient maturity for the task can push the younger too fast, both physically and emotionally. The consequence may be an insecure emotional base for the achievement of future goals. Everyone needs his or her own time and space in order to grow into his or her own person.

When it is time to begin the study of dance, the child who has been nurtured and feels secure in the early years will be the best equipped to handle the discipline required of eight- to twelve-year-olds for the foundation of serious dance study. A child at this age is anxious to please no matter what is demanded; as much as can be safely tolerated in a balanced manner that includes fun may be structured into the daily schedule.

Balanchine's theory of child development—not unlike the Eastern philosophy of child rearing—was for children to be close to their parents, permitted dependence and sharing until the age of eight, when they should be told they have grown up enough to face discipline and begin their independence with the study of dance.

While some educators feel there are advantages in predance classes for younger children (as mentioned in earlier chapters), provided sufficient attention is given to avoid harming bones that are not yet sufficiently ossified before the age of eight, other educators feel that children should be permitted to play, run, bike, skate, or engage in sports activity until that age, when the Balanchine doctrine can be put into effect. This does not mean that complete freedom should be allowed a child to do as he or she pleases. A gradual increase in mastering small tasks and challenges should begin at an early age until the grown-up point. Of course, separate classes are called for in the case of siblings, and parent and child. Separation and independence are the developmental goals.

In an emotionally healthy blood relationship, talent is nurtured and supported as a source of pride. There is an absence of rebelliousness, or a need to prove that one sibling is better than another, or just as good. One rebel in the family or classroom can destroy the harmony and must be handled by the teacher by discussing the matter with the parents of a rebel, or by not permitting that person to take classes in the school. That might be incompatible with the economics of running a dance school, and especially difficult if the rebel is very talented, but the unpleasantness must be faced by parents and teacher. Excuses to avoid the issue of disharmonious behavior or its influence on other students cannot be ignored.

Early patterns of behavior can become so obscure, so covered with defenses, conditioning, and false reasoning, that considerable professional effort may be required to change reactions and to trace the origins of the disruptive portions of a rivalry. Each case of success or failure in achieving a happy and healthy relationship is a separate and individual matter.

Some of the indications that all is not going well are quarrels that become public. Rivals become irritable and provoke one another, or they may withdraw from each other completely. Competition onstage or in the classroom becomes obvious since it is a more acceptable area for mutual conflict than private confrontation. Rehearsing or working together becomes strained. Prolonged depression that causes dysfunction should be given professional attention.

On the healthy side, some of the positive elements to inaugurate for separate needs and personal space are the establishment of different environments of work, play, and friends for each sibling. But what happens in reality is that the pull to reunite because of finances, circumstances, family needs, or just the emotional need to be together keeps rivals coming back—sometimes for good reasons, sometimes to judge each other, sometimes on an uncomfortable or disturbed basis. An evaluation should be made of what is in one's control over what has been the fantasy of the parents (or others). What has been unhealthy or destructive in the past should be recognized, forgiven, and every effort made to gain distance from its influence—not an easy task.

Talented siblings share a double jeopardy unless they support, nurture, and separate their lives and egos. Separating the professions is not necessary if they have pursued the profession out of love for it, not parental prodding or other reasons. Often, siblings and rivals are unable to accept the fact that others make inevitable comparisons between them that must be *discarded as opinion* not necessarily based upon fact. It should be remembered that no matter what genes are shared, what schools, teachers, circumstances, friends, relations, or parents, no one can share another's reactions, interactions, or time frame. The big question for each is "What are *my* reasons for sharing the same profession?" If the answer is a free choice based upon a love for dance, there is no problem. If that is not the case, the relationship and one's happiness and progress are placed in a precarious balance.

COMPETITION

Because we tend to think of ourselves as intelligent, adult, and fair-minded, we are reluctant to admit feeling envious or jealous of our competitors. Yet, at some time in a classroom or rehearsal, everyone has felt threatened by the talent or opportunities given to others. Unless we recognize, admit, and cope with these feelings, envy and jealousy may immobilize our actions.

It's a question of the degree to which you will let the feelings go. Admitting envy may result in helpful and positive imitation of the qualities in the person envied. Or it may help us reinforce efforts in our own behalf. But when envy is not utilized and is permitted to grow into jealousy, we may blind ourselves with resentment, and stifle our progress with an unreasonable evaluation of the advantages we attribute to the object of our jealousy. The tension created by competition can be stimulating, but becomes offensive and self-defeating when it creates discomfort, unfairness, and hostility by excluding cooperativeness and consideration for others. Everyone has seen hotly competitive dancers who push to the front line of a class, crowd others on a diagonal, or place themselves under the nose of a director at an audition.

You'll be noticed if you are good enough to spin like a top, pick up combinations at a glance, remember everything created at the last rehearsal, or possess any other obvious attractions without being irritating.

Competition provides a healthy learning experience when it does not defeat self-confidence. A test of any kind reveals only what the dancer has achieved at a given moment in comparison to others. It does not guarantee future advantages. It's not easy to be objective about yourself or your work in a competitive situation, but you learn most when you learn from others, but compete only with yourself. And there has to be a certain amount of joy in the process, a feeling of elation, excitement, and satisfaction. If there isn't, you have to face the blocking fears and frustrations.

It would be helpful to make a realistic assessment of a competitive situation that includes exactly how, when, where, and why you do or do not do well. Try to meet the favorable conditions in your assessment each time as you strengthen the weaker elements. In this way, you can plan your strategy and meet your expectations without berating yourself. Redefine winning, remembering that no one performance is going to change the course of your life. Whatever the outcome of any contest or audition, you have "won" by trying your best, independent of what others say or think. Redefine failure as not trying, and success as giving your best. If the outcome is upsetting to others, they will have to deal with that themselves. If you stay in touch with your feelings, you'll be able to trace the source of an upset and come to terms with it as a course of action or changed attitude.

While the fear of failure followed by the embarrassment of facing friends or peers may dissuade you from taking a competitive risk, to some the fear of winning may be just as riveting. Many dancers blessed with new roles and destined for stardom are big self-doubters. They fear they are not good enough and that they might fail to meet the expectations placed upon them. Rather than lose harder battles after easier wins, they may never allow themselves to be as good as they could be or permit too high a rise in their rank. Because new roles showcase inadequacies and invite comparison, the pressure of good opinions, sometimes a strong motivator, can become overwhelming. The unconscious way out of this predicament is sometimes to permit oneself to become overly fatigued—a reliable and excusable environment for injury—to resort to substance abuse or overeating, or to lessen the performance level until eased out of the limelight.

The dancer should put aside the anxiety of being replaced when too tired physically or mentally to continue a rehearsal schedule. You cannot play Russian roulette with your body. Understudies are the business of the administration and directors, not the dancer's. Don't permit anyone, including yourself, to suggest guilt when you have reached and indicated your limit. You have not lost your one and only chance for success. Have the courage to tell your director that in order to assume your new responsibilities to the best of your ability and to maintain an enthusiastic attitude and self-confidence, you have reached a limit. That, too, is not an easy task, but if you create a history of reliability and high performance levels, you will be respected for knowing your potential and not considered a self-limiting performer.

POLITICS

The word itself often conjures up images of shady deals made in smoke-filled rooms. We use politics to explain mysterious decisions, unexpected moves, and unforeseen changes in casting or reviews. When used as an explanation, it leaves us feeling cheated, bewildered, and the helpless victims of destiny. A vague feeling in a classroom or rehearsal makes us think something is happening that has not been stated as policy or has occurred before. Something in the atmosphere has changed. Did you say or do something that tossed you out of favor with the group, you wonder? You may be cast out for good reasons, the butt of bias, or unjustly accused of disloyalty, or just misunderstood. If you think so, you will have to ask for an explanation from your ballet master, ballet mistress, director, or teacher.

But ever since you first placed your feet into a tight and frightened first position, you have known that there are some decisions that affect your life over which you have no control, and often do not have the right to question.

At times, a political situation may be the result of forceful manipulation or indirect maneuvers by someone seeking an unfair advantage. It takes talent to politic successfully and it's best left to those born to intrigue. In such a situation, you just have to live through it until an announcement of policy is made. If you have done your best every day, you have no need to feel threatened. There is no denying it is uncomfortable. Wait for the results to be presented. Anything you hear before an official announcement is based upon gossip—often passed along and padded with personal opinion—and is not reliable. Don't add to these unsubstantiated opinions.

People in authority always have the advantage in a political situation, especially if you let them. As a performer, you can question a decision you think unfair by going to the artistic director or management. You may indeed be the victim of favoritism. But as a member of a company class—the classes given to members of a company each day during a rehearsal period—you may not be getting the attention you deserve. Without knowing why and what you can do about it, and being angry at not getting the attention or opportunities you want, you may react by feeling it's no use trying, by skipping the class altogether, by arriving late to rehearsals with garments in disarray, by withdrawing, by playing the rebel, or, in a more subtle way, by indulging in pyrotechnics at the expense of taste and artistic development. A performer who feels out of favor should consult a neutral person who has been invited to observe the class or go directly to the teacher. Together it can be determined if the performer's attitude toward corrections has been resentful and discouraging to the teacher, if the performer has felt and shown superiority to the corrections, or if he or she has truly been ignored.

The company teacher may favor only the most obviously talented or the most obviously weak despite the fact that everyone has the right to improve.

If you feel you cannot continue in a company, change. That may not be the answer. If you change companies or studios too often, or use the excuse of politics for your lack of progress too frequently, you may be setting a self-destructive pattern instead of coping with the real and uncomfortable issues everyone in every profession must face. These upsets are not exclusive to the dance world, they are inherent in the human condition. Unless you take each into consideration as it emerges, they grow and will follow you wherever you go.

12

Taking Part in Your Future

In our introduction, we outlined the perfect course for a performing career. We stated the perfect situation for training, the perfect climate for emotional development, described the best career advantages, and chose the perfect friends, parents, and lovers.

Hopefully, somewhere in this imperfect world, someone has enjoyed that perfect life. Until we hear of such a case, let's admit that perfect conditions are a fantasy.

Getting back to reality, however, it is possible to improve several areas. Better training is available almost everywhere in the United States; career opportunities and scholarships have increased; good physical and psychological health care is accessible in the major cities. As for your relationships, those you will have to work out for yourself. The prerequisite for taking control of almost any condition is the desire to do so. That means instead of blaming dance, your background, your training, parents, or friends, you must accept the responsibility for your choices and for making changes, taking risks, becoming more flexible, and for persevering toward your goal.

The performing artist's enemies are folklore, mythology, the exaggerations and inadequate information given in the media, societal conditioning, and the performer's own mental inertia. The fears that dancers once had concerning medical attention are no longer necessary. Sports medicine, as a separate discipline from general medicine, has created a spin-off—dance medicine. Although there is still a need for health insurance to cover free-lance performers, dance clinics and caring doctors are available. (See Appendix A.) A national network for psychological counseling for performers has been created. Because the medical profession is permitted to advertise, be sure to check the credentials of cross-over practitioners who are certified to provide care in one aspect of health, but give advice in another aspect—such as those who offer dietary advice; those who create a dependency by promising freedom from injury with preventive care; or those catering to the need to be pampered. Your local county medical association is the best source for names of properly licensed professionals. The PACH health survey shows that 50 percent of the medical profession may tell you that an injury requires that you stop dancing. If you should meet this situation, consult your local sports clinic for a second opinion.

Physical therapy for dancers is also available. And here, too, sports clinics have specially trained therapists, if you do not live in an area with specialized clinics or therapists for dancers. Remember, dance is not dangerous; poor training is.

In the area of training, teaching levels have improved everywhere. Although dancers are reaching a high level of technical proficiency at an earlier age, any gaps, omissions, postponements, or delays in training can be repaired. Perhaps that speedier training enjoyed by young dancers today has been at the cost of emotional and artistic development—components that are best experienced at the same time as technical mastery. Channel your energy to this end if you find weaknesses, and order your life to mend your emotional and technical difficulties as soon as possible.

Just a few short decades ago, dancers performed in conditions that would not be acceptable today. Travel conditions were miserable and stages hard and dangerous. Although AGMA (the American Guild of Musical Artists) has provided specifications for the large performing arts stages, many are still unsuitable for dance, despite the availability of portable stages and surfaces that are now part of every traveling company's baggage.

CONTRACTS

One of the most colorful but not always amusing sides of the history of dance in America is the number of ways promoters, "impresarios," and outright con men of the past avoided payment to performers. Most unfair of all were the turn-of-the-century managers of the vaudeville circuits in various parts of the United States.

Agreements between performer and management have ranged from courtly handshakes and flowery contracts written in French to complex legal transactions with today's superstars.

The union which negotiates contracts for concert performers today—in dance companies and operas—is the American Guild of Musical Artists. Broadway dancers are covered by Actors Equity and nightclub dancers by the American Guild of Variety Artists, while every performer is covered by the American Federation of Television and Radio Artists (AFTRA). Your union depends upon what kind of theater you work. Many times you will have to belong to more than one union if your work pattern covers two kinds of theaters—concert hall and television, for instance.

The American Guild of Musical Artists (AGMA) issues a number of contracts based upon the number of travel weeks, rehearsal weeks, and the professional standing of a company. Performers are no longer punished with losing roles for union activism, although a large theater like the Radio City Music Hall never permitted its ballet performers a contract from the 30s to the day it closed its doors in the 80s. About 50 percent of the performers working under a modified AGMA contract in regional companies are under twenty years of age.

AGMA issues a standard contract to large companies but negotiates and modifies its stance on various issues like rehearsal pay for smaller companies. If you have any questions concerning *any*

Handling money in a profession that is seasonal can be tricky. But there are some rules in your favor and some protection available. Although tax laws change frequently, here is a list of some items which you should keep receipts or a daily diary for and discuss with your accountant.

Dues and initiation fees to unions
Trade and casting publications
Agents' fees
Coaching, vocal and musical lessons, dance classes (keep records)
Acting, coaching for a specific role
Music, study records, drama materials
Stage wardrobe, rehearsal clothes
Maintenance of wardrobe and rehearsal clothes
Makeup and dressing room supplies
Stage wigs
Hair care and coloring for stage
Rehearsal studio rentals
Accompanists
Depreciation (list property separately)
Piano tuning and instrument repairs
Rent allocation as professional studio
Telephone service
Home telephone allocation
Outside telephone expense
Photos and résumés
Offices and mailing expenses
Promotion and publicity
Tickets for promotion and study
Entertainment expenses
Special material
Local transportation between rehearsals, shows, making rounds
Professional gifts
Backstage gratuities
Tax preparation

Travel Expenses
Hotels and food, per diem, if paid by artist, not management
Laundry and cleaning
Transportation

Car rental
Taxies, bellhops, porters, maids, trunk, baggage

Medical Expenses

Miscellaneous doctors
Dental
Opticians and glasses
Medical travel
Prescription drugs
Clinics, hospitals
Blue Cross, Blue Shield
Insurance individually paid

Check to see if your therapist and physical rehabilitation or workout place has medical approval as a deduction.

The best source for finding a certified public accountant is through a performer's recommendation. Or you can call your state's Society of Certified Public Accountants. It is not wise to do your own tax forms since you might be called for an audit and would be at a disadvantage in representing yourself. Nor should you go to a quick tax center. They might not be aware of all your privileges and would not represent you at an audit.

The cost of the service should vary according to factors like the income of the applicant and the amount of work to be done. For that reason, it is a good idea to keep consistent records and thorough accounts. Make it a habit to keep your financial records in good order.

Don't be fooled by an accountant who acts smart and promises to do great things for you with his bag of tricks. You'll be holding that bag and he will be the one to disappear. Should you be called in for an audit, go over your tax return with your accountant, making sure that you have all pertinent material, and then let your accountant represent you. It will not likely be a pleasant experience, but if you have all your facts and a good accountant to represent you, you will eventually have a fair adjustment.

contract, call the AGMA office at 212-265-3687, or write to them at 1841 Broadway, New York, NY 10023.

If you intend to sign a contract that is not a standard AGMA agreement, you should be warned to check the following conditions: Be sure to have in writing permission from your parent company if you are performing during a layoff or vacation as a guest artist. Determine what your fee is going to be for the performance(s) in writing. Ask when you will receive your prepaid round-trip ticket. Determine who will book you into a first-class hotel. Find out if you have a taxi and meal allowance, if you have to bring your own costumes or wig, or if there is a rental allowance.

Send your copy to AGMA if you like. They'll look it over and will probably suggest you sign your own contract rather than give the power of attorney to anyone else. Let your agent send out photos and pay as you go along so you will not be asked to pay a percentage of your fee for publicity. Determine the percentage you pay your agent in advance.

INSURANCE

Let us assume that your solo engagement or group contract does insure you against injury on the job, but not while getting to the theater. Find out if the policy of the company to which you are traveling covers your trip. If it doesn't it might be time for you to invest in a general liability insurance policy.

The Ruben Company, 112 E. 61 Street, New York, NY 10021, specializes in insurance for entertainers, producers, and promoters. The dance teacher as well should consider liability insurance to protect him or herself and pupils.

Consult a library copy of *Best's Manual* for ratings on insurance companies in your area. Don't get superstitious about injuries, travel arrangements, or slippery floors. Find out about your coverage and then forget about it. Enjoy your new engagement.

THE REAL WORLD OF DANCERS TODAY

Dancers a short time ago did not enjoy the esteem of the public as they do today. Although the unemployment line is still a ritual in a performing career, recognition and approval have added to the dancer's income and security. At the same time, increased popularity has created misinformation concerning dance as perceived on television, MTV, on talk shows, and in films such as *The Turning Point, Fame,* and *Saturday Night Fever.* While films have always inspired young people to consider a theatrical career, they were viewed as make-believe, while television presentations appear to be more a literal, real, and honest view of a theatrical life. Those youngsters attracted to dance by these presentations have little or no concept of the years or kind of training necessary to achieve what appears to them to be so easy, spontaneous, and primarily a physical achievement. Would-be dancers who begin their training in high school or college face the shock of physical self-abuse and disappointment.

Although joining a major ballet or modern dance company is the goal of students in official schools with a company, many are unable to adapt to professional life without previous experience. The standards and pressures are too much too soon. Young performers in the recent past had the opportunity to learn their craft, refine their talents, and collect inner strength through stock companies, musicals, Hollywood films, nightclubs, concert dance, operetta or opera companies. A variety of styles were encompassed and eventually the goal of joining a major ballet or modern dance company was reached. Recently, a professional dancer who appeared in *A Chorus Line* failed an audition when he was asked to do a mazurka. He had never learned this basic dance step nor had ever been required to learn a mazurka in a previous job. While his training was probably condensed and limited to jazz dance so he could get a job (and he was probably a better jazz dancer than dancers of the past of his age), his job opportunities began and ended with the jazz steps he knew. A well-rounded education in a good school leads to a longer career.

Even more sadly limiting is the career of a well-trained performer who lacks emotional stability, whose talent is lost in despair, discouragement, or disintegration. Although performing offers a safety valve for pent-up rebellion, anger, or hostility, the full use of one's potential cannot be reached, nor is there much happiness for this artist. Although the conflicts of perfomers may seem different from those of the general population, they are not unusual, unique, or psychologically untreatable. Findings show that when the performer enters into therapy, he or she responds with the same dedication, concentration, and willingness to follow suggestions that made a good student or performer. They tend to commit themselves to the end of the therapy as well. Finding release from conflicts, they realize that their talent is not being endangered but sustained, and their progress tends to be swifter, to a fuller expression with greater joy. Of course, some performers *want* to be released from the profession so they may become creative in another aspect of their development. In either case, it is important to accept the fact that dance is not to blame for problems.

EIGHT WAYS TO TAKE CHARGE

You have a right to reach your potential whatever your geographical location, financial status, or background. The following factors have surfaced so consistently in the lives of successful artists, they might be called rules or standards by which you may judge your progress. Don't make the mistake of thinking they do not apply to you.

1. *Prepare properly* in the study of dance whether you plan to become a professional or not. The argument for the best training is the same as that for learning to swim or drive a car properly—you may never become an Olympic star swimmer or a race-car driver, but you might need to know how to do either or both of these things very well in an emergency. The emergency in dance is your safety. Good training

lessens the possibility of injury, accidents, and discomforts later in life.

It costs as much for good training as it does for poor training, and takes as much time. Lost time in a young person's training in dance cannot be recouped to the same degree as in other disciplines. The body does not permit it.

2. *Order your life, study, and stick to your priorities.* There is science in the art of dance as there is art in science. The science of dance is based upon immutable principles of anatomy, physics, and gravity. These principles are in the correct execution of the syllabus of every dance discipline. The syllabus cannot be rushed since it takes mastery over every principle to reach the next. Mastery requires order and daily renewal as well as the extension of effort. The goal is to acquire control and coordination of the body as an instrument, while the mind is left free to express the emotional content of the material.

Don't be reluctant to start over to repair bad habits. Refresh and rethink your understanding of basic principles regularly. Read descriptions of familiar steps as well as new steps in some of the excellent textbooks now available.

3. *Find a balance.* Eliminating other interests or relationships at any age level can topple your sense of proportion. Of course, your responsibilities to parent, school, dance, job, progress, and friends or lovers have to be balanced in your life in various proportions, then reevaluated every now and again when you feel the need. But balance is the key word. Your task as a performer is to reflect life in a bigger-than-life projection. The more you avoid interaction with non-dance persons, the less you will know about how others feel, and the less you will feel yourself. Reach out to the good in others, to those talented in other areas of life.

In a professional school near Boston, where students lived and had academic studies as well as arts training, a young man in his early teens was the most popular boy in the school. He was a talented pianist who could never say "no" to a request from another student to be their accompanist. He loved the activity. Soon his academics suffered and he became extremely fatigued trying to be everyone's first choice because of his talent.

Fortunately, because the school was small enough for the teachers to meet frequently and exchange evaluations of each pupil, the young man was found out. His music teacher spent the next lesson introducing the class to the little black daily diary that every busy student should carry every day. The entire class was asked to plan out one day of their lives and to schedule each activity. After some discussion, it was found that most students worked too hard at one study or another, left insufficient time for rest and proper meals, and no time for "hanging out"—doing whatever that meant to their peer group.

The teacher wisely explained the theory of balance in order to achieve the most from each activity and how balance revives the spirit, a valuable lesson if the schedule is kept.

4. *Reevaluate frequently.* Don't berate yourself for not having the current fashion image or preferred figure. Take calculated risks with a new role, new job, new type of dance study. Don't ever settle for what others think of your talents. Don't place limits on your goals. Enjoy as far as you go, and go as far as you enjoy. Integrate those fantasies with reality. Face the unexpected. Let your life and talents evolve from your inner direction.

5. *Create your own style, life-style, and individuality.* If you find you cannot reach the next level of your plan, find a new place to reach. Or if you have been limiting yourself with negative opinions, lack of support from others, or have become depressed or immobilized with fear or indecision, reaffirm yourself. Promise yourself that whatever anyone says, thinks, or does to you, you will seek your good, successful, and happy existence and that you will correct your attitude whenever you meet these conditions. Get professional help. Well-meaning amateurs consume your time. Walk away from

sickness in others until you are able to make suggestions without personal involvement.

6. *Dedication freely given is not at the cost of comfortable living, good relationships, or good health.* Success should bring greater ease, a bigger sense of emotional security, and robust endurance and strength. Deprivation in any area indicates an unrealistic, uncreative, or destructive solution. Solving some of these problems may mean facing the limits of your talents. Then you will have to become content with that, or change course into a more creative outlet that will use your experience, training, and dedication.

7. *Take responsibility for the conditions of your work.* You inherited the benefits of the efforts of others to correct misdoings by managements, inequitable pay, deplorable work and travel conditions for performers. Now maintain those gains as you find solutions by joining with others to improve whatever you find unsuitable, lacking in dignity, or disrespectful. Whatever your station in the profession, you are neither above nor beneath the effort. By participation, you are in some control over the rules by which you work and live. Don't give up your right to affect legislation.

8. *Face the inevitable changes in your career as a continuation of your development.* When you decide to stop dancing because of an injury, a limit of your capacity, or unwillingness to face internal changes within an organization, expect a period of loss from performing. You will mourn. You will also feel a lack of self-esteem and feel inadequate in the nonperforming world. You have not yet learned how many assets you have and the extent to which your past experience is superior to most educations in providing you with the means for the continuity of your career.

If you have developed interests along the way, you know where you might seek a challenge, where you need further education, or where to seek help.

Above all, don't stop dancing. Admittedly, this is difficult to do when you fall short of your professional standard. You need to exercise at every age and dance will be far more interesting than riding a stationary bike, swimming, or bounding through an aerobics class. You'll be the best again in your class. Stay lithe, healthy, and flexible.

Dance will never leave you even when you leave dance. The most beautiful of all the arts will still be there whenever you see the movement of a swaying flower, watch a child or pet run at top speed, go to a performance, or respond inwardly to music at a concert. Dance may leave your body, but it will never leave your mind and heart. Weren't you lucky to be able to be some part of dance, whatever fate gave you in time and talent?

Appendix A: Performing Arts Health Centers and Clinics in the United States

Although medical professionals with unusual understanding for the needs of performing artists have always been known to inside circles, new knowledge, therapies, clinics, and professionals have emerged throughout the United States to provide additional ways and sources for treatment.

Groups that provide services for dancers frequently offer reduced rates and are a division of the hospitals' sports clinics for reasons of cost effectiveness. While initial visits may be lower in cost, operations or treatments by a specialist may not be at reduced rates. Clinics and hospitals very often justify payment for service by encouraging research papers on dance injuries and dance problems for publication in scientific journals. Grants are given for this purpose to help amortize the cost of treatment and bring good press to the hospital.

Doctors with private clinics, although they face the same financial difficulty in providing service for uninsured artists, very often absorb the cost of treatment because of their personal and professional interest in dance. But remember, it is unethical to list famous patients in printed material and it is an unconscionable practice to jeopardize a performer's job or public image or contract by revealing the need, past or present, for treatment.

Many schools and companies now recognize the value of a contractual agreement with a medical professional to provide seasonal examinations and preventive measures. Seminars, lectures, and group psychological counseling sessions are contributing factors in preventing injuries and in anticipating emotional distress. Many physical therapists who adhere to realignment and strengthening procedures are on-the-scene faculty members.

The Center for Dancemedicine at *St. Francis Memorial Hospital in San Francisco* emerged as a division of the Center for Sports Medicine in 1983. Open at all times with a staff of eight doctors, the center charges a small fee for initial diagnostic visits and on an insurance rate or sliding scale basis for subsequent visits. Physical therapy is Pilates-based body conditioning. James Garrick, M.D., a pioneer in sports and dance medicine, provides orthopedic services for the San Francisco Ballet and San Francisco Ballet School as well as several modern dance, jazz, and aerobic groups. Psychiatrist Douglas Anderson, M.D., conducts seminars on anorexia nervosa and bulimia at the hospital.

The Century Park Chiropractic Office of Frederick Ruge, D.C., and Walter Schacht, D.C., opened its doors in 1983 to dancers at reduced rates. Office hours are 8 A.M. to 6 P.M. weekdays, although Ruge will go on the set or on location if required. Address is 9911 W. Pico Blvd, Los Angeles, CA 90035.

The L.A. Dance Clinic, founded in 1983, is a private office open Monday 6 to 7 P.M. for "serious" dancers who have made an appointment to see orthopedist Daniel M. Silver, M.D. A Laban Movement analyst and a physical therapist are staff members. Fees are on a sliding scale. The clinic gives seminars with internationally known doctors and participants may register for credit from the University of California/L.A. All fees are donated to the clininc's Dance Injury Research Fund. Address is 10921 Wilshire Blvd., Suite #LL-7, Westwood, Los Angeles, CA 90024.

The Cleveland Clinic provides professional services for members of the Cleveland Ballet and the School of the Cleveland Ballet. A contractual arrangement provides preseason, midseason, and post-season examinations. John Bergfeld, M.D., head of sports medicine, has been a celebrated speaker at dance medicine seminars. The clinic is open to dancers 8 A.M. to 5 P.M. Mondays through Fridays. Address is 9500 Euclid Avenue, Cleveland, OH 44106.

The West Hartford Physical Therapy and Sports Medicine Associates in contractual agreement with the School of the Hartford Ballet provides assessment and treatment of common dance injuries once a week at no cost to members of the Hartford Ballet. Counseling is also available. The school is at 308 Farmington Ave., Hartford, CT 06107.

The Children's Hospital, headed by Lyle Micheli, M.D., has extended hours once a week with a staff donating time to dancers of the Boston Ballet and the Boston Ballet Summer School. Fees are on a reduced basis. Micheli has done much research, particularly in analysis of injuries frequent in various modern dance techniques.

The Hospital for Joint Diseases has long been providing treatment to performing artists. Victor Frankel, M.D., heads the orthopedic department. Fadi Bejjani, M.D., has been a researcher and analyst of injuries to musicians. Address is 301 E. 17 St., New York, NY 10003.

Performing Arts Center for Health (PACH), created in 1981, is a referral service created to provide physical and psychological information to performing artists. PACH conducted the first survey on the physical and psychological health of performers, created a reduced-rate dental project, a podiatric project, and formed the first psychiatric clinic for performing artists, headed by Judith R.F. Kupersmith, M.D., at NYU-Bellevue Hospital, 30th Street at First Avenue. For referrals for pyschological counseling outside the New York City area, contact PACH, 357 W. 55 St, New York, NY 10019.

Appendix B:
Suggested Reading

W/hile a performance is the usual inspiration for a career in dance, books can reaffirm technical principles, open new philosophical doors, encourage, and set an example for everyone determined to live a theatrical life.

Whatever the reason for reading books on dance and whatever the outcome, dance literature published and reprinted in the past few decades has made it possible to know the history of dance in detail from its ancient beginnings, through the courts of Europe, its proliferation into the New World, and into our own lives today.

The following books are available on loan or to read in the research division of the Dance Collection, New York Public Library for the Performing Arts, Lincoln Center, New York City. The Harvard Theatre Collection in Boston is also a source for rare and out-of-print books on dance, and the library at the Irvine campus of the University of California is another good source. Books may be purchased from the Ballet Shop, 1887 Broadway, New York, NY 10023. They will send you a catalog. Other books and reprints are available from Dance Horizons, a subsidiary of Princeton Book Company (P.O. Box 57, Pennington, NJ 08534), or by mail order through the Dance Book Club, 12 West Delaware Avenue, Pennington, NJ 08534.

Videotapes are not recommended as teaching tools since they tend to encourage imitation of the performing artists. Harm to the body may result from a misunderstanding of the material represented or from a desire to make too rapid progress before muscularly possible. In places where live performances are not frequent, however, videotape performances can provide example and inspiration.

BALLET

New York City Ballet
A Catalogue of Works: 1984, Balanchine.
Portrait of Mr. B. Photographs and essays, Lincoln Kirstein, Viking.
Balanchine's New Complete Stories of the Great Ballets, Balanchine, ed. by Francis Mason, Doubleday, 1954.
Balanchine: A Biography, Bernard Taper, Times Books, 1984.
George Balanchine, Don McDonagh, Twayne, 1983.
The Nutcracker, Jack Anderson, 1979.
Ballet in Action, Walter Terry, 1954.

American Ballet Theatre
American Ballet Theatre, Charles Payne, Knopf, 1979.
Inside American Ballet Theatre, Clive Barnes, Hawthorn, 1977.
Giselle and Albrecht: American Ballet Theatre's Romantic Lovers, Doris Hering, Dance Horizons, 1981.
Stars of American Ballet Theater, Fred Fehl photographs, Dover.

Other Ballet Companies
The One and Only: The Ballet Russe de Monte Carlo, Anderson, Dance Horizons, 1981.
John Cranko, Stuttgart Ballet, in German, 1971.
National Ballet of Canada, University of Toronto Press, 1978.

Ballet in Australia. E. H. Pask, 1982.
Bejart by Bejart, Comgdon and Lattes, 1979.
Traumwege, John Neumeier, Hamburg Ballet, 1980.
The Royal Ballet—The First Fifty Years, A. Bland, 1981.
The Dancer's Heritage, 1960–77, Ivor Guest.
The Romantic Ballet in Paris, Ivor Guest, Dance Books, Ltd. (London).
The Romantic Ballet in England, 1972.
The Ballet of the Second Empire, Ivor Guest.
Fanny Elssler, Ivor Guest, Dance Books, Ltd. (London), 1970.
Jules Perrot, Master of the Romantic Ballet, Ivor Guest, Dance Horizons.

Famous Performers

The Divine Virginia, biography of Virginia Zucchi, 1977, Ivor Guest.
Fanny Elssler in America, Allison Delarue.
The Romantic Ballet, Theophile Gautier.
Echoes of American Ballet, Lillian Moore, Dance Horizons, 1976.
Baryshnikov: From Russia to the West, G. Smakov, 1981.
Bravo Baryshnikov, A. Le-Mond, 1978.
Baryshnikov at Work, 1976.
Nijinsky, Richard Buckle, 1971.
The Diary of Vaslav Nijinsky, Romola Nijinsky, 1936.
Diaghilev: His Artistic and Private Life, Arnold Haskell.
Nijinsky Dancing, Lincoln Kirstein, 1975.
Rudolf Nureyev, Craig Dodd, 1982.
Nureyev: Aspects of a Dancer, John Percival, 1975.
Nureyev, Alexander Bland, 1962.
Erik Bruhn, Danseur Noble, John Gruen, 1979.
Frederick Ashton and His Ballets, D. Vaughan, 1977.
The King's Ballet Master: A Biography of Denmark's August Bournonville,
    Walter Terry, 1979.
The Memoirs of Enrico Cecchetti, Olga Racster.
Robert Helpmann, Katherine Sorley Walker, 1957.
Unsung Genius, Jack Cole, Glenn Loney, 1984.
Shawn the Dancer, Katherine Dieser, 1933.
Auguste Vestris, Sergie Lifar, 1950.
Pavlova, Her Life and Art, Keith Money, 1982.
Flight of the Swan, a Memory of Pavlova, Andre Oliveroff.
Pavlova, Repertoire of a Legend, John and Roberta Lazzarini.
Anna Pavlova, Cyril Beaumont, 1938.
The Art of Margot Fonteyn, Keith Money, 1965.

Margot Fonteyn, Autobiography, 1975.

Makarova: A Dance Autobiography, Gennady Smakov, 1979.

Martha Graham, Barbara Morgan, Morgan and Morgan.

Dance to the Piper and Promenade Home: A Two-Part Autobiography, Agnes de Mille, DaCapo, 1951.

American Dances, De Mille.

Fifteen Years of a Dancer's Life: Loie Fuller, Anatole France, Dance Horizons, 1913.

Split Seconds: A Remembrance, Tamara Geva, 1984.

Denishawn: The Enduring Influence, Jane Sherman, Wesleyan, 1983.

Isadora Speaks, Franklin Rosemont, 1981.

My Life, Isadora Duncan.

Judith Jamison: Aspects of a Dancer, Olga Maynard.

Lydia Lopokova, Milo Keyes, St. Martins, 1982.

Total Education in Ethnic Dance, La Meri, Dance Books, Ltd. (London), 1977.

Branislava Nijinska: Early Memoirs, Irina Nijinska, 1981.

Ruth Page: An Intimate Biography, John Martin, 1977.

Days with Ulanova, Albert E. Kahn, 1962.

The Story of Ballet, Joan Lawson, 1976.

Dance Through the Ages, Walter Sorell, Grosset & Dunlap, 1967.

World History of the Dance, Curt Sachs, Norton, 1937.

Stuart Masques and Renaissance Stage, Allardice Nicoll, 1980.

The Bolshoi Ballet, Helene Obolensky, 1975.

Era of the Russian Ballet, N. Roslavleva, 1979.

The Great Russian Dancers, Gennady Smakov, Knopf, 1984.

Ballet or Ballyhoo, Barbara Barker, Dance Horizons.

The Ballet Called Swan Lake, Cyril Beaumont, Dance Horizons.

Letters from a Ballet Master, Arthur Saint-Leon, Dance Horizons.

Michel Fokine and His Ballets, Beaumont, Dance Horizons.

Theatre Street, Tamara Karsavina, Dance Books, Ltd. (London).

Ballet Textbooks

Letters on Dancing and Ballets, Jean Georges Noverre, Dance Horizons. A classic.

Basic Principles of Classical Ballet, Vaganova, 1934. The first textbook on Soviet technique.

Theory Manual and Practice of Classical Theatrical Ballet, Beaumont. Textbook for Cecchetti technique.

The School of Classical Dance, Kostrovitskaya. Update of the Vaganova classic.

Ballet Technique for the Male Dancer, Nikolai Tarasov, Doubleday. First textbook for male ballet dancers based upon Bolshoi system.

The Bournonville School, Kirsten Ralov, Dance Books, Ltd. (London).

Nicolas Legat, Andre Eglevsky, Dance Horizons.

The Code of Terpsichore, Carlo Blasis, Dance Horizons. The first textbook on professional classical ballet.

Pas de Deux, Nikolai Serebrennikov, Dance Books, Ltd. (London). Textbook on partnering based upon the Kirov system.

Orchesography, Thoinot Arbeau, Dover. First textbook, 1588, based upon court dances and manners.

New and Curious School of Theatrical Dancing, Gregorio Lambranzi, Dance Horizons. 1716 work for character and comedy dances.

Dance in Ancient Greece, Lillian Lawler, University of Washington Press.

Dance as a Theatre Art, Selma Jeanne Cohen. Dodd, Mead. Dance history from 1581 to the present.

Jewish Dancing Master of the Renaissance: Gugioelmo Ebreo, Dance Horizons. Fifteenth-century dance.

Classes in Classical Ballet, Asaf Messerer, Princeton Book Company. Contemporary Moscow pedagogue.

Historical Dances, Melusine Wood, Dance Books, Ltd. (London). Twelfth to nineteenth century.

Ancient Egyptian Dances, Irene Lexova, Dance Horizons.

Dancing Mania of the Middle Ages, Hecker.

MODERN DANCE

The Delsarte System of Expressions, Genevieve Stebbins, Dance Horizons. Early pioneer in expressive movement.

Every Little Movement, Ted Shawn, Dance Horizons.

The Modern Dance, John Martin, Dance Horizons.

Preclassic Dance Forms, Louis Horst, Dance Horizons.

Barton Mumaw: Dancer, Mumaw and Sherman, Dance Horizons. From Denishawn to Jacob's Pillow.

Mary Wigman: The Language of Dance, Walter Sorell, Wesleyan. About the first modern dancer.

Transformations: The Humphrey-Weidman Era, Eleanor King, Dance Horizons.

Gordon Craig on Movement and Dance, Rood, Dance Horizons, 1977.

Hanya Holm: A Biography, Walter Sorell, Wesleyan, 1965. Biography of another early modern dancer.

Doris Humphrey: An Artist First, Selma Jeanne Cohen, Wesleyan, 1972.

Inside Dance: Essays by Murray Louis.

Frontiers of Dance: The Life of Martha Graham, Walter Terry.

Martha Graham: Portrait of the Lady as an Artist, LeRoy Leatherman.

Modern Dance: Techniques and Teaching, Shurr and Yocom, Dance Horizons.

JAZZ

Anthology of American Jazz Dance, Gus Giordano, Orian.

Matt Mattox Book of Jazz Dance, Elizabeth Frich.

Jazz Dance: An Adult Beginner's Guide, Helena Andres, Prentice-Hall.

Jazz Dance: The Story of American Vernacular Dance, Marshall and Jean Sterns. The classic jazz dance history.

TAP DANCING

Tops in Tap, Ann Miller.

Tap Dancing: A Beginner's Guide, Trina Marx, Prentice-Hall.

The Encyclopedia of Tap.

DANCE THERAPY

The Thinking Body, Mable E. Todd, Dance Horizons. The first textbook on body principles for movement.

Awareness Through Movement, Moshe Feldenkrais.

Theory and Methods in Dance Movement Therapy, Lewis Bernstein.

The Effective Dance Program in Physical Education, Furst and Rockefeller, Princeton Book Company, 1981.
Dance Therapy for Dancers, Beryl Dunn.
Human Movement Potential, Lulu Sweigard, Harper and Row. Another pioneer and classic volume.

CHARACTER OR ETHNIC DANCE

Character Dance, Jagen Pagels, 1983.
Spanish Dancing, Helen Wingrave.
Dictionary of Spanish Dance, Matteo. A definitive resource.
El Arte del Baile Flamenco, Alfonso Puig, 1985.

BALLROOM, RELIGIOUS, AND COUNTRY DANCE

Ballroom Dancing, Alex Moore, 1983.
Castles in the Air, Irene Castle. Biography.
Square and Folk Dancing, Hank Greene.
The Gospel According to Dance, Giora Manor, 1980.
Liturgy as Dance and the Liturgical Dancer, Cardyd Dietering, 1984.

MIME

The Italian Comedy, Pierre Duchartre, 1966.
Mimes on Miming, Bari Rolfe.
All About Mime: Understanding and Performing the Expressive Silence, Marvene Loeschke.

Index

Salt, in diet, 82–83
Scholarships, 22, 25, 28, 30
Schools of dance, 3–4, 13–28
Science of dance, 223
Sebaceous glands, 124–25
Self-destructive behavior, 157–58
Self-esteem, 154, 190; and anorexia nervosa, 77, 79; and bulimia, 80
Seltzer, 86
Semiclassical hairdos, 132–33, 134
Sensitive skin, 126
Separation, and relationships, 155
Sesame dip, 72
Sexual development of dance students, 26
Sexual relationships, 155–56, 177–81
Shoes, 54, 62, 138–40; for dance class, 28
Sibling rivalries, 207–10
Skin care, 124–30
Sleep, 87–89
Sleeping pills, 170
Smoking, 150–53; and vitamins, 70
Social development of dancers, 26–27, 166, 176
Sodium, in diet, 82–83
Soft shoes, 139–40
Sore feet, 61
Sore muscles, 62–65
Souffle, 72
Splinters, 61
Sports, and dance, 91
Spotting, visual exercises, 121–22
Sprains, 59
Stability, emotional, 186
Stage fright, 44–46
Stage hairdos, 131–34
Stage makeup, 100–107; and contact lenses, 124
Steroids, 65
Stresses of dancers, 43–52, 145–73, 185–205
Stretching, before warm-up, 64, 115
Students of dance, 2–10, 221–23; body care, 53–89; dietary practices, 74–75; and drug abuse, 46–52; stress reactions, 43–46
Subcutaneous tissue, 124
Submissive behavior, in relationships, 177
Success, 185–86, 225; and drug abuse, 169; early, 147–49; fear of, 212
Suction surgery, 99–100
Sugar, 71; and energy, 84
Suggestibility, 45
Summer dance courses, 23
Sweat glands, 125

Swimming, 114–15
Syllabus, for dance education, 16
Symptoms: of drug abuse, 50, 171; of stress, 44, 203–5

Tax-deductible expenses, 218–19
Taylor, Paul, 37–38
Teachers of dance, evaluation of, 20–21, 24
Teeth, 140–41; cosmetic bonding, 108
Teig, Donald S., 121–23
Testing schedule, for dance schools, 16
Therapy, psychological, 167, 187–203, 216
Tobacco, 49, 51, 150–53
Toenails, grooming of, 59–60, 137
Toes, shape of, 63
Tofu dip, 72
Toxic shock syndrome (TSS), 67
Training for dance, 1, 216, 221–23. See also Schools of dance
Tranquilizers, 52, 169
Travel: jet lag, 142–44; nutrition in, 69; water supply, 85–86
Tremaine, Joe, 38
Tuition costs, 27–28
Turnout of hips, of male dancers, 63, 90–91
Turns, visual exercises, 121–22

Underbase, cosmetic, 102
Union contracts, 217–20
Union rules for auditions, 30

Valium, 169
Vasicka, Alis, 66, 67
Vegetables, 69, 71
Venereal disease, 179–81
Ventilation of exercise rooms, 19, 151
Verdon, Gwen, 39
Visualization of movements, 123, 188
Vitamins, 74–75; dietary supplements, 69–70; food sources, 71
Volatile substances, 50–51

Warm-up period, 64, 115
Washington, George, 92
Water, in diet, 83–86
Water retention, premenstrual, 67, 83
Water-soluble vitamins, 74–75
Weight control, 47, 67; and anorexia nervosa, 76
Working conditions, 216–17, 225

Yogurt, and travel disorders, 86
Young children, and dance training, 13–15

About the Authors

Marian Horosko and Judith R. F. Kupersmith, M.D., attended the School of American Ballet and were members of the New York City Ballet in the 1950s. Horosko, now an editor at *Dance Magazine,* lives and works in New York City. Kupersmith is a practicing psychiatrist currently living in Louisville, Kentucky. Both authors are cofounders of PACH, the Performing Arts Center for Health, where, at New York University/Bellevue Hospital, Kupersmith headed the first psychiatric clinic for performers. In 1986 Dr. Kupersmith established a PACH clinic in Louisville.